Field Guide to the Sandia Mountains

Field Guide to the Sandia Mountains

Edited by Robert Julyan and Mary Stuever
Gerald Sussman, book project manager

University of New Mexico Press   Albuquerque

© 2005 by the University of New Mexico Press
All rights reserved. Published 2005
Printed in Singapore by TWP America, Inc.

11   10   09   08   07   06   05   1   2   3   4   5   6   7

A co-publishing venture between the University of New Mexico Press
and the New Mexico Friends of the Forest, now known as
Friends of the Sandia Mountains; P. O. Box 1832, Tijeras, New Mexico, 87059.

LIBRARY OF CONGRESS CATALOGING-IN-PUBLICATION DATA

Field guide to the Sandia Mountains / edited by Robert Julyan and Mary Stuever.
     p. cm.
    ISBN 0-8263-3667-1 (spiral paperbound : alk. paper)
    1. Natural history—New Mexico—Sandia Mountains.
    2. Sandia Mountains (N.M.) I. Julyan, Robert Hixson. II. Stuever, Mary.
    QH105.N6F54 2005
    508.789—dc22

                                        2004026468

A NOTE ABOUT SAFETY

Safety is an important concern in all outdoor activities. No guidebook can alert you to every hazard or anticipate the limitations of every reader. Thus, the trails and activities described in this book are not representations that a particular place or activity will be safe for your party. When you engage in any of the activities described in this book, you assume responsibility for your own safety. Under normal conditions, these activities require the usual attention to traffic, road, and trail conditions, weather, terrain, the capabilities of your party, and other factors. Keeping informed regarding current conditions and using common sense are the keys to a safe, enjoyable outing.

Adapted from *Best Hikes with Children in New Mexico*,
by Robert Julyan (The Mountaineers Books, 2004).

Book design and composition by Kathleen Sparkes
Cover and frontis photos of the Sandia Mountains ©William Stone
Other photos and illustrations in book as noted on page 253.

This book was typeset using the Utopia and Berthold Akzidenz Grotesk families
Body type is Utopia 9/12
Display type is Berthold Akzidenz Grotesk

Contents

Sections used for identification are color coded as indicated below.

Foreword

Fifty years ago, more or less, I first was made aware that Sandia Mountain was something magical-mystical, and not merely for the solid physical reasons a lot of us like to live in Albuquerque.

I was a reporter then. The murder of a state policeman had drawn me to the Laguna Reservation to check out a tip. Far to the east I noticed a glow in the night sky and mentioned it.

"That's the signal Spider Grandmother sends to show her people the way home," said my Laguna friend, grinning at me. "Or, if you prefer a more scientific explanation, the lights of Albuquerque are reflecting off the clouds Turtle Mountain gathers above herself."

Most of those providing information about our Sandia Mountain in this book will be devoting their essays more to the hard facts and less to the spiritual. Since my knowledge of the hard facts about our mountain is derived mostly from hearsay, I'll pass along some of the accumulated information that I've heard from folks I know in the Native American community about its role in their spiritual history.

For example, while the Hispanic invaders called it *Sierra Sandia,* possibly in recognition of the watermelon pink the light of sundown paints it, the Navajo name for it is *Dzil Naayisi,* "Spinning Mountain." Zunis revere it as the origin site of their Home Fire Society. The Rio Grande Pueblo peoples have always called it Turtle Mountain. In the distant past, when their ancestors reached this Glittering World in their Genesis journey, their Spider Grandmother spirit advised them to search for a place to settle when they found a mountain that reminded them of a turtle. Seen from a couple of directions, our mountain does that.

Another of the appeals of Sandia Mountain to folks like myself is what one can see from the crest. On the more than 300 clear nights this high, dry climate provides per average year, the view from the top includes the lights of more than half of New Mexico's population—from Los Alamos, Santa Fe, and environs to the north to the spreading sprawl of communities up and down the river below.

By day, it's a landscape rich in history. On the western horizon, about eighty miles away, rises what we latecomers call Mount Taylor, honoring Zachary Taylor, hero of the Mexican War and twelfth president of the United States. To Navajos, however, it is *Dootl'izhii Dziil,* "Turquoise Mountain," one of the four sacred mountains of the Diné world. We look upon it as an extinct volcano. For the Navajos, it is the handiwork of First Man, one of the tribe's important spiritual figures, who built the Turquoise Mountain of materials he brought up from the previous world far below. He then decorated it with turquoise, pinned it to the earth with a magic knife to keep it from flying away, and made it the home of spirits called Turquoise Boy and Yellow Corn Girl.

But that's only the start of the story. Other landmarks one sees from Sandia Crest have their own list of legends. About forty miles to the northwest one sees the flat-topped core of a long-retired volcano jutting above the skyline. That's Cabezon Peak, or *Tse Naajiin* to the Navajos. Mythologists know it as the head of Walking Monster, the first of the evil beings killed by the Navajo Hero Twins, while geographers describe it as one of the largest volcanic stumps of its kind anywhere. If one stares southwest, one sees the jagged outline of the Sierra Ladrones, "Thieves Mountains," on the horizon. Named because robbers and rustlers would take refuge in these remote, forbidding mountains, they are the focus for numerous tales and legends.

Sandia Mountain itself provides its share of claims to fame. It is the product of a rift, one of those cosmic events in which a section of the earth's crust is stretched and split, with the center subsiding to form a deep valley. At the same time, geologic forces raise the rims of this valley upward. Geologists who measure such things report that one must drill some twenty thousand feet into the bed of the Rio Grande to reach the same strata of stone one finds on Sandia Crest, which is another mile above the river.

Stone underfoot along the Sandia Crest is rich in marine fossils, providing evidence that this area was once beneath an ocean. Now aquatic life is limited to the narrow river a mile below and includes the rare silvery minnow and a few brown trout in its irrigation canals.

To change the subject to anthropology, consider that evidence has been found that some of the very earliest humans in North America camped in a cliffside cave in the Sandias. Chipped stone and bone artifacts, found under a mineral deposit on the cave floor, were believed to have been left behind by hunters years before men of the Folsom Culture were hunting their Ice Age animals.

Our mountain also offers interesting botanical and meteorological features. For example, its flora varies noticeably as one climbs from its foothills, roughly a mile above sea level, to the crest, more than two miles. One can also note the plant variation between the cooler, wetter east slope and the sun-blasted west slope.

An interesting weather phenomenon also occurs when a low-pressure system causes clouds on the east side to pour over the Sandia Crest like a slow-motion Niagara Falls.

I leave specifics about the natural history of our mountain to the experts in this book, but I do want to pass on two points. First, in the proper season thousands of ladybugs cluster on shrubs in the Sandias, making us wish they had instead chosen our gardens, where they would wipe out aphid infestations. Second, people sometimes forget that conditions are much cooler at ten thousand feet than in Albuquerque. Dress for and expect lower temperatures in the mountains.

—*Tony Hillerman*

Forest Service and Sandia Pueblo Management Agreement

A unique situation exists in the Sandia Mountains, where the U.S. Forest Service and the Pueblo of Sandia share in the management of the northern portion of the west face of the Sandia Mountains, and Pueblo members have special rights. In 2003, Congress passed legislation creating the T'uf Shur Bien Preservation Trust Area within the Cibola National Forest and Sandia Mountain Wilderness and resolving litigation involving the Pueblo's claim to the Area. As stated in the act, the purpose of the legislation was "to recognize and protect in perpetuity the rights and interests of the [Sandia] Pueblo in and to the Area; to preserve in perpetuity the national forest and wilderness character of the Area; and to recognize and protect in perpetuity the longstanding use and enjoyment of the Area by the public."

The Area continues to be administered as part of the National Forest System, while also recognizing the Pueblo's interests in the Area, including its members' longstanding traditional and cultural uses. These uses include the right of Pueblo members to bow hunt throughout the entire area and to hunt with rifles in and around the Piedra Lisa tract. Other persons hiking or recreating within the Area should be respectful and appropriately cautious of Sandia Pueblo members' special rights in the Area and should take care not to disturb cultural activities of, or cultural objects left by, Pueblo members or members of other Indian tribes utilizing the area with Sandia Pueblo's permission. Regulations resulting from the Wilderness Act, which designated the Sandia Mountain Wilderness in 1978, still apply to the Area, as well as other federal laws and regulations existing at the time the legislation was passed in 2003.

CHAPTER 1

Introduction

Robert Julyan and Sue Bohannan Mann

This most beautiful backdrop a city ever had.
—Phillip B. Tollefsrud (Memorial plaque at
Elena Gallegos picnic area)

On my breakfast walk from UNM's old Hokona dorm to the dining hall, I always looked to the Sandia Mountains and absorbed a mood for the day. As a green freshman in 1949, I found comfort in scanning the peaks hidden among cloudy blankets. Some days, they seemed sleepy, as if they wanted to stay in bed. However, on the evening trek to dinner, they came alive, bathed in vivid pink, orange, and mauve tints, as well as a mixture of watermelon hues, betokening another day's perfect ending. My moods were inextricably tuned to the mountains.
—Sue Bohannan Mann, A Friend of the Forest

The Sandia Mountains continue to set the day's mood for many New Mexicans. Indeed, in this part of the state the Sandias are a commanding presence, not only physically but also reaching deep into people's lives in other ways as well. Recreation is an example. For the approximately seven hundred thousand New Mexicans who live within thirty miles of the mountains—approximately a third of the state's total population—the range serves as a friendly wild backyard, one they visit often. Some people take the tram to the Sandia Crest, some drive to the top on the Crest Highway, NM 536. Others are simply walkers, hikers, climbers, runners, mountain-bikers, downhill and cross-country skiers, hang-gliders, bird-watchers, trackers, meditators, and many more—all enjoying the many miles of trails in the mountains. By the hundreds they come each day, natives and new-comers alike, seeking recreation and renewal. Each year more than two million visitors take advantage of the mountains' easy access.

For the Cibola National Forest and the Sandia Ranger District, the challenge lies in protecting the area's natural qualities while meeting the ever-increasing demands made upon the resource. The Sandia Ranger District is the smallest Forest Service district in New Mexico, consisting of the Sandia and Manzanita Mountains (a subrange immediately south) and totaling 100,555 acres. At the time the Sandia District was created in 1908, fewer than fifteen thousand people lived in Albuquerque. In 1921 the Sandia Mountains were designated a game refuge, and firearms were banned. During the late 1930s, hardy souls began skiing on the eastern slope of the Sandia Mountains where the Sandia Peak Ski Area is now located. Their greatest challenge may have been driving there—on muddy dirt roads.

Today, with Albuquerque having approximately five hundred thousand people and with development surrounding the mountains, the District meets its modern challenges by fostering an understanding of natural systems and learning to co-exist with wildlife. Rangers urge visitors to volunteer and actively participate in helping make the Sandia Mountains a place to be visited, enjoyed, and improved by all who come here. (See "Leave No Trace" below.) The more people appreciate and understand the mountains, the more they will respect and care for them. This guide is but one expression of that belief.

About This Book

This book is the quintessential "labor of love"—love for the Sandia Mountains, and love for the many aspects of the mountains. It was conceived by the Sandia Ranger District and New Mexico Friends of the Forest (FOF), a nonprofit volunteer group of private citizens who have come together to support the Sandia Ranger District in their management of the mountains. The idea was to create a field guide that in one book would include several subjects but cover a single, relatively small, but very important area—the Sandia Mountains. Not intended as an exhaustive reference, it rather seeks to introduce visitors to the features and species they are most likely to encounter here.

Leading the project was Gerry Sussman, Sandia Ranger District volunteer who retired to New Mexico and the Sandias following a long career with Oxford University Press. He worked with the Sandia Ranger District, New Mexico Friends of the Forest, the New Mexico Museum of Natural History, the University of New Mexico (UNM) Press, and others, to assemble a committee of experts in various subject areas. At first, they were led by Mary Stuever, who worked on a similar guide for Philmont Scout Ranch. When she left town Bob Julyan assumed the role and guided the book to completion, though she remained involved throughout the project.

Within the larger committee were subject-oriented subcommittees, each responsible for text and illustrations for its subject, such as wildflowers or mammals. Sometimes committee members had professional training in their fields; more often they were passionate amateurs with years of field experience not only in their subjects but also in the Sandias. All were volunteers, and all made a major commitment of time and effort to the project.

Early in the process UNM Press became involved. As David Holtby, UNM Press associate director and editor-in-chief, explained, "We saw this as an opportunity to do regional publishing—to bring to light material that needed to be there, that wasn't there, and that could only come about through a collaborative effort."

Reasoning that the *Field Guide to the Sandia Mountains* would be a community resource, the Friends of the Forest and UNM Press sought community support to offset costs and keep the book affordable. The fundraising included a photo contest, which resulted in the color photos used on the book's covers.

Getting to Know the Sandia Mountains

Vegetation Zones

Whether hiking up the craggy western face, traveling to Sandia Crest by car, or riding the tram, visitors pass through four vegetation zones, determined primarily by latitude and altitude. This change in vegetation varies as much as if you were driving along the California Coast from San Diego north to British Columbia, about 1,500 miles.

Other factors, especially slope and direction of exposure, will also determine where specific plants within these zones occur. Vegetation on cool, moist, north slopes can vary dramatically from that on sunny, arid, south-facing slopes. Add to this the diversity of soil and disturbance history and it is easy to understand why there are hundreds of plant communities throughout the mountains. Perhaps the best way to become familiar with the major vegetation zones is by taking a drive to the crest on the Sandia Crest National Scenic Byway, NM 536—known in this book as the Crest Highway. Look for Sandia Ranger District signs labeling the vegetation zones and their elevations. The elevations below are for the east side. The same tree species will tend to be found about two hundred feet higher on the mountains' west side, which is drier and more exposed.

Piñon-Juniper

In the Sandias, from the foothills at approximately 6,000 feet to 7,500 feet, is New Mexico's most widespread vegetation type, the piñon-juniper woodland. Within this zone, summers are hot, winters somewhat mild. Precipitation is modest, and evaporation is high. Plants in this zone have adapted to hot, arid conditions and include many species of cacti such as cholla, hedgehog, and prickly pear. Shrubs, flowers, and grasses at this elevation play an important role by holding the loose soil in place, which prevents erosion during rain runoff. Other characteristic plants are alligator juniper, chamisa, Apache plume, Gambel oak, and, near water, box elder, and cottonwood.

PINE FOREST
Also known as the Transition Zone, this zone, 7,500 to 8,200 feet, has mild summers and cold winters, often with substantial snowfall. Here ponderosa pines become predominant, replacing piñons and junipers. Other typical plants are Gambel oak, New Mexico locust, and riparian willows. Numerous wildflowers bloom in this life zone, which has the greatest species diversity on the mountain.

MIXED CONIFER
Also known as the Canadian Zone and the Fir-Aspen Belt, this zone, from 8,000 to 9,800 feet in the Sandias, is dominated by Douglas-fir, white fir, subalpine fir, Engelmann spruce, and common juniper, as well as Rocky Mountain maple. These trees interweave with stands of quaking aspen, which turn the mountain from an early spring green to a rich gold in autumn. Aspens are common in sunny disturbed or transition areas. In the summertime, you may see a sego lily, or one of the many bright penstemons, wild geraniums, columbines, and orange-rust wallflowers. Summers here are cool, winters cold, and at this elevation the mountains receive significant moisture.

SPRUCE-FIR
This is the highest, coldest, moistest, windiest part of the mountains. Here Engelmann spruce join white fir, corkbark fir, and Douglas-fir as dominant species. The very hardy and long-lived limber pines also are here. Wolf currant is a common shrub. Summers are cool, winters long and cold, and at this elevation the mountains receive significant moisture.

National Scenic Byway and Roadside Geology
Ever since a road was first carved to the Sandia Crest in 1927, this route has been popular with motorists. Now part of the Turquoise Trail, the Crest Highway was designated a National Scenic Byway in June 2000 by the U.S. Federal Highway Administration. It stretches 13.6 miles and climbs 3,814 feet from its beginning at NM 14 in Sandia Park. As you drive, the highway takes you on a dramatic journey of natural and geologic history.

Most of the rocks along the byway are sedimentary formations, laid down in ancient seas. Soon you'll pass Tinkertown Museum, part of the mountains' human history, and a little farther the Doc Long Picnic Area, also a part of that history. At approximately two miles from NM 14, just before the Doc Long Picnic Area, at Auto Tour Stop 7, you'll pass the "Great Unconformity," where igneous granite rocks 1.4 billion years old underlie sedimentary rocks a mere 300 million years old. The Great Unconformity represents a gap in the geologic record of 1.1 billion years!

As you pass Tejano Canyon at 7,800 feet, keep your eyes open for gray, tassel-eared squirrels collecting acorns from Gambel oaks growing on the south-facing slopes, as well as for mule deer. Soon you'll pass the Tree Spring Trailhead (8,480 feet), named for a nearby natural spring, which originated from under a stump. The water from the spring is now collected in a stone drinker and provides water for wildlife year round. Just beyond the Sandia Peak Ski Area (8,600 feet) is the turn-off for Balsam Glade. The area is heavily visited during autumn, when the aspen leaves turn a deep shimmering gold, and appear to dance in the deep green arms of neighboring firs.

The region around Ninemile Picnic Area (9,200 feet) is notable to bird watchers. Look for the dashing deep-blue of the Steller's jay and the flash of the yellow-rumped warbler, as well as the black-headed grosbeak.

At the 10K Trailheads, the byway passes into the spruce-fir belt, an area similar in vegetation and climate to Hudson Bay, Canada. Temperatures here can be 20 degrees cooler than those at the start of the byway—even in the summer! Next stop, the crest!

Higher, past the Ellis Trailhead, notice the power lines that hang across the roadway (10,500 feet). The poles supporting these lines were specifically designed to serve as a perch for hawks, falcons, and other raptors.

From the crest at 10,678 feet, over two miles above sea level, you have a commanding view of central New Mexico. Below to the west is the Rio Grande Rift Valley and on its west side numerous volcanic structures. Beyond is Mount Taylor—like the Sandias, sacred to Native Americans throughout the region. To the east is the Estancia Valley, once a large Pleistocene lake. To the northeast are the San Pedro Mountains, Ortiz Mountains, and Cerrillos Hills. Farther north are the snow-capped Sangre de Cristo Mountains. And to the south the Manzano Mountains point toward still other ranges along the Rio Grande.

One mile below you to the west is the Rio Grande and the Rio Grande Rift. It's this great crack in the Earth's crust that caused the valley below to subside and the Sandia Mountains to lift up. It's one of our continent's great geological dramas, one still continuing.

From the vantage point of the crest, looking north and south over the western escarpment, the Great Unconformity is unmistakable — the 300-million-year-old Pennsylvanian marine limestone lying like a watermelon rind atop a heart of gray-pink igneous granite, 1.4 billion years old. And both rocks are much older than the Sandias themselves, mere upstarts at only 10 million years old.

Sandia Mountain Wilderness

The year 2003 marked the twenty-fifth anniversary of the Sandia Mountain Wilderness, created in 1978 by an act of Congress. In 1982, the Forest Service added 7,000 more acres to the Sandia Wilderness, bringing its total to 37,877 acres. Today, a well-developed network of trails provides access to tiny streams, hidden waterfalls, forested glades, and other surprises and delights of wild nature.

LEAVE NO TRACE

As ever more people use America's wild lands, it is increasingly important to minimize your impact by adopting an ethic known as "Leave No Trace." This responsibility is even more urgent in the heavily used Sandia Mountains. "Leave No Trace" really isn't difficult. It just means adopting some fairly simple habits and practices:

Plan and prepare. Repackage and store food in reusable containers, and have on hand bags in which to pack out garbage and trash.

Trails. Stay on designated trails, walking single-file in the middle. Don't take shortcuts on switchbacks. Try to stay on durable surfaces.

Camp. When camping in the backcountry—there are no formal Forest Service campgrounds in the Sandias—choose, where possible, already established campsites, preferably those where the soil already is bare. Camp at least two hundred feet (about seventy adult steps) from water sources. Control pets. Take everything you bring into the wilderness out with you—and take out at least some of other peoples' trash. Also, check to see what wilderness restrictions might be in effect.

Fires. Best of all, don't build a fire; use a portable stove. If you do build a fire, use only established fire rings. Don't scar the landscape by snapping branches off live or dead trees or shrubs. Completely extinguish your fire, make sure it's cold before departing, remove all unburned trash from the fire ring, and scatter the cold ashes over a large area. If you want to build a fire in an area where no fire ring exists, build a "mound fire": create a mound of mineral soil, build the fire on this, then scatter everything when done. Also, be sure to check with the Forest Service regarding current fire restrictions.

Sanitation. The recommended method of disposing of human wastes is the "cat hole," dug six to eight inches deep at least two hundred feet away from water sources. Cover and disguise the cat hole when you're done. Toilet paper should be used sparingly and packed out (sealed in double plastic bags) or use a natural alternative. Don't contaminate water sources with soap, food, or human waste.

Trash. All trash, especially food scraps, should be packed out. Most trash, including paper, doesn't burn well in a fire, and ends up being scattered by wind or animals.

Wild animals. Don't attract them. Don't feed them. Don't approach them or touch them. This not only disrupts wildlife ecology and encourages animals to become dependent on humans, it also exposes people to the possibility of bites and infection by animal-borne diseases, such as plague. Hang your food supplies out of reach, and do food preparation and clean-up away and downwind from your camp.

Tread softly. In arid regions, the soil often acquires a protective "crust" that once disturbed leaves the soil vulnerable to erosion. Watch for these.

Leave what you find. Leave plants, rocks, and cultural artifacts as you found them so others can enjoy them.

Enjoy the Mountains–Safely

Though the Sandia Mountains have been described as an urban wilderness, they are a wilderness nonetheless, as scores of injured or lost people discover each year. The precautions one should take regarding the mountains' weather are described in this book's weather section, but here are some other tips for exploring the Sandias safely:

- Tell someone where you are going—and when you expect to return. Take a cell phone if you have one.
- Familiarize yourself with the mountains and carry a map and compass.
- You can augment these with a Global Positioning System (GPS) unit.
- Stay on the trail, unless you are familiar with the terrain and cross-country navigation.
- Take water, food, and warm, protective clothing, as well as materials for building a fire (in emergencies only). Learn the symptoms and treatment of hypothermia.
- Learn to prepare for heat and sun exposure; wear hats, sunscreen, drink water often, avoid strenuous exercise during the hottest part of the day, learn the symptoms and treatment of heat exhaustion, dehydration exhaustion, and heat stroke.
- Don't underestimate the mountain.

Become Involved/Give Back to the Mountains

By becoming involved in this guide, we committee members have deepened our appreciation of the Sandia Mountains and reaped the satisfaction that comes with giving something back to the mountains that have given so much to us. This is available to each of you as well. In addition to its own volunteer programs, the Sandia Ranger District coordinates a wide variety of programs sponsored by groups such as New Mexico Friends of the Forest, New Mexico Volunteers for the Outdoors, Friends of Tijeras Pueblo, the New Mexico Mountain Club, the Sierra Club, Nordic and alpine ski clubs, the Audubon Society, the New Mexico Geological Society, the Wildflower Club and the Native Plant Society, and many more. Becoming involved in these organizations is like recapturing the excitement of discovering the mountains for the first time.

CHAPTER 2

Ecology of the Sandia Mountains

Robert Julyan

This book primarily is an introduction to the various individual elements found in the Sandia Mountains—hummingbirds, black bears, granite, butterflies, and so forth. But as you consider these, you should always remain mindful that they make up an overall ecosystem that is greater than the sum of its parts. Hundreds of plants and animals—as well as countless microbes, soil types, moisture systems, and more—all are linked to create the miraculously complex entity we know as the Sandia Mountains. In the introduction to his *Flowering Plants of New Mexico* (third edition), Robert DeWitt Ivey defined an ecosystem thus: "It is a self-sustaining system, making its own food and recycling its own wastes. What happens to any one part ultimately affects all parts. . . . Like an organism, it heals its own wounds and sicknesses."

It's an interrelated system of checks and balances, feedback loops, correction mechanisms, and responses to change, but despite this daunting complexity a few general concepts can help us recognize what we see in the Sandias. First is the arrangement of plant species into zones on the mountains in response to elevation and associated temperature and moisture conditions. Because plants form the base of the animal food chain, the plants within a zone also determine the animals that live there. For example, birds and mammals that depend upon piñon nuts and juniper berries, such as piñon jays and white-throated woodrats, will be found in the piñon-juniper zone.

In the introduction to this book we discuss the progression of vegetation types you encounter as you ascend the mountains' east side to the crest. Here also is a chart of these vegetation zones. Unfortunately, the actual plants and animals within these zones have not seen this chart and don't necessarily follow it, so their on-the-ground occurrences vary enormously.

The second important concept is that plant communities evolve in a succession over time in response to disturbances, such as fire, clearing, grazing, and so forth. Beginning with bare soil, plant communities go through a series of stages, each replacing the previous one until a mature and self-perpetuating forest is established. Driving this succession is shade-tolerance as the forest evolves toward species whose seedlings can grow in the shade of the trees above them.

As an example, imagine a lightning strike at the crest igniting a small fire in a stand of mature mixed conifers. Suddenly sunlight is able to reach the forest floor that previously had been in shade. Sun-loving wildflowers appear, as well as various shrubs. After a time, aspens sprouting from root shoots occupy the area. Beneath their canopy, shade-tolerant seedlings of spruce and fir begin to appear.

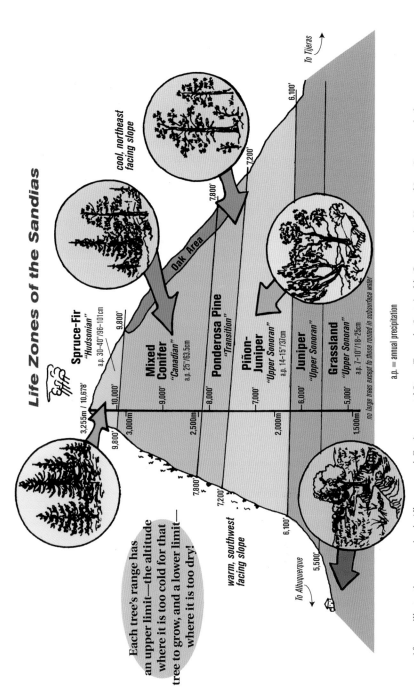

Life Zones of the Sandias

cool, northeast facing slope

Oak Area

Spruce-Fir "Hudsonian" a.p. 30–40"/96–101cm

Mixed Conifer "Canadian" a.p. 25"/63.5cm

Ponderosa Pine "Transition"

Piñon–Juniper "Upper Sonoran" a.p. 14–15"/37cm

Juniper "Upper Sonoran"

Grassland "Upper Sonoran" a.p. 7–10"/18–25cm

no large trees except to those rooted in subsurface water

a.p. = annual precipitation

3,255m / 10,678'
10,000'
9,000'
8,000'
7,000'
6,000'
5,000'

9,800'
3,000m
2,500m
2,000m
1,500m

9,800'
7,800'
7,200'

7,800'
7,200'
6,100'

6,100'
5,500'

warm, southwest facing slope

To Albuquerque

To Tijeras

Each tree's range has an upper limit—the altitude where it is too cold for that tree to grow, and a lower limit—where it is too dry!

After an illustration appearing in Albuquerque's Environmental Story: Toward a Sustainable Community, Hy and Joan Rosner, 3rd ed., 1996.

10

Eventually, after perhaps fifty years, the mixed-confer forest will have returned—until another lightning strike, or powerful gust of wind, or clearing by humans.

Because such a plant community, if left undisturbed, is the end of succession, it is called a climax community. The accompanying chart shows the climax forests for the various elevations in the Sandias. Yet in reality, plant succession is a far more complex and dynamic process than is suggested here, and the factors that influence it are many and often subtle.

Plant succession is occurring now throughout the Sandias. You can observe it in the western foothills in the Albuquerque Open Space, where grasses and shrubs are returning to lands that once had been grazed. You also can observe it at the North 10K Trailhead, where shrubs such as raspberries are colonizing an area cleared by humans. By learning the climax forest types for each elevation and by being aware of the stages plant communities go through to reach climax forests, you will soon come to appreciate that the life of the mountain is constantly changing and adapting, just as are human societies.

In addition to reflecting elevational and successional variation, the plants and animals of the Sandias also respond to a third set of changes—those of the seasons. From the rosy finches of the arctic arriving at the crest in late November to golden eagles migrating northward past the HawkWatch site in March, from the dappling of hillsides by evening primrose flowers in May to the appearance in the fall of purple *tunas* on prickly pear cacti, from the arrival of mourning cloak butterflies and the swarming of ladybugs in spring to the disappearance of rattlesnakes in winter—from the grandest scale to the smallest, the cycles and rhythms of seasons in the Sandias are an endless source of fascination and wonder for those who love these mountains.

All these—elevation, natural succession, and the cycles of the seasons—are manifestations of the never-ending dance of nature in which the individual plants and animals in the mountains participate—as do we.

CHAPTER 3
Weather in the Sandia Mountains

Paul E. Stubbe

Latitude, elevation, seasons, and a north-to-south orientation of the mountains are the primary determinants of weather in the Sandias. Sandia Crest, at 10,678 feet in elevation, receives an average annual precipitation of 30 inches. The eastern foothills receive an average of 14 inches and the western foothills even less, 8.4 inches. Precipitation varies greatly throughout the year, with summer having significantly more precipitation than winter. The Sandias generally receive almost half of the yearly total during July, August, and September. Thunderstorms are very common in the summer, because the mountains create a vertical movement of unstable moist air. During late afternoon and evenings, tall cumulonimbus clouds continually develop and create brief storms of rain and lightning usually accompanied by high winds; however, clouds can form in all seasons over the Sandias. Summer rains frequently evolve from tropical air masses that move to the eastern slopes of the Sandias. Westerly storms, originating over the Pacific, lose most of their moisture over mountains to the west and thus have little influence on rainfall in the Sandias.

Generally, snow begins to fall on the crest in October and can remain on the ground until June, particularly at the higher elevations, on north-facing slopes, and in deeper canyons. Even on a sunny August day snow showers can develop at the higher altitudes in the afternoon. Snowfall at the crest can exceed one hundred inches in a year.

On the crest, measurements reveal over thirty inches of precipitation in some years and as low as thirteen inches in others. The Sandias are reservoirs of moisture that hold winter snows and summer rains, particularly at the upper elevations. Much of the heavy rain from summer storms becomes surface runoff, while a gradually melting snow pack releases more moisture to the ground-water reservoirs. Ground water flows through cracks and crevices of rocks and may appear again as surface water through a series of springs throughout the mountain or remain underground. Surface water travels downward in streams, particularly after heavy rains, but eventually it too becomes part of the ground water.

Temperatures also vary widely throughout the year and within any given day. Elevation and season of the year are the most important temperature determinants. July is normally the warmest month and January the coldest. The average temperature gradient on the Sandias usually ranges from 3 to 5 degrees Fahrenheit for every one thousand feet of altitude. Temperatures at Sandia Crest can be 15 to 20 degrees, or more, lower than the western foothills and Albuquerque on a hot summer day. Cloudless skies and low levels of water vapor and heat-absorbing

Lenticular Clouds

Moist air carried by the prevailing westerlies must rise significantly to get over the ten-thousand-foot Sandias and thus lenticular clouds often form over the mountains. These attractive smooth clouds, resembling curved flakes of flint, result from moist air briefly condensing at the crest before descending.

gasses in the air at higher altitudes cause temperatures to decrease sharply when the sun goes down. Cold, wind, and dampness are a dangerous combination. Heat loss, or hypothermia, is one of the most serious problems for hikers in the Sandias any time of the year.

The Sandias are aligned north to south, with east and west flanks. Maximum temperatures on the west flank are higher than those on the eastern slopes, because the sun's rays on the east come in the morning when temperatures start to rise from nighttime minimum temperatures. By the time the sun's rays reach the west flank, the air has been warming since sunrise. The air is already warm when the sunlight becomes most intense. Also, forest density affects temperature.

To Learn More:

Benedict, Audrey DeLella. *A Sierra Club Naturalist's Guide: The Southern Rockies.* San Francisco, Calif.: Sierra Club Books, 1991.

Tuan, Yi-Fu, Cyril W. Everard, and Jerold G. Widdison. *The Climate of New Mexico.* Santa Fe, N.Mex.: State Planning Office, 1969.

CHAPTER 4

Fire in the Sandia Mountains

Sam Beard and Mary Stuever

Fire in the Southwest Ecosystems

Since the dawn of time, lightning has started most wildfires. Over many millennia, fire has influenced the life cycle of plants and animals and plant and animal communities. The fire cycle of a forest leads from bare ground to new meadows to vigorous seedlings and saplings, then to trees, then fast-growing closed tree stands, and finally mature and old-growth forests. Since the arrival of people to this region more than ten thousand years ago, humans have also started wildfires both accidentally and intentionally.

On average in the Southwest (Arizona and New Mexico) under pre-European settlement conditions, piñon-juniper and desert grasslands burned on a 5- to 30-year cycle depending on the history of wet and dry periods and the accumulation of vegetative materials. Fire in the ponderosa-pine and oak elevation zone burned at a low intensity on a 7- to 15-year cycle. Forests in the fir-aspen zone burned on a cycle of 60–250 years or greater.

Wildfires in the Sandias

In the Sandias, topography has played an important role in the mountain's fire history. Due to the rocky, drier environmental conditions found on the west front of the mountains, fires have not been able to spread readily. The gentle east slope, however, lends itself to landscape-scale events.

In a preliminary tree-ring study, dendrochronologists Chris Baisan and Tom Swetnam of the University of Arizona have given us a glimpse of the fire history of the Sandia Mountains over the last six hundred years. Prior to Spanish settlement, the limited tree-ring record indicates a higher fire frequency than that expected from natural ignition and an increase in fires during wetter conditions. This pattern suggests that humans had a role in setting some of the fires.

Whereas, throughout the Southwest, wildfires have been excluded in most forests for over one hundred years, the Sandia story points to two hundred years of limited fire activity. The area's early settlement history may explain this anomaly. With the increased prosperity of Spanish settlements in the late 1700s, some landowners were grazing as many as two million head of livestock, primarily sheep, in the area by 1800. This grazing pressure would have severely limited the availability of grasses that provide the fuel for fires to spread.

After the devastating fires of 1910 in the western United States, fire was viewed as destructive and dangerous. In addition to the reduced fuel loading from excessive grazing, fires were actively suppressed. By the time responsible

The fire of July, 1967, burns on the west side of the Sandias.

grazing strategies increased grass availability, fire-fighters had developed suppression tactics that resulted in most fires being extinguished within the first
twenty-four hours. Only in the past fifteen years has that policy been reevaluated.

Now that approximately one hundred thousand people live adjacent to the
Sandia Mountains, fire that is viewed as a necessary part of the forest ecology is
also viewed as a serious threat to people and must be carefully used and watched
and suppressed when necessary. In addition, as fires generally spread faster
uphill, most fires if left unattended would burn to the crest, where significant
economic investment has been made in radio and microwaves towers.
Therefore, the opportunity of reintroducing a natural role for fire in the Sandias
is particularly challenging.

Most of the wildfires in the Sandia Mountains are caused by lightning strikes. In a typical year on the Sandia Ranger District, twenty to twenty-five wildfires occur; most are contained before exceeding two acres in area. Visitors can easily view forest regeneration, succession, and black snags in two wildfire areas. On July 2, 1967, a fire consumed the trees in one of the canyons on the steep west side of the mountains. To look down into this canyon from the ridgeline, hike one mile north of Sandia Crest on Crest Trail 130. To visit the second area, in Capulin Canyon, burned in the Cooper Fire in June 1990, drive two miles from Balsam Glade Picnic Area down State Road 165 or drive up State Road 165 six miles from Placitas. This fire burned on both sides of the road and was human-caused. Bottle rockets were found in the area where the fire started.

Although landscape-scale fires have not occurred in modern history, the Sandias have experienced large fires in the past. Tree-ring records as well as stand replacement dating have indicated that the Sandias had significant fires in the mid-fifteenth century and the mid-eighteenth century. Oral histories and vast fields of Gambel oak on the north side of the Sandias also hint of a large fire in the early to mid-1800s.

Present Forest Conditions

The present forest condition of dense groves of small trees was caused by suppression of wildfire during the twentieth century and reduction of grass fuels due to livestock grazing in the nineteenth century. Previously, low-intensity fires in the pine forest killed many of the small saplings and burned out accumulations of forest litter, which resulted in open, park-like forests of mostly large trees.

With recent multi-year drought conditions, today's overly dense forests are primed for a large, catastrophic fire. Therefore, it is especially important to prevent fires from igniting during extreme fire conditions. Recently, the Cibola National Forest has closed the forest to public access when the fuel conditions are so dry that a fire would travel rapidly and cover a large area.

Fuel Breaks in the Sandia Mountains

Wildfires in forests with high fuel loads tend to be high-intensity fires, which can consume whole stands of trees and frequently homes. To protect homes and the forest along the wildland-urban interface (WUI) around the Sandia Mountains, a two-hundred-foot-wide fuel break has been mechanically cleared for several miles on the east slopes of the Sandias. You can see a fuel break by hiking one-half mile along a closed road east of the entrance to Cienega Picnic Area. Prescribed fires are also used to reduce fuel loads, and piles of slash (downed limbs) from the thinning projects are burned or chipped. Fuelwood permits are also sold to reduce fuel loads in these areas.

Role of Aspen in the Fire Cycle and Aspen Regeneration Projects

In the higher elevations of the Sandia Mountains, aspen trees are an important pioneer species of the forest, usually the first tree species to appear after a fire or logging project. Aspen trees sprout from suckers in the ground, cloning themselves and creating some of the largest living organisms in the West. As the aspen grove grows, it provides the needed shade to allow young fir and spruce trees to take hold. Spruce and fir often only sprout in the shade of other trees. The spruce and fir trees grow larger and eventually shade out the sun-loving aspen trees. The aspens will die and fall only to reappear after a fire or a logging operation opens a place to the sun.

Wildfire suppression has reduced the opportunities for new aspen groves, and the acreage of aspen forests has declined significantly. Some foresters say up to 60 percent of the aspen groves have died in the Southwest. In the Sandia Mountains, the Crest Aspen Regeneration Project was initiated to increase the number of aspens and to provide additional important wildlife food. Wildlife specialists have identified 221 animal species, including deer, elk, rabbits, rodents, and birds, that feed on aspen buds, twigs, and bark. Large trees are removed through small logging operations in patches of five to thirty acres, followed by either a pile burning or broadcast burning to provide ideal conditions for aspen regeneration through sprouting. You can visit young groves at the following three sites along the Crest Highway: (1) west of Ellis Trail about one-half mile north of the highway, (2) uphill from the South 10K Trailhead parking lot, and (3) below the North 10K Trailhead parking area.

East Mountain Interagency Fire Protection Association (EMIFPA)

EMIFPA was organized after two relatively small fires and a large one occurred almost simultaneously in 1989. The Coyote and Raven fires in the Manzanita Mountains south of I-40 burned at the same time. The Armijo Fire in the Sandia Mountains near Sandia Park occurred a day or two later. The Coyote Fire was devastating, completely burning approximately 480 acres. (Any fire over 100 acres is classified as a large fire.) These fires were not only a serious threat to the communities on the east side but also severely stretched the resources of firefighting agencies. Authorities recognized the need for cooperation among the various firefighting organizations along the WUI (wildland-urban interface) on the east side of the mountains. By 2003, EMIFPA was made up of twenty-seven federal, state, municipal, and private agencies concerned with wildfire protection and suppression in all areas adjacent to the Sandia Mountains and the Sandia Ranger District, including not only the East Mountain area but also Placitas to the north, Albuquerque to the west, and Isleta Pueblo to the south.

CHAPTER 5

Geology of the Sandia Mountains

Jayne Aubele, Larry Crumpler,
James Deal, Spencer Lucas, and Paul E. Stubbe

Building a Mountain

Have you ever wondered why mountains are present in some regions and not in others? At first sight, all mountains may look alike, but if you look a little closer you will see that each mountain tells its own geological story.

Mountains can be formed in many ways. Some are built by volcanoes, while others are produced by the folding or crumpling of rocks as though you were pushing a rug from two sides. But the Sandia Mountains are the result of a third and unusual mechanism: rifting.

A rift occurs when the Earth's crust is thinning and splitting apart, producing a long, linear, topographically low area with well-defined margins. Much of New Mexico's landscape, topography, biodiversity, and "geodiversity" are related to a rift. In fact, there would be no Sandia Mountains if it were not for the rift, because the Sandias are the raised eastern margin of the rift at Albuquerque. This rift extends from southern Colorado to northern Mexico and has been called the Rio Grande Rift, to honor the river, but the rift came first and then the river took advantage of the low linear valley and flowed down it to the south.

The Rio Grande Rift is geologically young and still forming, and so are the Sandia Mountains. As the rift has dropped downward, the margins of the rift have lifted up, especially the eastern margin. The Sandias, and the long chain of mountains to the south (the Manzanita, Manzano, and Los Pinos Mountains), have all been lifted up and tilted toward the east, like a trap door opening upward with its hinges on the east. That is why the Sandias' steep western face looks so different from the gently sloping eastern face. (See diagram page 20.)

Young Mountains

The Sandias are geologically young, as mountains go, though the rocks comprising them are very, very old. Before about 10 million years ago, there were plains and low hills where the Sandias are today. Ten million years sounds old, but in the span of 4.6 billion years of geologic time, it is practically "yesterday." It is important to understand that the Sandias are not part of the Rocky Mountains. Geologically, the two are very different mountain ranges. The Rockies were formed by folding and crumpling of the entire western United States at the end of the age of dinosaurs (about 65 million years ago) and extend south into New Mexico, ending with the Sangre de Cristo Mountains east of Santa Fe.

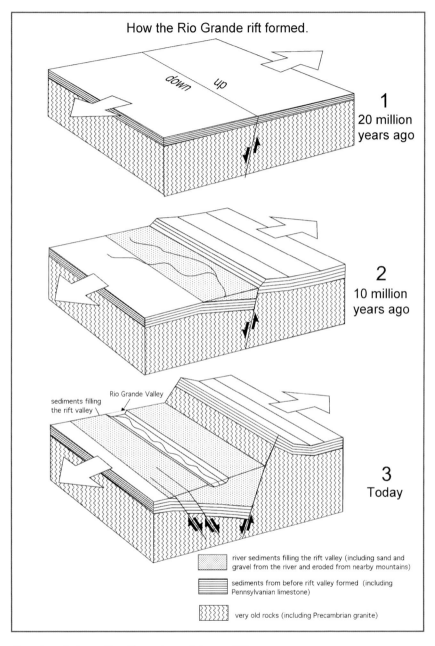

How the Rio Grande rift formed.

down   up

1
20 million
years ago

2
10 million
years ago

sediments filling
the rift valley

Rio Grande Valley

3
Today

river sediments filling the rift valley (including sand and gravel from the river and eroded from nearby mountains)

sediments from before rift valley formed (including Pennsylvanian limestone)

very old rocks (including Precambrian granite)

Drawings interpreting three stages (at 20 million years ago, 10 million years ago, and the present) of the formation of the Rio Grande Rift at Albuquerque.

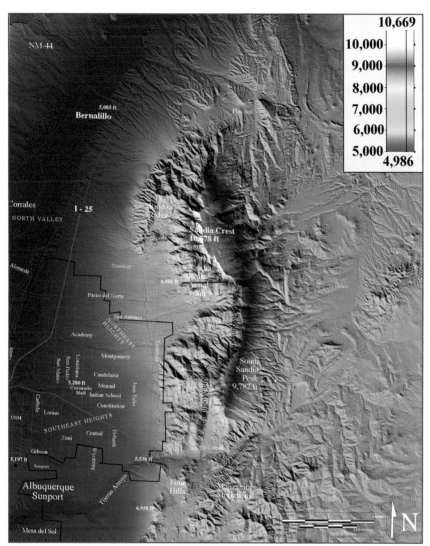

General topography of the Sandia Mountains. Colors relate to general bands of elevation; blue represents around five thousand feet, white represents around ten thousand feet.

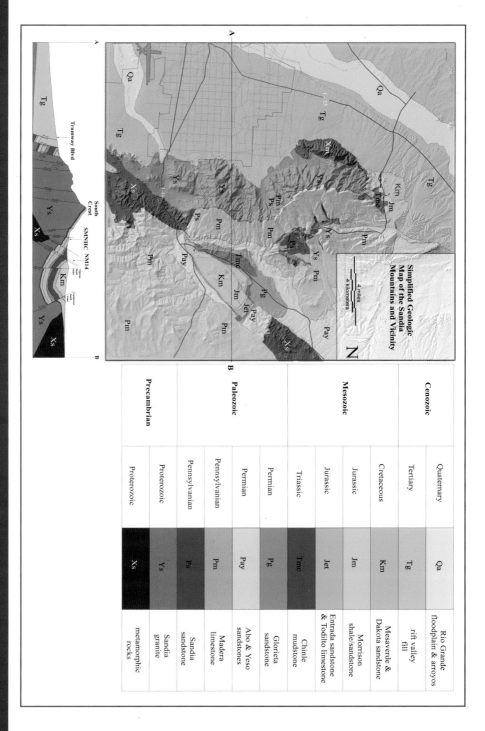

Simplified Geologic Map of the Sandia Mountains and Vicinity

Cenozoic	Quaternary		Qa	Rio Grande floodplain & arroyos
	Tertiary		Tg	rift valley fill
Mesozoic	Cretaceous		Km	Mesaverde & Dakota sandstone
	Jurassic		Jm	Morrison shale/sandstone
	Jurassic		Jet	Entrada sandstone & Todilto limestone
	Triassic		Tmc	Chinle mudstone
	Permian		Pg	Glorieta sandstone
	Permian		Pay	Abo & Yeso sandstones
Paleozoic	Permian		Pm	Madera limestone
	Pennsylvanian		Ps	Sandia sandstone
	Pennsylvanian			Sandia sandstone
Precambrian	Proterozoic		Ys	Sandia granite
	Proterozoic		Xs	metamorphic rocks

1.7 Billion Years of History

A geologic map tells a story of what has happened to a particular region through-out time, with each color representing a different rock layer; the map also shows the areas where the rock is exposed at the surface. Next to the map, the various rock layers shown in the map are "stacked" with the oldest on the bottom and the youngest on the top.

In the geologic map of the Sandias, a staggering amount of time—1.7 billion years—is represented. The oldest rocks are the metamorphic rocks (1.7 billion) and the Sandia granite (1.4 billion). Deposited on top of these ancient rocks is a series of rock layers, like a layer cake. As the mountains lifted up and tilted toward the east, the entire stack of rock layers tilted down to the east as well. If you were to walk in a straight line up and over the Sandias, west to east, you would notice that, from the foothills on, the rocks are very old until you reach the crest, and then the rock layers become generally younger and younger as you travel east-ward, down the slope of the Sandias from the crest. (See diagram page 22.)

The Mystery of the Missing Rocks and the Great Unconformity

As you approached the crest from the west, you encountered a geologic mystery. The Sandia granite is about 1.4 billion years old. Deposited directly on top of it and just below the crest is the soft, slope-forming Sandia Formation overlaid by the hard, cliff-forming Madera group that represents the bottom of a 300-million-year-old ocean. So . . . where are the rock layers that were formed between 1.4 billion years ago and 300 million years ago?

Geologists call such time gaps *unconformities,* and the Sandias are such a world-class example that they have called the gap here the *Great Unconformity.* It is readily seen from anywhere west of the crest as the subtle line where the mas-sive, unlayered granite and the cliff of layered sandstone and limestone meet. What happened to the missing rocks?

Though it is possible they were never deposited, in fact, New Mexico's envi-ronment has changed many times during those 1.1 billion years, and any rocks formed then could have been eroded away before the sea laid down the Sandia Formation and the Madera limestone. (See diagrams pages 24–25.)

Page 22: Simplified geologic map of the Sandia Mountains. The colors (and letter designations) show the location of the rock types from each geologic time period. The geology is superimposed on a shaded relief map. Compare this map to the topography shown on page 21; the contact between the Sandia granite and the Madera limestone is at the topographically high Sandia Crest.

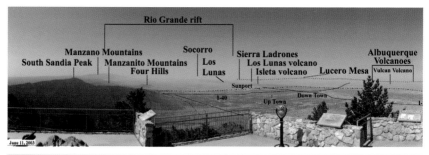

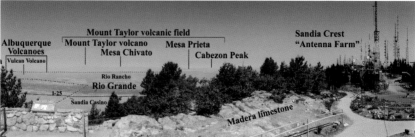

Panoramic view from Sandia Crest showing all of the geologic landscape features visible in a 360° sweep.

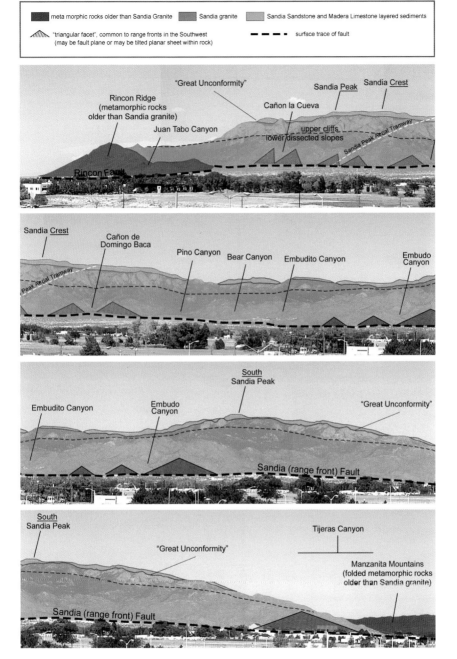

Panel 1:

"Great Unconformity"

Sandia Peak Sandia Crest

Rincon Ridge (metamorphic rocks older than Sandia granite)

Cañon la Cueva

Juan Tabo Canyon

upper cliffs

lower dissected slopes

Sandia Peak Aerial Tramway

Rincon Fault

Panel 2:

Sandia Crest

Cañon de Domingo Baca

Pino Canyon Bear Canyon Embudito Canyon

Embudo Canyon

Peak Aerial Tramway

Panel 3:

South Sandia Peak

Embudito Canyon

Embudo Canyon

"Great Unconformity"

Sandia (range front) Fault

Panel 4:

South Sandia Peak

Tijeras Canyon

"Great Unconformity"

Manzanita Mountains (folded metamorphic rocks older than Sandia granite)

Sandia (range front) Fault

The view from Albuquerque. The west face of the Sandias with colors and lines showing rock type and the location of faults. Colors are the same as shown on page 22 and pages 27–30. The Rincon fault is one of the major rift boundary faults along which the Sandias have been lifted up. The triangular facets between drainage patterns are common in young mountains and may represent movement along faults or erosion along tilted rock.

Don't Take It All for Granite

Many rocks and rock layers of different types and ages are interwoven into the fabric of the Sandias, rocks much older than the mountains themselves. Igneous rocks can be thought of as primary, or first-generation, rocks. They are formed directly from molten material from deep below the Earth's surface. They either cool slowly underground to form rocks such as the Sandia granite, or they are erupted onto the surface by volcanic activity to form rocks such as the black basalt of Petroglyph National Monument on the West Mesa.

Sedimentary rocks are secondary, or second-generation, rocks. They are mostly made up of eroded fragments of first-generation rocks or debris of once-living organisms that are then deposited as layers of sand, silt, clay, or calcite-rich sea-floor mud. These layers ultimately become sandstone, siltstone, shale, and limestone.

If either an igneous or a sedimentary rock is subjected to high pressure and temperature, that rock can be changed into a very different rock called a metamorphic rock. Sandstone when metamorphosed becomes quartzite; shale becomes slate; volcanic lava flows become a rock called greenstone; and granite becomes a rock called gneiss (pronounced "nice"). Examples of all these rocks are found in the Sandias.

Think of a rock as a "time machine" that records what the world was like long ago. Every rock represents both a time period and a past environment. For example, if you have seen sand dunes, you are looking at sandstone in the making. A few million years from now, a geologist will interpret that sandstone as having been formed in a desert environment. In the same way, a geologist today can read the rocks to interpret the environments of the past. As you see the different rocks in the Sandias, driving through Tijeras Canyon, climbing La Luz Trail, or traveling to the crest by tram or road, "read" the rocks as a geologist would.

Pages 27–30: Guide to common rocks of the Sandia Mountains showing their typical appearance as outcrops along the highways or trails and in a close-up view. Colors are the same as shown in diagram page 22.

Geologic Map color	Rock Unit Name	Outcrop View	Hand specimen view	Brief description of the rock
Ps	Pennsylvanian Sandia sandstone			Sandstone, limestone, and claystone grades into the Madera limestone and may represent a change in the environment from seashore to seafloor.
Ys	Proterozoic Sandia granite		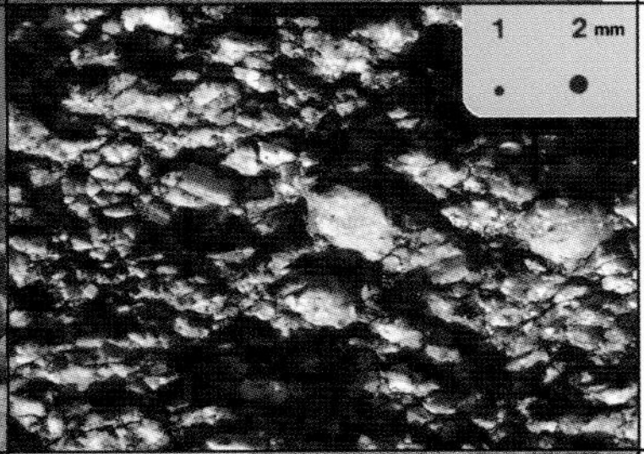	The Sandia granite is very old and formed deep under ground as a large intrusion called a batholith. When the mountains were formed by uplift, the granite was brought to the surface. The Sandia "granite" is actually classified by geologists as a sub-type of the "granite family" of rocks called biotite-monzonite or granodiorite. The Sandia granite contains large crystals cf a pink feldspar mineral, shown here in the hand specimen view.
Xs	Proterozoic metamorphic rocks		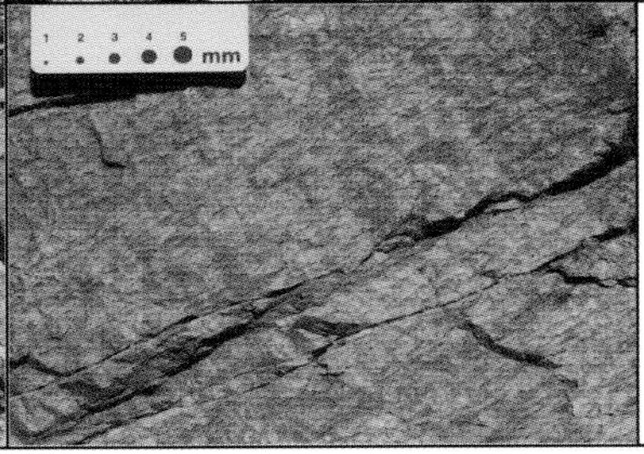	Very old rocks in Tijeras Canyon and the Rincon Ridge that have been altered due to heat and pressure. Many show linear banding. Some rock types represent very old sedimentary rock such as the quartzite in Tijeras Canyon (metamorphosed sandstone), and others may represent old igneous rock (metamorphosed to gneiss) or old volcanic rock (metamorphosed to greenstone). The gneiss of Tijeras Canyon is shown here.

Pm	Pay	Pg	Geologic Map color
Pennsylvanian Madera limestone	Permian Abo & Yeso sandstones	Permian Glorieta sandstone	**Rock Unit Name**
			Outcrop View
			Hand specimen view
Gray limestone with abundant marine fossils. Deposited at the bottom of a very ancient sea.	Red sandstone deposited by rivers and along the edge of a marine environment.	Well-sorted beach and shoreline sandstone.	Brief description of the rock

	Tmc	Jet	Jm
Geologic Map color			
Rock Unit Name	Triassic Chinle mudstone/sandstone	Jurassic Entrada sandstone & Todilto limestone	Jurassic Morrison shale/sandstone
Outcrop View			
Hand specimen view			
Brief description of the rock	Red mudstone deposited in a swampy floodplain environment. Contains some ledges of sandstone and shale, and abundant pieces of petrified wood.	Sandstone deposited in a Sahara-like sand sea (Entrada) and limestone and gypsum deposited within a large saline lake (Todilto). (The gypsum layer at the top of the Todilto limestone is shown here.)	Green-gray and maroon mudstone, with sandstone and shale, deposited over an extremely large floodplain associated with many rivers.

Km	Tg	Qa	Geologic Map color
Mesaverde & Dakota sandstone	lower Pleistocene to Miocene rift valley fill	Rio Grande floodplain & arroyos	Rock Unit Name
			Outcrop View
			Hand specimen view
Sandstone and shale deposited by an ocean that covered much of western North America during this geologic period. May represent seafloor, beach, or shoreline environments. Includes thin layers of coal.	Sandstone, sand, gravel, cobbles, and boulders eroded from mountains surrounding the rift valley and deposited as fill within the rift valley.	Loosely consolidated sand and gravel deposited by the river.	Brief description of the rock

Orbicular Granite

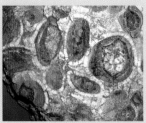

The Sandia Mountains are among the few places worldwide where you can find orbicular granite. Its name comes from minerals in the granite being arranged in spherical nodules that resemble eyes and are called "orbs," or "orbicules." They are one to five inches in diameter and appear to float in the regular granite. Each orb consists of a core of typical granite surrounded by a zone of dark-colored mica alternating with the mineral feldspar, and finally with an outer shell of feldspar. Orbicular granite is extremely rare even in the Sandias; if you find some, please take only photographs.

Igneous Rocks

GRANITE

Granite is formed by the slow cooling of large bodies of molten rock, or magma, that solidify underground and never reach the surface. Ancient granite forms the core of many mountain ranges throughout the world. In fact, Sandia granite is one of the oldest rocks visible at the surface in New Mexico; it is around 1.4 billion years old.

The Sandia granite consists primarily of quartz, two kinds of the mineral feldspar (pink and white), and a dark brown mica called biotite. The pink feldspar helps to give the Sandia granite its pinkish overall appearance. As the granite weathers and erodes, the quartz and feldspar form the sand that is deposited in the arroyos and foothills at the western base of the mountains. Within this sand, you will find black sand that clings to a magnet. This is the mineral magnetite weathering out of the granite.

Although we think of granite as being very hard and durable, the rock actually begins to weather and erode as soon as it is exposed at the surface. The Sandia granite is easily eroded, forming rounded boulders on the west and south and fragmented outcrops on the road to Sandia Crest on the east.

PEGMATITES AND APLITE DIKES

Large areas of the Sandia granite and the metamorphic rock of the Rincon Ridge (the ridge east of Sandia Pueblo in front of the main mountains) are cut by long, linear fractures in which molten rock later solidified to form dikes. The larger dikes in the Sandias are a specific kind called *pegmatite*. As molten granite cools and adjusts to becoming solid rock, the fractures that occur are filled by large crystals of quartz, feldspar, and a translucent mica called muscovite. The pegmatite dikes can also contain less-common minerals such as garnet, tourmaline, beryl, or pyrite (fool's gold). Very large pegmatites in other mountain ranges are sometimes mined for valuable minerals but not those in the Sandias.

If you hike along the Sandias' western foothill trails, you will see many small pegmatite dikes cutting across the granite oriented east-west, northwest, or northeast. From I-25, with late afternoon lighting, you can see large white lines cutting through the darker metamorphic rocks of the Rincon Ridge. These white lines are pegmatite dikes, up to three thousand feet long and ten feet wide.

Also common are *aplite dikes.* These are thinner than pegmatite dikes and are filled by fine, sugary crystals of quartz and feldspar.

Sedimentary Rocks

LIMESTONE

At the Sandia Crest, you are standing on rock that is now more than ten thousand feet above sea level, but you are also walking on the bottom of an ancient sea that covered most of New Mexico about 300 million years ago, during the geologic time period called the Pennsylvanian. At that time, New Mexico was located almost on the equator—and of course at sea level. Only a few islands and hills stood above the sea, and the Sandia Mountains did not yet exist. It was during this time that the Madera limestone upon which you are standing was laid down.

Limestone originates in the calcium carbonate shells of marine animals: clams, snails, plankton, and many others. When these animals die, their shells accumulate on the sea bottom, and their organic body parts decompose. What remains is the calcium carbonate of the shells. Over time, with the addition of calcium carbonate precipitating out of the sea water, the shells eventually become limestone.

All limestone you find in the Sandias will contain marine fossils, and with searching you can discover some. The most common fossils found at the crest are *crinoids* (CRY-noids), animals resembling plants whose stalks look like stacked poker chips; *brachiopods,* which superficially resemble clam shells; *gastropods,* or snails; *horn corals,* which appear in the limestone as curved or grooved cones; and *bryozoans,* whose long, rectangular fossils resemble a net or grid. But most of the shells and shell fragments comprising the limestone are microscopic, thus the Madera limestone usually looks gray and smooth.

SANDSTONE

When rocks erode, some minerals within the rock survive (quartz is particularly hard and durable) and become small, nearly indestructible sand fragments. This sand is moved, usually by water but sometimes by wind, and accumulates (geologists like to say it is "deposited") somewhere such as in a river bank, lake shore, or dune field. Over a long time, the sand grains are buried and compressed and cemented together by clay or calcite—and become sandstone.

As you hike the trails or drive along the roads you may see whitish, tan, and

Fossils from the Madera limestone: **A.** *Crinoid stem fragments; these discs were originally part of a stem that attached the animal to the sea floor.* **B.** *Horn coral* (Lophophyllidium); *a solitary coral.* **C.** *Brachiopod* (Neospirifer); *one species of a varied and common fossil group.* **D.** *Bryozoa* (Fenestella); *small colonial animals.* **E.** *Gastropod* (Amphiscapha); *characterized by a single coiled, unchambered shell.* **F.** *Brachiopod* (Derbyia); *the two valves of the shell are always slightly different in size and shape. Scale: single large crinoid disc is one-half inch in diameter.*

buff sandstone or red sandstone. In general, the red sandstones were formed about 290 million to 200 million years ago during the geologic periods known as the Permian and Triassic, when what is now central New Mexico was covered by flat meandering rivers and muddy plains. You can see the Permian-age red rocks (Abo and Yeso sandstones) at the intersection of I-40 and NM 14 just north of the village of Tijeras. The Triassic red sandstone (Chinle formation) forms the red soil and rolling hills north of the town of Cedar Crest along NM 14.

The whitish to tan or buff sandstones generally were formed 208 million to 65 million years ago (during the Jurassic and Cretaceous geologic periods). These time periods covered the heyday of the dinosaurs to their end. During this long span of geologic time, New Mexico's environment changed many times, and with each change, a different color or type of sandstone was deposited.

During the Jurassic Period, this area was first a Sahara-like desert with wind-blown dunes (Entrada sandstone), then a great saline lake (Todilto limestone and gypsum), then a river lowland (Morrison sandstone-mudstone). And then, during the Cretaceous Period, the sea covered what is now New Mexico once again, and this area was a sandy beach with intermittent mud flats and tidal pools on the edge of an encroaching ocean. The tan to buff sandstones from this time period (Mesaverde and Dakota sandstones) can be seen in outcrops along NM 14 between the village of Tijeras and Cedar Crest.

Metamorphic Rocks

Rocks can metamorphose, or change, if they are put under stress as in mountain-building or faulting, or if they are near a body of magma. After metamorphosis, a rock takes on a totally different character.

All of the metamorphic rocks of the Sandias are very old; they range in age from 1.4 to 1.7 billion years. This means that they represent parent rocks (the original rocks prior to metamorphism) that are even older than the Sandia granite dated at 1.4 billion years old. Great places to see metamorphic rocks in the Sandias are Tijeras Canyon, Rincon Ridge, and especially the west side of the Forest Service road leading to Juan Tabo Picnic Area.

GNEISS AND SCHIST

When granite is metamorphosed, it becomes *gneiss,* which looks a little like granite but instead of having a random salt-and-pepper appearance, it usually appears to be banded or layered with alternating dark and light lines. The metamorphic rock called *schist* also looks a little like gneiss, but it has a shiny satin or silk-like appearance caused by the stacking of platy grains of white mica, or muscovite.

QUARTZITE AND GREENSTONE

When ancient sandstone is metamorphosed it becomes a very hard light-colored rock called *quartzite.* When you drive east through Tijeras Canyon on NM 333 (old US 66), you may notice a high-standing ridge, crossing the canyon near a large curve in the highway near the I-40 underpass, that shows a gray color along the ridge line. This quartzite ridge was once a thick layer of sandstone.

When ancient lava is metamorphosed it can become the very evenly colored dark-green rock called *greenstone.* The Sandias are *not* volcanic mountains, so the presence of very old greenstone in Tijeras Canyon tells us that lava flows once occurred in this area long before the mountains formed.

Faults and Other Complexities

The metamorphic rocks of Tijeras Canyon and the Rincon Ridge east of Sandia Pueblo form a sort of halo of rocks around the Sandia granite. They represent a complex of ancient sedimentary and volcanic rocks, and a very long and complicated geologic history, involving faults.

A fault is simply a fracture in the Earth's crust along which rocks on either side have moved. Faults exist everywhere, but some are larger and more active than others. Frequently, faults in the crust form lines of weakness that are reactivated again and again over geologic time. The fault that marks Tijeras Canyon is actually a zone, oriented northeast-southwest, of several related faults. Geologists have evidence that the Tijeras fault zone is actually much older than the Sandia Mountains, and present-day Tijeras Canyon simply marks the trace of the fault's latest movement. In general, this fault zone has moved in a type of "shear" motion that has dragged and

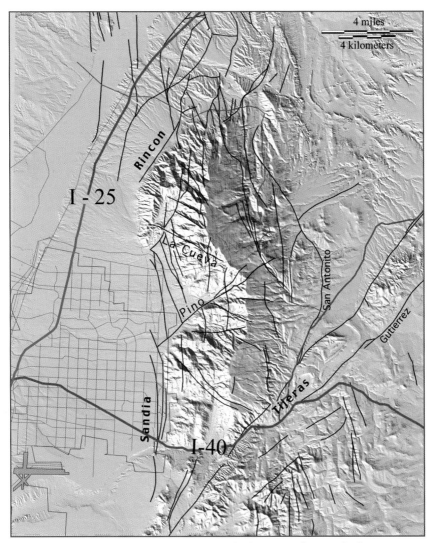

Shaded relief map of the Sandias showing the location of major faults.
In general most of the north-south oriented faults are normal faults,
with rocks on the east side of most faults uplifted above rocks on the
west side. The Rincon fault is one of the major rift boundary faults.
The Tijeras fault is part of a very old fault zone along which the rocks
have sheared past each other horizontally.

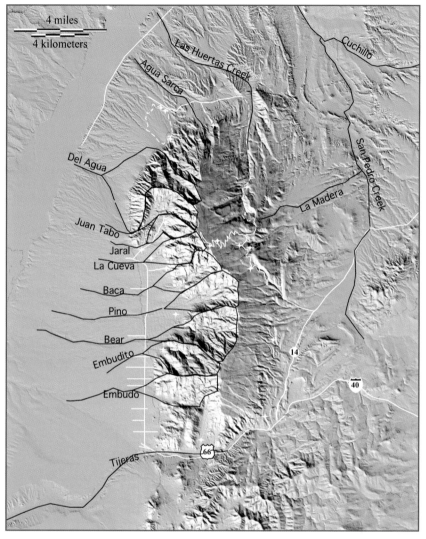

Shaded relief map of the Sandias showing the major drainage canyons.

offset rocks of different types—very appropriate for a canyon named for the Spanish word for scissors!

The Rincon Ridge is a mass of rock that has been dragged up along the boundary fault of the west side of the Sandias. You can see the line of the fault zone in the fault map and in the geologic map, where the rock units suddenly change, and the Sandia granite stops abruptly against the metamorphic rocks. (See map page 35.)

Snow, Springs, and Arroyos

Water, necessary for life, also has shaped the topography of the Sandias and determined where people have settled and how they have used the mountains. As rain and snow fall on the Sandias, the water wears away the rock through erosion. The water also finds a way into or between the rock layers and begins to travel down through the mountain to the level of the surrounding plains. This underground water can be forced upward and onto the surface to form a spring. There are many springs, fed seasonally by snow melt, on the mountains' east flank because the water is following along the rock layers that are tilted to the east. A few springs, such as Cienega Spring, have actively formed deposits of travertine, rock produced by the evaporation of water containing dissolved limestone.

Water running off the Sandia Mountains' granite surface has carved arroyos and canyon systems that sometimes are short and very steep, especially on the west side. Each canyon or arroyo ends in an alluvial fan of loose surface sediments carried by water and deposited at the mountains' base.

As you approach the Sandias and Albuquerque along I-25 from the north, you will notice an inclined slope leading from the river to the base of the mountains. Much of Albuquerque is built on that slope, which is called a pediment. It consists of the uplifted bedrock at the foot of the Sandias and a series of coalescing alluvial fans of sediment eroded off the mountains, which geologists know by the Spanish word *bajada*. (See map page 36.)

Minerals of the Sandia Mountains
(see also chapter 8, "Human Presence in the Sandia Mountains")

More than a thousand years ago, prehistoric people living near the mountains were the first human users of the Sandias' geologic resources. Today's hikers have found scrapers and projectile points. Some of these were carried from as far away as Pedernal and Polvadera Peaks near Abiquiu in northern New Mexico, but many were made locally from chert nodules found in the limestones of the Sandias.

The arrival of the Spanish on the North American continent began the European quest for precious metals, particularly gold and silver, in the mountains of the Southwest. Archives in Mexico and Spain report five lost mines in this region, with gold, silver, and other precious metals extracted from the Sandias. The remnants of smelters from that period provide further evidence of early mining activity. The names of mines and deposits offer a sense of romance and wonder for what could have been a "big strike": *La mina de ventana* (window) or *La mina de la escalera* (ladder)—both "lost"—and from more recent times, mines named Blue Sky, Capulin, La Madera, La Luz, Shakespeare, Longfellow, Ortiz, and York.

The Sandias on Mars!
The geologist Larry Crumpler, among the contributors to the *Field Guide to the Sandia Mountains*, was also the only scientist from New Mexico on the 2004 Mars project that landed two rovers on the red planet. The project surveyed and named many rocks on the surface, and one was dubbed Sandia (guess who proposed that name!). Well, why not? Mars is red— just like the inside of a watermelon!

Gold, silver, copper, lead, and zinc were the principal metals taken from mineral deposits in the mountains. Barite and fluorite were also mined. Occasionally, the modern hiker will find small pieces of the copper minerals malachite (dark green) and chrysocolla (often mistaken for turquoise) scattered on a ridge near an old prospect. The reality, however, is that the Sandia Mountains have produced only small amounts of economically valuable minerals.

The most important economic resource of the Sandia Mountains area is limestone used to manufacture cement. While there is abundant limestone in the Sandias, much of it is in National Forest and Wilderness-designated land and much contains too many impurities for the manufacturing process. The most accessible limestone is in the Tijeras region, where a large cement plant is located south of the town of Tijeras and readily seen from I-40 and from many of the hiking trails on the south end of the mountain. Other minerals needed in the manufacture of cement are available from nearby sources.

At one time, small manufacturers made lime (calcium oxide) for plaster and agricultural uses from the same limestone that is used today to produce cement. Remnants of a few old lime kilns still stand in Tijeras Canyon. Shale and clay from the Sandias have been used for making bricks. Rocks from the mountains have been used for construction of dwellings or for landscaping, but the Sandia granite, although beautiful, is not durable enough for decorative building purposes. Thin seams of coal occur locally; one is visible in the road cut opposite the Doc Long Picnic Area. These seams are just a few inches thick, discontinuous, and scattered. Farther north, near the now-abandoned mining town of Hagan and east of Tijeras, coal reserves were mined intermittently until the 1930s.

Reading the Rocks along Highways and Trails

La Luz Trail

The road to this trailhead takes you between the Rincon Ridge, with its old meta-morphic rocks, and the main mass of Sandia granite to the east. As you climb the switchbacks you can see the power of erosion. The rounded boulders you see around you are connected to the bedrock in most cases and are being formed by erosion around an unweathered core. Spires and canyons have been eroded into the granite. Finally, quite close to the top, you will begin to see the layered ledges of the Sandia formation and Madera limestone. You have now walked across the Great Unconformity, from rocks that formed 1.4 billion years ago to rocks that formed 300 million years ago; and you are now in an ocean environment.

Page 41: Geologic map along La Luz Trail showing rock types and locations of faults and dikes along the trail. Colors are the same as shown on page 22.

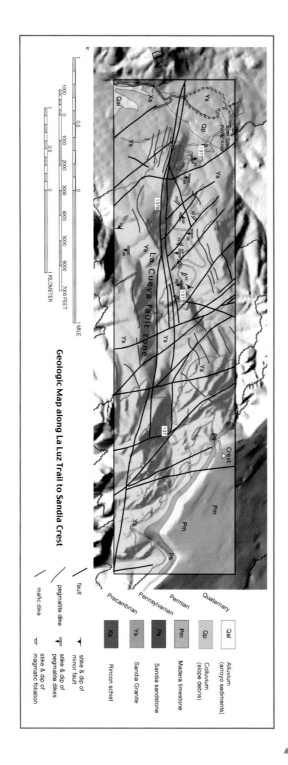

Geologic Map along La Luz Trail to Sandia Crest

fault

pegmatite dike

mafic dike

strike & dip of minor fault

strike & dip of pegmatite dikes

strike & dip of magmatic foliation

Precambrian

Pennsylvanian

Permian

Quaternary

Ks — Rincon schist

Ys — Sandia Granite

Ps — Sandia sandstone

Pm — Madera limestone

Qp — Colluvium (slope debris)

Qal — Alluvium (arroyo sediments)

Tram Route

When you walk up the steps to the tram entry level you are walking up the scarp formed by movement along the eastern margin fault of the Rio Grande Rift. The Sandias lifted up along this fault. The last large movement of the fault occurred several thousand years ago. From the tram, look down as you start the ascent, and you will see the spheroidal boulders (tors) of granite produced by erosion at the base of the mountains. As you travel higher, the granite has been eroded into thick spires and ridges that follow fractures produced along joints in the rock. Keep an eye out for pegmatite dikes cutting through the granite. Near the second tower, to the north, is a landslide scar where approximately four thousand tons of rock slid away in 1936. To the south, you can see the large canyons formed by water and the alluvial fans they have deposited. As you go over the Great Unconformity, brush- and tree-covered ledges are formed by the layered sedimentary rocks at the crest. At the top, you can look down the line of the mountains forming the eastern margin of the rift and across the rift to the west. The Albuquerque volcanoes mark the center of the Rio Grande Rift at Albuquerque.

Page 43: Shaded relief and topographic contour map (top) and geologic map (bottom) along the Aerial Tram route showing rock types and locations of faults and dikes. Colors depict the rock types in same colors as shown on page 22.

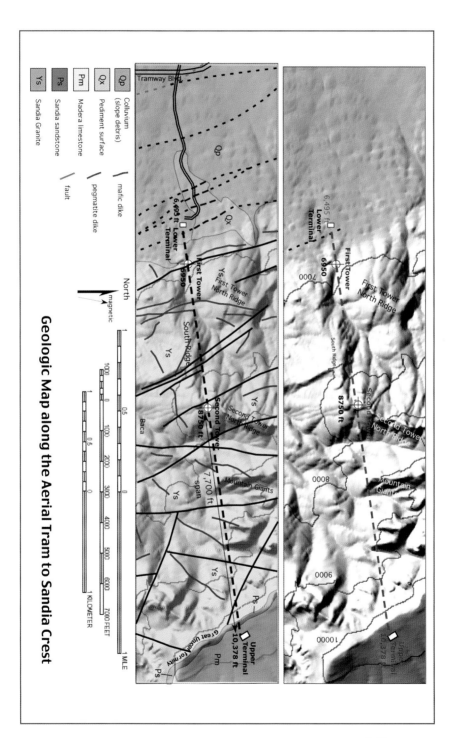

Geologic Map along the Aerial Tram to Sandia Crest

Legend:

- Qp — Colluvium (slope debris)
- Qx — Pediment surface
- Pm — Madera limestone
- Ps — Sandia sandstone
- Ys — Sandia Granite

- mafic dike
- pegmatite dike
- fault

Tijeras Canyon

The spherical boulders of Sandia granite at the entrance to Tijeras Canyon, driving from Albuquerque, are residual boulders formed by weathering along joints or fractures. Most of these boulders are still attached to the bedrock beneath the surface and grade downward into solid granite. When you drive through Tijeras Canyon you are following the trace of a very old fault zone that has moved rocks side by side in a shearing movement. Just past Carnuel, you will see the metamorphic rock called gneiss and a mile beyond, near the I-40 underpass, gray quartzite (metamorphosed sandstone) cuts across the canyon to form the top of a large ridge visible on both sides of the highway. Between here and Tijeras, you will see a few road cuts that look very dark in color; these are formed in greenstone (metamorphosed basalt). The Sandia granite and the metamorphic rocks of Tijeras Canyon are some of the oldest rocks in New Mexico (ranging from 1.7 to 1.4 billion years old). Within these rocks are small, dark-colored igneous dikes called "mafic dikes" that are much younger (Tertiary Period). At Tijeras, the red slopes to the north mark the mudstone and sandstone of the Abo formation. These red rocks were deposited by rivers moving lazily along a flat plain, during the age of reptiles about 270 million years ago, before the age of dinosaurs began.

Page 45: Shaded relief map with rock types, faults, and dikes shown along the route of I-40 through Tijeras Canyon (from just west of Carnuel to just east of Tijeras, N.Mex.). Colors are the same as shown on page 22.

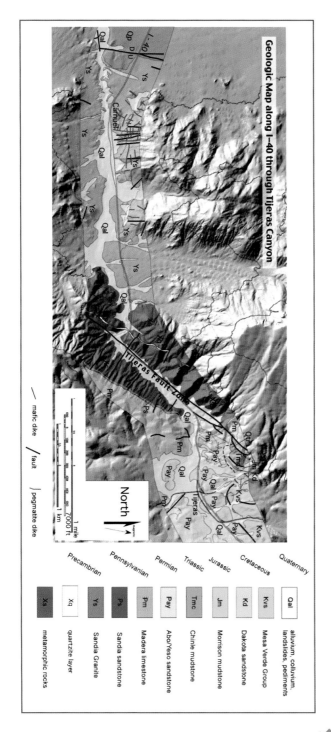

Geologic Map along I-40 through Tijeras Canyon

North

1 mile
7000 ft
km

⟋ mafic dike
╱ fault
⫽ pegmatite dike

Precambrian
Pennsylvanian
Permian
Triassic
Jurassic
Cretaceous
Quaternary

Xs — metamorphic rocks
Xq — quartzite layer
Ys — Sandia Granite
Ps — Sandia sandstone
Pm — Madera limestone
Pay — Abo/Yeso sandstone
Tmc — Chinle mudstone
Jm — Morrison mudstone
Kd — Dakota sandstone
Kvs — Mesa Verde Group
Qal — alluvium, colluvium, landslides, pediments

45

NM 14 and Crest Highway

Between Tijeras and Cedar Crest, a number of faults have moved and displaced rock units so that you are suddenly driving through outcrops of yellow sandstone from the Cretaceous period (the end of the age of dinosaurs). As you drive farther north, you will go past sandstone, limestone, and gypsum from the Jurassic Period, and near Cañoncito you will drive through a valley eroded into the red Triassic shale of the Chinle Group. This rock represents lowland river deposits.

When you turn onto the Crest Highway you will move backward in time. The red sandstone here is Permian Abo formation again, the same rocks you saw near the village of Tijeras, and as you drive higher you will continue to move back in time to the sandstone and limestone deposited at the bottom of the Penn-sylvanian-period sea about 300 million years ago. A major fault called the Barro Canyon fault causes an outcrop of the Sandia granite to suddenly appear. This fault broke the gradual eastern slope of the Sandias and lifted up a kind of minia-ture version of the crest in this location. As you continue to drive, however, you are back in the limestone. In general, as you drive up the road, you will notice the limestone layers tilt down toward the east and mark the gentle eastern flank of the Sandias, although in at least one location a small fault has dragged the lime-stone upward so that it tilts toward the west for a short distance. At the Sandia Crest parking area you can take a good look at this limestone and its abundant fossils. On the crest you are standing at the bottom of an ancient sea. And beneath you on the west face lies the gap in time called the Great Unconformity and the Sandia granite, some of the oldest rock in New Mexico.

Page 47: Shaded relief map with rock types and faults shown along the route of the highway to Sandia Crest from its intersection with NM 14. Colors are the same as shown on page 22.

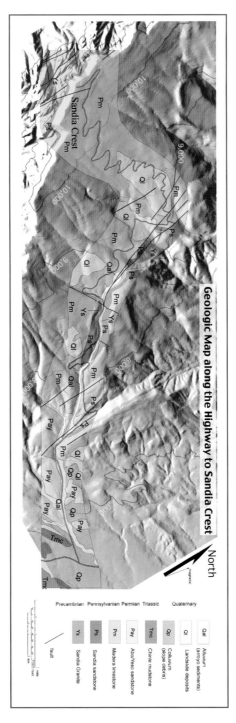

Geologic Map along the Highway to Sandia Crest

North
magnetic

Sandia Crest

Precambrian Pennsylvanian Permian Triassic Quaternary

Ys	Sandia Granite
Ps	Sandia sandstone
Pm	Madera limestone
Pay	Abo/Yeso sandstone
Tmc	Chinle mudstone
Qp	Colluvium (slope debris)
Ql	Landslide deposits
Qal	Alluvium (arroyo sediments)

fault

47

To Learn More:

Arnold, John, Jayne Aubele, and Dave Hafner, eds. *TimeTracks: A Journey through the Natural World.* Albuquerque, N.Mex.: Museum of Natural History and Science, 2001.

Bauer, Paul W., Richard P. Lozinsky, Carol J. Condie, and L. Greer Price. *Albuquerque: A Guide to Its Geology and Culture.* Socorro, N.Mex.: Bureau of Geology and Mineral Resources, 2003.

Chronic, Halka. *Roadside Geology of New Mexico.* Missoula, Mont.: Mountain Press Publishing Co., 1987.

Crumpler, L. S., Joan Newsom, and Jayne Aubele. "Albuquerque's Geoscape." Imágenes de la historia natural no. 1 (poster). Albuquerque, N.Mex.: Museum of Natural History and Science, 2004.

Kelley, Vincent C. *Albuquerque: Its Mountains, Valley, Water and Volcanoes.* Scenic Trips to the Geologic Past No. 9. Socorro, N.Mex.: Bureau of Geology and Mineral Resources, 1982.

Kelley, Vincent C. and Stuart A. Northrup. *Geology of Sandia Mountains and Vicinity.* Memoir 29. Socorro, N.Mex.: Bureau of Geology and Mineral Resources, 1975.

Pazzaglia, Frank and Spencer Lucas, eds. *Albuquerque Geology.* Albuquerque, N.Mex.: Geological Society Fiftieth Annual Field Conference, 1999.

Flora of the Sandia Mountains

Introduction

Mary Stuever, Helen Haskell, Pearl Burns, and Tom Ferguson

They are a life form so unlike our own. They remain rooted their whole lives—in some cases centuries—in exactly the same spot. They ooze sap rather than blood. If they talk or have forms of communication, those escape our notice. Yet they are so familiar. They are so much a part of our lives that we take them for granted. They are plants. A kingdom unto their own. A fascinating world of life so intimately connected to sunlight, earth, water, and sky.

Plants are the fabric all other life exists upon, and learning their interrelationships with mammals, birds, insects, and microbes opens a world of fascination. Throughout the ages, human knowledge of plants has been essential for survival. They give us food, medicine, and inspiration. We even cultivate them. Understanding where plants grow unlocks a subtle key to comprehending the ecological world around us.

Although the word "flora" conjures up a clean concept of plants, there are other organisms presented here that are not part of the plant kingdom. For example, the puffball, as a mushroom, falls into the fungi kingdom; and old man's beard, a lichen, is a combination of two different kingdoms—fungi and protists. Our human tendency is to put things into neat categories, but nature isn't always as simple.

The Sandias are home to over five hundred species of flowering plants as well as many other organisms. This section on "Flora" offers a tiny glimpse at this vast world. We start and end with under-appreciated, little-known, "not-quite" plants we often overlook. These organisms are vital to the functioning of the ecosystem. Starting with cryptobiotic soil, chapter six introduces us to fungi, lichens, parasites, and saprophytes, as well as the often-ignored plant families of mosses and grasses.

Chapter seven provides an introduction to some of the Sandias' most commonly seen or asked-about wildflowers. Though most of these plants are forbs, this section includes some stunning flowers that are found on shrubs, vines, and cacti.

The next two chapters introduce the area's trees and shrubs. Chapter eight covers the evergreen, conifer (or cone-bearing) trees and shrubs, such as pines, firs, and junipers. Chapter nine describes many of the broadleaf trees and shrubs, most of which are deciduous, meaning they lose their foliage during the winter. Those shrubs with distinctive blossoms are also featured in the wildflower section.

In the final flora chapter, we explore the world of tree diseases—another realm often unnoticed but having an active role in defining our forest environment.

The plants and other organisms in this section are identified by common names, which can vary from region to region or person to person. The scientific name *(Genus species)* allows for one worldwide name for each species; however, as our knowledge of plants expands, these names may shift as well. We have provided synonyms for some of those plants that have been known by other names. We also include the common name for the plant's family. Learning the relationship of plants within families can greatly enhance one's understanding of the plant kingdom.

CHAPTER 6

Grasses, Fungi, Lichens, Mosses, and Others

Helen Haskell

Cryptobiotic soils

Some of the soils in the Sandias, especially in the lower areas, look "crusty." This crust is extremely important and is a combination of cyanobacteria, lichens, and mosses. Together, these organisms protect the soil from erosion and are collectively referred to as cryptobiotic soil. The cyanobacteria make fibers in the soil that soil particles stick to, slowing erosion. The moss and lichen slow runoff and allow water to sink into the ground more readily. Cryptobiotic soils also allow grasses to take root and grow. Take a closer look if you find these soils, but avoid treading on them because they are very delicate. One footprint can cause long-term damage to this fragile part of the forest.

Fungi

Fungi are among the most primitive and inconspicuous life forms in the Sandias—and among the most essential, like the foundation of a house. It is an apt analogy, because like a foundation fungi function primarily underground. The fungi we see in the forest, such as mushrooms, usually are only the fruiting bodies of the fungi. The main body of the organism exists within the soil as a filamentous network, known as a mycelium.

Mushrooms, yeasts, and "toadstools" are all types of fungi. Along with bacteria they are the decomposers in the ecosystem. Instead of obtaining food through photosynthesis like plants, fungi and bacterial saprophytes extract their energy from decaying plants and animals and in the process serve the vital role of turning these organisms into component parts of the soil. Unlike plants, fungi do not have leaves, roots, or flowers, and they reproduce by spores instead of seeds. Many animals in the Sandia Mountains eat fungi, including deer, insects, squirrels, and other rodents.

Some fungi have symbiotic relationships with plants such as oaks, orchids, and pines. These fungi grow on the roots of the plant and take up minerals from the soil in exchange for starches and sugars manufactured by the plant. This is known as mutual symbiosis. So as you are hiking, wondering where all the decomposers are, think about how many thousands are hidden beneath your feet.

Mushrooms are easy to find here, if you look at times and places of adequate moisture, such as after spring snowmelt and summer rains. They come in a variety of shapes, sizes, and colors. Puffballs are usually stalkless and resemble a ball, breaking open when ripe to disperse spores. Gill mushrooms resemble those we

Old Man's Beard

You may have heard the term "Spanish moss" used for the gray-green lichen dangling from tree limbs in the Sandias, but in fact Spanish moss is a different plant altogether. A relative of pineapples, true Spanish moss usually is found in the southern forests of the United States—not in the Sandias. Our "Spanish moss" is more accurately called "old man's beard."

commonly buy at the supermarket. Ink caps are a common example. Pore mushrooms, such as the shelf fungi on trees, have a porous tissue instead of gills. Look on some juniper trees in the Sandia Mountains for a gelatinous orange jelly-like substance after a rainstorm. Nicknamed "fire fungus," it resembles orange flames and is known as a rust.

Many mushrooms are poisonous.
***Never* gather and eat *any* wild mushrooms without adequate training.**

Lichens

Hiking along the Sandia trails or even exploring the picnic areas, look around closely on rocks and trees. Lichens are a combination of two organisms—a fungus and an alga, or a fungus and cyanobacteria (blue-green algae). Usually found in water, on land an alga lives within a fungus, photosynthesizing and providing both organisms with food. The fungus provides the algae with a home, along with collecting water and minerals. This mutually beneficial relationship is known as symbiosis. The approximately fourteen thousand known lichen species worldwide come in many different colors and textures. Lichens only grow where the air is clean, and will not survive in areas of significant air pollution.

In the Sandia Mountains you will often see lichens growing on rocks and tree bark. Although the lichens attach to bark, they are not dependent upon it for nutrients and do not harm the tree in any way, though they do fix nitrogen and thus contribute this important nutrient to the soil. Lichens may be more abundant on dead trees as the loss of canopy (leaves/needles) provides more light for the lichen. They also contribute to the decay and nutrient recycling of dead matter. Lichens growing on rocks may over time slowly break apart the rock by depositing crystals of acid. Most lichens grow very slowly, and their size can correlate with their age.

Here in the Sandias many birds, including hummingbirds, will use lichens in their nests. People have used lichens for many years for dyes, food, and medicines. A well-known lichen in these mountains is known as "old man's beard" (*Usnea* sp.).

Left, antler lichen. Right, antler lichen with fruiting bodies.

Shelf lichen.

Rock lichen.

Left, chamisa gall. Right, oak gall.

Mosses

Moss is the small, almost carpet-like plant that according to myths only grows on the north side of the tree and thus can be used to determine direction in the forest. But why might moss often be found on this side of the tree? Here in the northern hemisphere, the sun follows a southern route in our sky. Therefore, the north side of a tree has the most shade. Moss thrives in a moist, cool environment. Where there is more shade, there is less evaporation. Hence, moss is more commonly found on the north-facing sides, but this is not a reliable indication of compass direction.

Moss is a very ancient plant. It is extremely hardy and can survive long droughts, appearing dead and dry but greening up quickly following a rain. One way mosses reproduce is by spores rather than seeds, and because the spores of some species take many years to germinate, mosses are slow to reproduce and thus should not be disturbed when hiking. Because mosses tend to grow on decaying matter, they are among the primary colonizers in plant succession.

Saprophytic Plants

Saprophytes are plants that do not contain chlorophyll and so do not photosynthesize. Instead, these plants feed from thick beds of conifer humus and detritus. It is believed that they have a symbiotic relationship with a fungus that allows them to obtain nutrients from decaying matter. In the Sandias two of the most commonly seen saprophytes are pine drops *(Pterospora andromedea)* and spotted coral root *(Corallorhiza maculata)*.

Parasitic Plants

Like saprophytes, parasites contain no chlorophyll and do not photosynthesize, but unlike saprophytes, which live on dead plants, parasites feed on living tissue. In the Sandias, an example is Mexican squawroot *(Conopholis alpina* var. *Mexicana),* sometimes referred to locally as bear corn. It extracts nutrients from oak roots, in particular Gambel oak. Another group of parasites, the mistletoes, is discussed in chapter ten.

Galls

As you explore the forests of the Sandias, look closely at the leaves and twigs, where you may find some strange growths. These lumps can result from fungi or viruses but often are caused by insects laying their eggs on particular plants. The plants react by growing around the egg a "gall," consisting of layers of plant tissue that protect both the plant and egg. Galls come in all shapes and sizes. Chamisa, or rabbitbrush, has many galls from the picture wing fly; look for small spherical lumps on the twigs. Oaks have more galls than other groups of plants; look for the bright pink fuzzy galls found on oak leaves in the spring.

Grasses

When exploring the Sandia Mountains, it is easy to overlook one of the most important families of plants—grasses! The 128 species of grasses found in the Sandia and Manzano Mountains represent about 15 percent of the flora. These plants are an essential food source for native animals and play a vital role in holding the soil in place with their roots, helping to control erosion. People use grasses, too—Indian ricegrass for food and sideoats grama for making brooms.

Some conditions, such as overgrazing, fire, and tree succession can lead to certain plant species replacing others—an issue facing many ecosystems is the introduction of non-native species, and the Sandias are no exception. The most aggressive non-native grasses in the Sandias were intentionally introduced: as pasture grasses, for restoration after wildfires, for ski runs, and for roadside reclamation. So next time you are in the mountains, take a closer look at the grasses.

Piñon-Juniper Area Grasses

a. Blue grama *(Bouteloua gracilis)*
b. Sideoats grama *(Bouteloua curtipendula)*
c. Longleaf squirreltail *(Elymus longifolius)*
d. Galleta *(Pleuraphis jamesii)*
Red three-awn *(Aristida purpurea)*
Bristly wolftail *(Lycurus setosus)*
Black grama *(Bouteloua eriopoda)*
Indian ricegrass *(Oryzopsis hymenoides)*

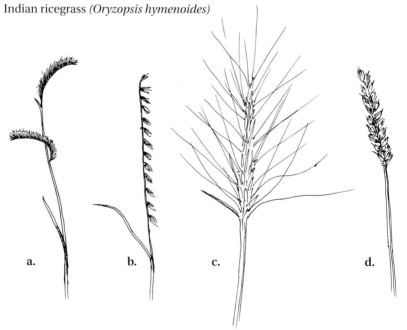

a.   b.   c.   d.

Ponderosa/Mixed-Conifer Area Grasses
e. Pine dropseed *(Blepharoneuron tricholepis)*
f. Foxtail barley *(Hordeum jubatum)*
g. Muttongrass *(Poa fendleriana)*
h. Mountain muhly *(Muhlenbergia montana)*
i. Arizona fescue *(Festuca arizonica)*

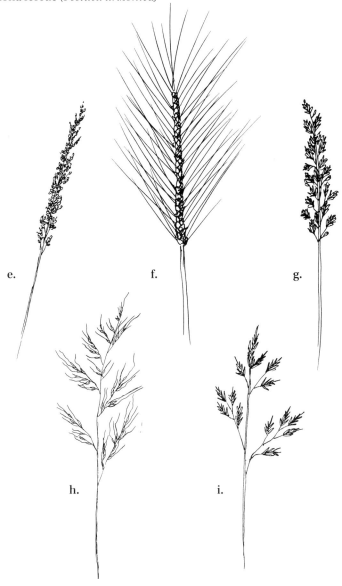

e.   f.   g.

h.   i.

Subalpine Meadows and Spruce-Fir (or Aspen) Forests
i. Fringed brome *(Bromus ciliatus)*
Parry's danthonia *(Danthonia parryi)*
j. Slender wheatgrass *(Elymus trachycaulus)*
Rocky Mountain trisetum *(Trisetum montanum)*
Interior bluegrass *(Poa interior)*

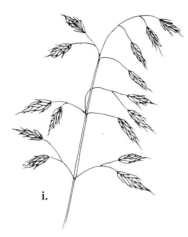

i.   j.

Non-native Species, Commonly Found on the Roadside
k. Cheatgrass *(Bromus tectorum)*
Orchardgrass *(Dactylis glomerata)*
l. Kentucky bluegrass *(Poa pratensis)*
Tall fescue *(Festuca arundinacea)*
Smooth brome *(Bromus inermis)*

k.   l.

The Living Earth
In the Sandias as elsewhere, some of the most numerous and important components of the ecosystem often are the least visible. Scientists have estimated that within just 0.04 ounces of soil—not much more than a pinch—live as many as 4 billion individual bacteria, more than half the total number of human beings on Earth.

To Learn More:

Allred, K. W. *A Field Guide to the Grasses of New Mexico.* Las Cruces: New Mexico State University, 1997.

Arora, David. *Mushrooms Demystified: A Comprehensive Guide to the Fleshy Fungi.* 2nd ed. Berkeley, Calif.: Ten Speed Press, 1986.

Brodo, Irwin M. *Lichens of North America.* New Haven, Conn.: Yale University Press, 2001.

Ivey, Robert DeWitt. *Flowering Plants of New Mexico.* 4th ed. Albuquerque, N.Mex.: published by the author, 2003.

Chapter 7
Wildflowers

Pearl Burns, Tom Ferguson, and Jeanette Buffet

The earth laughs in flowers.
> —Ralph Waldo Emerson

Weed: a plant whose virtues have not been discovered.
> —Ralph Waldo Emerson

Introduction

The plants in this chapter are organized by flower color. When you find a picture that seems to match your plant, read the description to see if it corresponds to your observations. The illustrationson pages 62 and 63 and glossary on page 64 define the terms of flower parts and their shapes and arrangements as they are used in the descriptions.

Regular flowers have radial symmetry, with petals arranged like spokes on a wheel. The *irregular* flowers have bilateral symmetry, with two sides like people. All flowers are regular unless stated to be irregular. When petals are fused together along their edges to form tubes or cups, symmetry is determined from the petal lobes around the flower opening.

By our convention, leaves and flowers are either attached to a plant by *stalks*, or they are *stalkless*. All other supporting structures are termed branches, twigs, or stems. *Compound* leaves are divided into *leaflets* that, with few exceptions, lie in a common plane containing the leaf main vein, or *midrib*. Leaves along a stem do not lie in a common plane. Leaflet shapes are as varied as individual leaves. The flower *stamens*, *styles*, and other details may help confirm an identification. Dimensions of the plants and their parts are typical and not meant to be precise.

The stated growing ranges and blooming periods come from references and personal observations in the Sandias. Plant growth and blooming depend on the habitat, including elevation, slope orientation, soil type, the timing and amount of rain or snow, deviations from normal temperatures, and human impact. Plant growth can be vigorous in an ideal habitat or stunted in marginal areas.

Medicinal and food uses are mentioned for selected plants but should not be tried without consulting experts. Many plants that are highly toxic or poisonous, even in small quantities, appear similar to common medicinal or food plants.

Flower Illustrations

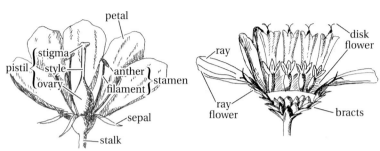

Typical flower parts   **Composite flowerhead**

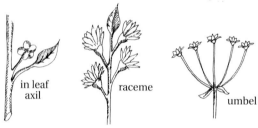

Flower arrangements

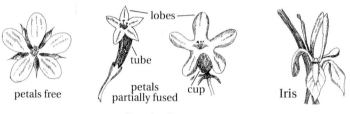

Regular flowers

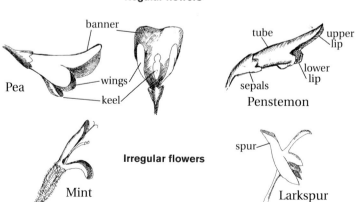

Irregular flowers

Leaf Illustrations

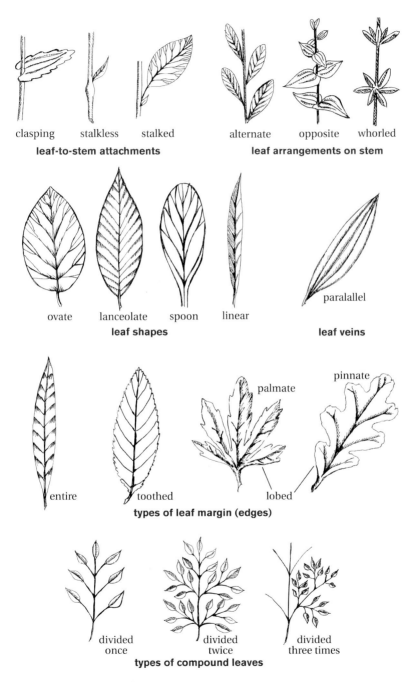

clasping   stalkless   stalked
leaf-to-stem attachments

alternate   opposite   whorled
leaf arrangements on stem

ovate   lanceolate   spoon   linear
leaf shapes

paralallel
leaf veins

entire   toothed   palmate   pinnate   lobed
types of leaf margin (edges)

divided once   divided twice   divided three times
types of compound leaves

63

Glossary

Some of the terms are illustrated in the drawings located on pages 62 and 63.

Anther: the portion of the stamen which contains the pollen

Axil: the angle formed by the stem and its leaf

Banner: the upper petal of a pea-type flower

Composite: a flower head consisting of disk and/or ray flowers—the head appears to be regular

Compound: divided into smaller similar parts as a compound leaf or compound umbel; compound umbels only occur in the Parsley Family

Disk flowers: in the Composite Family; the small regular flowers comprising the center of the flower head

Entire: with and unbroken edge—not lobed or toothed

Filament: supporting stalk of the stamen

Herb: a plant that is not woody; all above-ground parts die in winter

Irregular: flowers that are not regular in shape or whose petals are not alike (peas, mints, orchids, etc.)

Keel: the lower two petals, enclosing the reproductive parts of pea-type flowers, which resemble the keel of a boat

Lanceolate: shaped like the head of a lance, longer than wide

Node: a place, on the stem, where the leaf is attached, which may be swollen

Ovary: basal part of the pistil that contains the eggs that ripen into seeds when fertilized

Ovate: egg-shaped

Palmately compound: a leaf divided once with leaflets attached at a common point

Parasitic: depends on another living organism as a source of food

Pinnately compound: a leaf divided one or more times with leaflets on each side of a common vein

Pistil: the female part of the flower consisting of ovary, style, and stigma

Raceme: individual flowers with stalks attached along an unbranched stem

Ray flowers: in the Composite Family; the wide-flaring, irregular flowers that surround the disk like spokes on a wheel and are often mistaken for "petals"

Regular: the flower has radial symmetry; the petals or petal-like parts are equally spaced and alike

Rosette: a crowded whorl of basal leaves

Saprophytic: lacking chlorophyll; lives on fungi or fungal byproducts associated with decayed vegetable matter such as rotten wood and leaf mold

Sepal: a leaf-like structure below the petals, usually green, but sometimes colored and resembling a petal

Shrub: a woody plant usually with several main stems

Spike: individual flowers, without stalks, attached along an unbranched stem

Stamen: the male part of the flower consisting of filament and anther

Stigma: the tip of the pistil where the pollen is received

Style: the stalk that connects the stigma and ovary

Umbel: an arrangement of multiple flowers where all the individual flower stalks radiate from the same point on the flower stem

Whorl: three or more similar structures (leaves, bracts, flowers) encircling the stem

Wings: the two lateral petals in pea-type flowers usually enclosing the keel

64

Plants with Blue or Purple Flowers

Dayflower
Commelina dianthifolia •
Spiderwort Family

The large flower bracts distinguish this genus from others in the Spiderwort Family.
The intensely blue flower lasts only until noon on a sunny day. A single, 3-petaled, irregular flower rises out of an envelope of two united, 1 to 3-inch, tapered green bracts. Additional buds hidden in the bracts will emerge and bloom on subsequent days. Five or six yellow stamens and one long style curve outward. The alternate, linear, 6-inch leaves sheath the 16-inch-long stems at the swollen nodes.

Dayflowers are found in rocky soil among piñon-juniper and ponderosa pine trees between 6,500 and 9,000 feet. They bloom from mid-July through mid-September.

Rocky Mountain Iris
Iris missouriensis •
Iris Family

This plant is poisonous. The flower was named for King Louis VII of France, who used it as his emblem, Fleur-de-lis or Flower of Louis.
Large showy patches of iris can be seen in mountain meadows. The distinctive *Iris* flowers resemble the Dutch iris. All flower parts are pale blue to purple and look like petals. The 3-inch-wide flower blooms at the top of a 2-foot stalk. The basal leaves are linear, smooth, flat, and up to 20 inches long. Occasionally you may see a white iris.

Iris grows in moist mountain meadows from mid-May to mid-June above 7,500 feet.

Do Not Pick Wildflowers!

Please don't pick wildflowers. Unlike hybridized species cultivated for home and commercial uses, they wilt rapidly. Picking flowers reduces seed production and plant reproduction. Beautiful flowers like the fairy slipper, or calypso, orchid can be eliminated from the Sandias due to human impact. Enjoy your outing, and leave the flowers for everyone to appreciate.

Alpine Clematis
Clematis columbiana • *Buttercup Family*

This vine clings to other vegetation with its tendrils. The nodding 1- to 2-inch flowers have 4 spreading, pointed lavender sepals and many stamens. The flowers are long-stalked. The leaves are opposite on the stem and pinnately compound, divided twice, with leaflets usually in threes. The side leaflets are asymmetrical and irregularly lobed and toothed. Each of the many seeds has a long feathery tail. The result looks like a 2-inch fluffy feather duster.

This vine grows in wooded areas from 7,000 feet to 9,000 feet and blooms from mid-May through June.

Blue Flax
Linum lewisii • *Flax Family*

Blue Flax is used to reseed highway slopes after highway construction. The commercial flax fiber species is Linum usitatissimum.

When these flowers are backlighted by the sun, their sky-blue color is dazzling. Spindly 8- to 20-inch stems are topped by a few 1-inch-wide flowers. They have 5 broad, fragile petals and 5 short green sepals. The 5 stamens and 5 styles spread outward. The few leaves are short, linear, and alternate.

Blue flax blooms all summer from plains to high mountain meadows, in sunlight or partial shade.

Jacob's Ladder
Polemonium foliosissimum • *Phlox Family*

The leaves have a skunky odor.
In the woods, the pale- to medium-blue or white flowers catch your attention. They grow in loose clusters
on 8- to 18-inch stem tops. There are 5 broad petals
arising from the shallow cup with 5 stamens and a
3-pronged style. The inner part of the flower is a pale
yellow with darker lines. The sepals, upper stems, and leaves are lightly haired.
The lower stems and leaves may be smooth or hairy. The ladder-like alternating
leaves are odd-pinnately compound, with 9 to 19 entire leaflets.

This plant blooms through the summer months in damp woods or meadows
above 8000 feet.

Purple Geranium
Geranium caespitosum • *Geranium Family*

Richardson's geranium is similar but has pinkish flowers
with 5 wide petals. The genus name comes from Greek
geranos, or "crane," referring to the beak of the fruit.
This sprawling plant with a few reddish-purple flowers
may escape your attention, but take a closer look. Five
separated petals alternate with 5 shorter green sepals.
The long-beaked pistil and 10 stamens protrude. The pistil extends outward after
pollination to form the characteristic Geranium Family "storksbill." The 2-inch
leaves are mostly opposite and deeply palmately lobed.

These plants bloom from May to September, and are found up to 9,500 feet.

Verbena, Moradilla
Glandularia bipinnatifida • *Verbena Family*

The seeds do not grow the first year and will remain
dormant waiting for ideal growing conditions. Some
verbena species are prepared as a tea to treat cold
symptoms, settle the stomach, or act as a sedative.
Rose-purple tubular flowers facing upward in flat-
topped clusters cover low plants that may blanket a
field. Each flower is $^3/_8$ of an inch across, with 5 slightly irregular notched lobes.
The 1 to 3-inch leaves are opposite and pinnately compound, with leaflets deeply
and variously lobed. The stems are upright or sprawl and turn upward.

This plant grows in open areas up to 6,500 feet. It blooms in May and occasionally in late summer.

67

Spike Verbena
Verbena macdougalii • *Verbena Family*

Although Verbenas may be mistaken for mints, the foliage lacks the aromatic scent. Verbena is used as a tea for sedation, stomach problems, and to induce sweating.

Spiky roadside plants invite a closer inspection. Stout 2 to 3-foot stems terminate in long cylindrical flowering spikes up to ³/₄ inches in diameter. The irregular, ¹/₂-inch tubular purple flowers start blooming in a dense ring around the base of the spike. Only one flowering row is produced at a time. The 4-sided stems have opposite, lanceolate leaves up to 4 inches long, which are coarsely toothed and wrinkled.

This plant is found in mountain meadows, up to 8,000 feet, and blooms from June to September.

Franciscan Bluebells
Mertensia franciscana • *Borage Family*

Species of Mertensia *are grown domestically. They also are called lungworts due to an early belief that they could help cure lung disease.*

Little chiming bells dangle from the upper leaf axils on arching stems up to 3 feet tall. Usually blue, they may also be pink or white on the same plant. Their stalks and green sepals are hairy. The alternate leaves are entire and broadly lance-shaped. The lower ones may have long stalks, but those higher on the stem are stalkless.

These bluebells grow in moist places higher on the mountain, and bloom early in summer.

Harebell
Campanula rotundifolia • *Bellflower Family*

Also called "Bluebells of Scotland," this plant has been associated with witches. Navajos used them for protection. Scots called them witches' thimble. Some witches thought the flowers could change into hares and cause bad luck.

A meadow may be accented with these pretty, nodding, bell-shaped blue flowers. They hang on upright, slender stems about 1 foot high. These 1-inch flowers have 5 outward-flaring pointed lobes, and 5 short stamens. The few stem leaves are alternate, linear, and entire. The spoon-shaped basal leaves fall off at flowering time.

Harebells flower from June to September above 7500 feet.

Dwarf Lousewort
Pedicularis centranthera • *Figwort Family*

The plant is used as a sedative for children and as a tranquilizer for adults.

This ground-hugging purple lousewort is one of the earliest plants to bloom. The irregular tubular flowers are whitish with purple lips. The upper lip is a hood. The flowers nestle among the leaves, which emerge purple and mature green. The 2 to 6-inch leaves are pinnately compound with toothed leaflets. The stems are no longer than 6 inches.

This plant grows in juniper/pine woods up to 8,000 feet and blooms from March through June.

Dusky (Whipple's) Penstemon
Penstemon whippleanus • *Figwort Family*

This is a beardtongue penstemon as the sterile stamen is haired. The presence of hairs in the throat of the flower does not constitute a beardtongue.

These dark-purple irregular flowers blend into the background. They bloom in whorled clusters along the 1 to 2-foot stem. The tubular flower has a 3-lobed lower lip with long white hairs in the throat. The 2-lobed upper lip curls slightly upward. There are 5 stamens; one is sterile and haired. Tiny sticky hairs cover the flowers. The basal leaves are ovate to spatulate, and entire. The stem leaves are opposite, lanceolate, and stalkless.

Whipple's penstemon grows above 7,000 feet and blooms from July through mid-September.

Rocky Mountain Penstemon
Penstemon strictus • *Figwort Family*

Penstemons readily hybridize in a garden but rarely in wild habitats.

The royal-purple flowers attract your attention immediately. The irregular, funnel-shaped flowers grow in a raceme, facing outward, on one side of an erect stem. The flowers are distinctly 2-lipped with the 3 lower lobes hanging downward. There are 5 stamens; 1 is sterile with a somewhat dilated tip. The sterile stamen may or may not be slightly haired. The dark-green basal leaves are spatulate. The opposite, clasping, stem leaves are more lance-shaped. The plant is 8 to 30 inches tall.

This penstemon can be found blooming from June to August in open woods above 7,000 feet.

Low Lupine
Lupinus pusillus • *Pea Family*

This plant is poisonous.
If there seems to be a purple haze low to the ground, it may be the low lupine that is blooming. The small (1/2-inch), blue-violet irregular flower grows in short terminal racemes. It is a typical pea flower. The banner, which is broadest in the middle, has a square white eye. The 8-inch plant is branched from the base. The long-stalked palmate leaves are divided into 5 to 9 lanceolate leaflets that are 3/4 to 1 1/8 inches long. The stems, leaf stalks, and the undersides of the leaflets are stiff-haired.

Low lupine grows on sandy plains and dry slopes up to 7,500 feet and blooms from May to June.

Silvery Lupine
Lupinus argenteus • *Pea Family*

Argenteus means silvery. To minimize their heat and water loss, leaflets fold lengthwise at night. Lupines are poisonous. A greenish-yellow dye is produced from the plant.
Your attention will be attracted to a 2 to 3-foot-tall plant with blue to purple flowers in loose, elongated racemes. The 1/4- to 1-inch irregular flowers are typical pea flowers. There are several stems with alternate leaves palmately divided into 5 to 10 lance-shaped leaflets. The hairy leaflets are 1/4 to 1 inch wide and 1 to 2 inches long.

Lupines grow in moist conifer forests above 7,000 feet and bloom from late May through August.

Lambert's Locoweed
Oxytropis lambertii • *Pea Family*

This poisonous plant may make animals loco *("crazy") when eaten. The genus name, from the Greek* oxus *("sharp") and* trophies *("keel"), refers to the beaked keel. The genera* Oxytropis *and* Astragulus *are often confused.* Astragulus *has blooms on a leafed stem, and the keel is not beaked.*
Bright rose-purple pea-like flowers are in densely flowered racemes on 4 to 16-inch leafless stalks. The irregular 1/2- to 1-inch flowers have beaked keels. The long-stalked 3 to 12-inch basal leaves are odd-pinnately compound. The leaflets are entire, narrowly ovate to lanceolate. All parts, except the petals, are covered with silvery hairs.

This locoweed grows on the plains and mountain slopes above 5,000 feet, and is common at the crest. It blooms all summer.

Milkvetch
Astragulus spp. • *Pea Family*

This genus has many species. One produces a fleshy, plum-shaped fruit whose immature pods were often eaten by Native Americans. Some milkvetches contain poisonous alkaloids or toxic quantities of selenium.
Purple, pink, yellow, or white pea-like flowers, in spikes or racemes, bloom on leafed, branched, or single-stemmed plants. Plants vary from 4 to 18 inches tall. The leaves are odd-pinnately compound, usually with simple, smooth leaflets. Some plants may be very hairy. Milkvetches are variable with seed pods produced in many shapes and sizes.

Milkvetches grow up to 8,000 feet in dry open areas. Different species will bloom from May throughout the summer.

Leather Flower
Clematis bigelovii • *Buttercup Family*

Brownish-purple, urn-shaped flowers grow on this vine, which doesn't climb but uses other plants or shrubs for support.
The nodding, long-stalked, 1¹/₂-inch flowers have 4 petal-like parts that are edged with light gray hairs. The leaves are opposite on the stem. The 3 leaflets are net-veined and asymmetrically lobed. The seeds have long hairy tails, which give a plumed appearance.

Leatherflower grows in strong sunlight or shade. It blooms from May to August. Among other places, look for it along the North Crest Trail around 9,000 feet in elevation.

Monkshood
Aconitum columbianum • *Buttercup Family*

Bumblebees are supposed to enter the front of the flower to reach the nectar under the hood, leaving pollen on the reproductive parts. They have been known to cheat and just bite through the hood. A highly poisonous alkaloid is found throughout the plant.
What a delight to see these blue-purple blossoms. The unusual irregular flowers are in a raceme on a 1 to 3-foot single-stemmed plant. The upper sepal is shaped like a monk's hood or helmet. Two rounded sepals below the hood flare outward, and 2 narrower sepals dangle underneath. The large, alternate stem leaves have 3 to 5 deeply cleft palmate lobes.

Monkshood blooms in July and August in high, moist, partially shaded areas.

71

Plants with Green or Cream Flowers

Monument Plant, Deers Ears
Frasera speciosa • *Gentian Family*

The root is rumored to be useful for treatment of fungal infections, head lice, and scabies.

This plant begins as a basal rosette of long, simple leaves resembling the ears of a deer. It may take years, as many as 20 or more, for the plant to store sufficient food in the root to produce the single, thick, 2 to 7-foot flowering stem. The 1-inch greenish flowers have 4 petals facing outward. Their stalks emerge from sheaths around the stem, where long smooth leaves radiate in whorls. Each whorl along the stem has about the same number of leaves. From plant to plant, this number varies from 3 to 9.

The flowers emerge from mid-June to mid-August. These giants grow above 8,000 feet. They often crowd the meadows north of South Sandia Peak.

Virgin's Bower
Clematis ligusticifolia • *Buttercup Family*

The stems and leaves have a peppery taste and were chewed by Native Americans to relieve sore throats.

A profusion of dainty, creamy-white flowers cover this 10 to 20-foot-long, woody vine that drapes over fences, shrubs, or trees. The clustered, $3/4$-inch-wide flowers have 4 to 5 petal-like sepals. The unisexual flowers have numerous stamens or pistils. The opposite leaves are pinnately compound with 3 to 7 lanceolate leaflets. The 3-inch-long leaflets are coarsely toothed or lobed, smooth, or softly haired. As the seed matures, the style elongates into a feathery plume with a "feather duster" appearance.

Virgin's bower usually is found below 7,500 feet in canyons, arroyos, and roadsides from the desert to pine forests. It blooms all summer.

Mountain Spray
Holodiscus dumosus • *Rose Family*

A tea has been made from mountain spray roots. The wood is very hard and has been used to make bows, spears, and other items.

Sprays of many tiny, cream-to-pink flowers are in racemes at the stem tips of this shrub. The $1/5$-inch-wide flowers have 5 petals, 5 pistils, and 10 stamens. This shrub grows to 8 feet tall with spreading branches. The smaller branches have shredding bark, and the twigs are dark red. The alternate 2-inch leaves are oval and variously lobed with cottony undersides.

Mountain spray grows on rocky slopes and canyon walls at 6,500 to 9,000 feet and blooms from mid-June to mid-August.

Pinedrops
Pterospora andromeda • *Indian Pipe Family*

Pinedrops are saprophytic, living on decaying matter.
A tan-colored dye is produced from the plant.
Often seen as a rusty-brown dried plant with persistent seed
capsules, pinedrops grow as a single, erect 12 to 18-inch reddish-brown stem with yellowish-brown flowers. The $1/4$-inch
flowers grow in a raceme on downward-curved red stalks. The
fused petals form narrow-mouthed hanging bells. The alter-
nate leaves have been reduced to scales. All plant parts, except the bells, are covered
with sticky glandular hairs.

Pinedrops are found in conifer forests, primarily among ponderosa pine,
from 7,000 to 9,000 feet and bloom from July through September.

Fern-leaf Lousewort
Pedicularis procera • *Figwort Family*

Before the 2 to 4-foot flowering stalk is produced,
this plant is often mistaken for a fern.
A dense raceme of showy cream-colored flowers, interspersed
with hairy bracts, covers the flowering stalk. The irregular,
2-lipped flowers have red-brown lines. The upper lip is a
hood. The 3-lobed lower lip is shorter and wider. The flowers
progressively bloom from the bottom of the raceme upward.
The large and tapering basal and alternate stem leaves are
25 inches long or more, deeply pinnately lobed, evenly toothed, and fern-like.

This flower blooms from mid-July through August. This plant grows above
8,500 feet.

Figwort
Scrophularia montana • *Figwort Family*

A topical treatment made with this herb can be applied for fun-
gal infections, eczema, rashes, or hemorrhoids. Tea from the dried
plant can be imbibed for skin problems or as a mild sedative.
This robust herb constitutes the hummingbird delicatessen.
The tiny ($5/8$-inch-long) flowers contain nutrients that attract
these tiny birds. The irregular flowers are green with a brownish bill tilted a bit
upward. They grow in branched clusters at the ends of the stems. The plant grows
2 to 6 feet tall. The leaves are in opposite pairs or whorled in threes, fours, or fives
around the ribbed stems. They are large, broadly lanceolate, and evenly serrated.

This meadow plant usually blooms in early summer above 8,500 feet.

73

Plants with Pink or Red Flowers

Geyer's Wild Onion
Allium geyeri •
Lily Family

Nodding Onion
Allium cernuum •
Lily Family

Allium leaves and bulbs can be used as flavoring in soups and stews, or dried and stored as an emergency food. However, the poisonous death camas has been mistaken for an onion, but is easily distinguished. If it smells like an onion, it is an onion—and edible.

Dainty pink flowers grow in upright umbels on *Allium geyeri* and in nodding umbels on *Allium cernuum*. There are 6 petal-like parts. Those on *Allium geyeri* have pointed ends curving outward. The bell-like flowers of *Allium cernuum* have protruding stamens. The long, smooth leaves of both species are basal and very narrow. They smell like onions, particularly when crushed.

These onions grow above 6,500 feet, prefer sun, and bloom during the summer and early fall.

Calypso, Fairy Slipper Orchid
Calypso bulbosa •
Orchid Family

Although this orchid has chlorophyll, it is dependent on specific fungi in the soil. The calypso lures the bees by appearance and scent. It has no nectar.

What a treat to see these rare, delicate orchids blooming. The nodding, irregular flower has 3 sepals and 2 petals, all rose-purple, that spread up and out over the third petal, a slipper-like lip. A single flower grows on a 4 to 8-inch pinkish-brown stem. A basal, ovate leaf grows in the fall and may die the next year before blooming occurs.

In shady forests above 9,000 feet the calypso grows in the well-rotted understory. It blooms from mid-May to mid-June.

Spotted Coralroot
Corallorhiza maculata •
Orchid Family

Striped Coralroot
Corallorhiza striata •
Orchid Family

Coralroots lack chlorophyll and are saprophytic.
They grow from a cluster of coral-like roots, which
may remain dormant for years.

These two small orchids are similar and not eye-catching from afar. The outward facing, $3/4$-inch irregular flowers are in a raceme on an upright 8 to 17-inch pale yellow or reddish-brown stem. Three sepals and 2 petals spread upward and to the side. The third lower petal is a lip. The spotted coralroot has a white lip and purple dots on all the petals. Striped coralroot has lengthwise stripes on the sepals and petals. The leaves are sheathing scales.

Both species bloom in June and July from 7,000 to 9,500 feet.

Pinesap
Monotropa hypopithys •
Indian Pipe Family

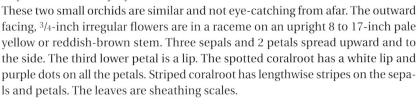

Pinesap lacks chlorophyll and is a saprophyte.
That bright-red, fleshy plant is pinesap. The short raceme of 3 to 10 flowers nods initially and then becomes erect with upward-facing flowers as the plant matures. The 3 to 5 narrow $1/2$-inch long bell-shaped flowers have twice as many stamens as petals. Multiple stems up to 12 inches tall grow from a tangled root system. The leaves have been reduced to scales.

Pinesap is found in conifer forests from 7,000 to 9,500 feet. It blooms from July through mid-August.

Fireweed
Epilobium angustifolium • *Evening Primrose Family*

Wind carries the tufted seeds aloft. A burned area may be covered with fireweed the next year. Following bombing during World War II, these plants appeared in London for the first time in generations. Fireweed tea is enjoyed around the world.

These bright magenta flowers readily catch your eye as seen along the roadside or in the meadows. The showy 1-inch flowers with 4 broad petals face outward on a raceme at the top of a single upright stem. They have 8 stamens and 1 protruding 4-pronged style. The leaves are alternate, lanceolate, and entire with a pale central vein. The red or green fruits are erect, linear pods.

Fireweed grows almost anywhere, especially in disturbed soil, and blooms from July to September.

Scarlet Gaura
Gaura coccinea • *Evening Primrose Family*

The primary pollinators of these plants are night-flying moths, which are attracted by the white flowers. These plants are common throughout the western and central U.S.

As you walk in the evening you may see these lacy white or pink flowers that have just opened. The next morning they have changed to pink and red. The 1/2-inch flowers on short racemes have 4 small petals spreading upward and 8 stamens projecting outward or drooping downward. They have a protruding style with a 4-lobed stigma. The alternate leaves are narrow and hairy. The fruits are upright pods with grooves.

These 6 to 18-inch-tall plants grow up to 7,500 feet in the piñon-juniper belt. They bloom from May through September.

Coralbells
Heuchera pulchella • *Saxifrage Family*

This species is a rare, cliff-loving plant that is narrowly distributed. It only occurs in the Sandia and Manzano mountains of central New Mexico.

Look along the cliff edges for these dainty, bell-shaped pink flowers. The 1/4-inch flowers have burgundy sepals and 5 projecting stamens. They grow in a dense raceme on 4- to 6-inch-long stems. The 3/4-inch palmately lobed and toothed leaves are clustered at the base of the plant. In the fall, the leaves turn a deep red.

Blooming starts in July and continues until frost. Coralbells grow in rocks and crevices above 8,000 feet.

Our Own Coralbells

Coralbells are small plants with dainty pink bell-shaped flowers that grow in only one place in New Mexico: the high cliffs of the Sandia and Manzano Mountains.

King's Crown, Roseroot
Sedum integrifolium • *Stonecrop Family*

King's Crown is high in vitamins A and C. The leaves and shoots can be eaten cooked or raw, and the rhizomes can be cooked alone or with other vegetables. It is relatively rare in the Sandias and should not be harvested.

Look at the rocky cliffs or outcroppings. See if you spot a dense, flat-topped cluster of tiny dark-red flowers crowning a succulent herbaceous plant. It is the king's crown. The stamens protrude. The short fleshy leaves are smooth, flat or round-ed, and crowded around the 4 to 8-inch stems. The fruits are reddish clusters of 5 spreading, pointed capsules.

Flowering is from late June through August.

Cliff Primrose
Primula rusbyi • *Primrose Family*

You might see these bright rose-pink flowers nestled in the cracks of the rocky cliffs or along La Luz Trail. The tubular flowers grow in umbels. The yellow-throated floral tube flares to 3/4-inch wide with 5 notched lobes. The basal leaves are hairy, toothed, and lanceolate. The upper stems, flowering stalks, and sepals can have a powdery, white coating.

Cliff primrose grows in the rocky outcroppings and damp slopes of the mountain above 7,500 feet and usually blooms in June.

Four O'Clock, Maravilla
Mirabilis multiflora • *Four O'Clock Family*

The root has been made into a poultice. A tea made from this plant acts as an appetite suppressant.

If you are hiking after "four o'clock" you may see these showy reddish-purple flowers that open late in the afternoon. The tubular flowers are held within a 5-lobed cup of bracts (modified leaves). The style and 5 stamens extend beyond the 5 united, notched petals. The opposite, entire, triangular leaves are on short stalks. This bushy plant grows up to 18 inches tall, and is often seen as a mound of sprawling stems.

The plant grows in open areas below 7,000 feet and blooms from mid-May through the summer.

Richardson's Geranium
Geranium richardsonii • *Geranium Family*

The genus comes from the Greek geranos, which means "crane" and refers to the elongated style.

In the woods, a pink or whitish flower catches your eye. There may be 1 or several flowers in a branched cluster. The 5 wide petals are white to pink with purple veins. The leaves are palmately lobed into 5 to 7 segments with pointed lobes. The stems grow to 1 to 2^1/$_2$ feet tall. The leaves turn red in the fall. The style elongates on the seedpod, giving it the appearance of a "crane's bill," another common name for this plant.

This plant grows above 7,500 feet in moist shaded or open woods and blooms in July and August.

Scarlet Gilia, Skyrocket
Ipomopsis aggregata • *Phlox Family*

Skyrocket was once placed in the genus Gilia, hence one common name. It may have a skunky odor, particularly when crushed.

Like little skyrockets or trumpets, the bright-red flowers grow in the upper leaf axils of stems that may grow to 2 feet tall. The 1-inch tubular red flowers have 5 flaring, pointed lobes, which often have yellow spots. The 5 stamens and single style may protrude a bit. This is another biennial plant that produces a basal rosette of leaves the first year. The second year the leaves are alternate on the stem and pinnately compound, divided into narrow segments.

Found on dry, open, or lightly wooded slopes from foothills to 9,000 feet, these attractive plants flower from May to October.

Wild Rose
Rosa woodsii • *Rose Family*

A strong rose scent accompanies these lovely pink roses. The 2-inch flowers with 5 wide pink petals and many stamens are scattered across this shrub, which grows as high as 5 feet. Prickles grow just below the stem nodes at the leaf axils. The alternate leaves are odd-pinnately compound, divided once, with 5 to 9 ovate leaflets having serrated edges.

This shrub grows in sandy or rocky soil up to 9500 feet and blooms from June through August.

Bergamot, Beebalm
Monarda fistulosa syn. Monarda menthifolia •
Mint Family

Bergamot has been used as spice, potherb, preservative, insect repellant, cold and flu treatment, and perfume. Species of this family often have an aroma, sometimes minty.
The attractive, dense cluster of lavender or pink irregu-
lar flowers draws your attention to this multi-stemmed 2-foot-tall plant. The tubular flowers are 1 to 1$^1/_2$ inches long, with a long, narrow upper lip and a 3-lobed lower lip. The style and two stamens protrude below the upper lip. The leaves are broadly lanceolate, 1 to 2$^1/_2$ inches long, uniformly serrated, and oppo-site on the square stems.

Flowering from July to October, this aromatic plant grows in moist canyons and meadows up to 8,000 feet.

Tree Cholla
Opuntia imbricata • *Cactus Family*

A joint will readily grow when planted. Cholla is an indi-cator plant of over-grazing. It has been planted as a living fence. The dried stems are woody, hollow cylinders with many elongated holes. They are used in craftworks.
When in bloom, this 1 to 6-foot-tall cactus is spectacu-
lar. The many-petaled, reddish-purple flowers are 2 to 3 inches wide. The chollas grow by adding cylindrical stem segments called joints. The number of spines on the prominent spine-bearing knobs is quite variable with fewer on new growth. The fruit is a yellow, fleshy, spineless, knobby, ovoid capsule.

Cholla is very common and grows in open dry areas up to 6,500 feet. It blooms from mid-May to mid-June.

Claret Cup
Echinocereus triglochidiatus • *Cactus Family*

Red-flowered Hedgehog
Echinocereus coccineus • *Cactus Family*

Bright red flowers grow from the tops of these two cacti, whose fleshy stems resemble upright grooved cucumbers with spines. The flowers have many wide overlapping 1 to 2-inch petals and a central column of styles surrounded by stamens. The claret cup has 5 or more alternating vertical grooves and ribs. The ribs have groups of 2 to 5 radial-spreading yellowish or grayish spines without a central spine. The shorter red-flowered hedgehog has 8 to 11 grooves with less-prominent ribs and 8 to 12 grayish, slender radial spines. A central spine, 1 to 3 inches long, is directed downward. Spines of claret cup are angular in cross-section while those of red-flowered hedgehog are elliptic in cross-section.

These cacti grow in desert-like environments up to 7,500 feet and bloom from mid-May to mid June.

Strawberry Cactus
Echinocereus fendleri • *Cactus Family*

The desert landscape is punctuated with showy, rose-pink flowers. Closer examination reveals that they are cactus blossoms. The upward-facing 3-inch flowers grow on the shoulders of the stems and usually extend well above the stem. The 3 to 4-inch cylindrical stems are thick. They may be clumped together in a low mound but are more often seen as a single stem in the Sandias. The fruit has small clusters of white spines. It ripens to a reddish hue.

Strawberry cactus grows in a desert-like environment up to 7,000 feet and blooms from mid-May to June.

New Mexico Locust
Robinia neomexicana • *Pea Family*

New Mexico locust is often planted as an ornamental. The thorns are a bane to hikers.

Along the Crest Highway, look for shrubs or small trees covered with many rose-pink flowers hanging in droopy racemes. These fragrant 1-inch pea-type flowers produce 2 to 4-inch-long pods. The leaves are pinnately compound with 9 to 23 ovate, entire leaflets that are about 1 inch long. Bristly hairs cover the sepals, smaller stems, and the 2 to 4-inch-long pods. A pair of opposing, sharp, reddish-brown spines grows on the stem where the leaf stalk is attached.

This showy shrub blooms from May to June at elevations up to 9,500 feet.

Paintbrush, Flor de Santa Rita
Castilleja **spp.** • *Figwort Family*

Several species of paintbrushes grow in the Sandias. The plant is partially parasitic, and at lower elevations uses the roots of a host plant, grama grass, to obtain water. Hovering insects and hummingbirds pollinate these plants.

Bright red or orange colors attract the eye. The color comes from modified leaves (bracts), not from the tubular flowers hidden among the bracts. The leaves are alternate, usually narrow, simple or lobed. The plant ranges from 6 to 24 inches tall.

Paintbrushes grow from sandy desert at 6,000 feet to the rich forest soils at the top of the mountain. The blooming season is from May to September.

Red Columbine
Aquilegia desertorum • *Buttercup Family*

Columbine comes from the Latin meaning "dove-like." It was thought that the flower resembled a circle of 5 doves drinking. Aquilegia *is from the Latin meaning "eagle" and refers to the talon-like appearance of the spurs.*

Bright yellow and red nodding flowers accent the woods. Five petal-like red sepals project forward. Five shorter, yellow petals extend backward into hollow red spurs $3/4$ to $1^1/4$ inches long. The stamens strongly project beyond the flower. The long-stalked 1 to $2^1/2$-inch leaves are twice pinnately compound with three lobed leaflets. This plant grows up to 2 feet tall.

Red columbine grows in moist areas of the mountain above 7,000 feet and blooms from June to mid-August.

Red Penstemon
Penstemon barbatus **ssp.** *torreyi* • *Figwort Family*

Red tubular flowers hang down from long stems. The irregular flowers have 2 upper lobes projecting forward and 3 curled underneath. They grow in a tall raceme on long stalks, and have 5 short green sepals. All species of this genus have 5 stamens, 4 with anthers and 1 without. The stalkless stem leaves are opposite, entire, smooth, and narrow, widening toward the end. The stalked basal leaves are more spoon-shaped.

Red penstemons grow in dry foothills or high on the mountain. They bloom from June to September.

Plants with White Flowers

Beargrass, Sacahuista
Nolina greenei •
Nolina Family

The fibrous leaves were used for sandal making.
Flour was made from the tuberous roots.

This interesting plant has either pinkish (female) or white (male) flowering stems rising out of a dense basal cluster of tough, flexible perennial leaves. The annual flower stem grows as high as 3 feet with many alternating dense racemes of flowers. The small flowers have 3 petals and 3 similar sepals. The leaves grow up to 3 feet in length and 1/2 inch in width and taper to a point. They are not spiny or sharp to the touch although they have small teeth along the edge of the leaf. This species is dioecious; each plant has either male or female flowers, but not both.

This hardy plant grows up to 7,500 feet. It blooms in May.

Banana Yucca, Datil
Yucca baccata •
Agave Family

Leaf fibers have been made into various items.
The flowers, fruit, and tender inner leaves are edible.
The root contains saponin, a substitute for soap.

Large clusters of 2- to 4-inch-long waxy flowers are partially nestled among the dense clump of leaves. The drooping flowers have 3 creamy white petals and 3 white-to-purplish sepals. The rigid, spine-tipped, concave leaves are about 1 1/4 to 2 inches wide and up to 3 feet long with curved fibers on the edges. The cylindrical, fleshy fruit is 4 to 8 inches long.

The banana yucca grows on dry hills and rocky slopes up to 8,500 feet and blooms in June and July. The fruit matures in September.

Soapweed Yucca
Yucca glauca •
Agave Family

Soaptree yucca (Yucca elata) *is the state flower of New Mexico but does not grow in the Sandias. The yucca root contains saponin, a soap substitute. The fibrous leaves have been made into brooms, rope, and sandals. The flowers and immature fruits are edible. Soapweed yucca has a cooperative relationship with the female yucca moth, which visits the flower at night, pollinates it, and deposits her egg in the plant's ovary. The developing larva feeds on the seeds of the yucca, apparently not diminishing the seed production.*
A flowering stalk of white, sometimes purplish, waxy flowers arises from numerous basal leaves. The 1- to 1^1/$_2$-inch-long flower has 3 sepals and 3 petals. The 8- to 24-inch-long spine-tipped leaves are seldom over ^{1}/$_2$ inch wide. The fruit is about 1^1/$_2$ inches long.

This yucca grows up to 7,500 feet in a desert-like environment. It blooms during May and June.

Mariposa Lily
Calochortus gunnisonii •
Lily Family

Calochortus, a Greek word, means "beautiful grass." Mariposa, a Spanish word, means "butterfly." Native Americans and early settlers ate the bulbs.
You won't fail to notice these attractive, white to purple-shaded, cup-shaped 2-inch flowers growing on slender stalks. The flowers have 3 petals, 3 green sepals, and 6 stamens. At the base of the petals is a purple band. In the center, yellow hairs attract pollinators. The 10-inch linear leaves alternate on 12-inch-tall stems.

These lilies are found in the upper mountain meadows and aspen forests above 7,000 feet and bloom in July.

False Solomon's Seal
Maianthemum racemosum • *Lily Family*

Star Solomon's Seal
Maianthemum stellatum • *Lily Family*

The berries, young shoots, and roots of various
Maianthemum *species have been used for food.*
The gently arching 1- to 2-foot stems of these plants terminate in dainty white flowers. The stalkless, alternate,
smooth leaves have parallel veins. *Maianthemum racemosum* has small branched
racemes of tiny flowers whose appearance is dominated by prominent white stamens. The shiny leaves are half as wide as their 3- to 6-inch length. *Maianthemum
stellatum* has one small sparse raceme of flowers with 6 narrow petal-like parts.
The leaves are about 1 inch wide and 6 inches long. The fruits are ¹/₄-inch berries.
   Both plants grow at higher elevations and bloom from May to July.

Stemless Evening Primrose
Oenothera caespitosa • *Evening Primrose Family*

*Deer, birds, and small rodents eat the flower and seeds
of this plant.*
Like scattered pieces of tissue, the showy stemless
evening primrose decorates the landscape. The 2- to
4-inch-white flowers have 4 wide petals that turn pink as
the flower fades. The petals are notched at the tip. The flowers have 8 stamens and
a 4-branched stigma. The lance-shaped, basal, 4- to 6-inch leaves may be entire,
toothed, or pinnately lobed. The flowers open at night, their fragrance attracting
the night pollinators. They may remain open until noon for other pollinators.
   The plant grows in dry and sandy areas up to 9,000 feet. Blooming occurs
mainly in May and occasionally all summer.

Fendlerbush
Fendlera rupicola • *Hydrangea Family*

*This shrub can be seen from the tram. The hard wood
has been used by Native Americans to make weaving
forks, arrows, and other items.*
The fendlerbush blooms gloriously. It is a lanky shrub,
up to 6 feet tall, with shredding bark. The 1- to 2-inch white flowers have 4 well-
separated spade-like petals that are raggedly toothed on the outer edge. There
are 8 stamens. The flower buds are rose-tinged. The leaves are in opposite clusters
at the branch nodes. They are entire, lanceolate, ³/₄ to 1¹/₂ inches long, and about a
third as wide.
   Fendlerbush grows in rocky canyons and on slopes up to 8,000 feet. It blooms
from May through June.

Mock Orange
Philadelphus microphyllus • *Hydrangea Family*

The species name means "little-leaf," which distinguishes the plant from Lewis' mock orange, the state flower of Idaho, with leaves twice as large. Several species of the genus Philadelphus *are often cultivated.*

The fragrance may greet you before you see the shrub. The fragrant white flowers have 4 broad, separate petals, many stamens, and a single style with 4 branches. This shrub may reach 5 feet in height. The reddish bark shreds gray as it ages. The shiny, leathery $1/2$- to 1-inch leaves are opposite on the branches. They are ovate and somewhat pointed, with smooth edges.

These shrubs grow in rocky soils from about 7,000 feet to 9,500 feet and bloom in June.

James' Cliffbush
Jamesia americana • *Hydrangea Family*

Clusters of white flowers at the stem tips and in the leaf axils contrast with the dark green of the leaves of this shrub. The $1/2$-inch white flowers have 5 wide petals, about 10 stamens, and a columnar center that opens into several styles as it matures. A mature shrub may be 6 feet tall in canyons, but is often smaller along the rocky crest of the mountain. It has rough reddish-brown bark that may be peeling. The leaves are opposite on the stems, ovate, and evenly serrated, with a rough upper surface and whitish hairs underneath.

This shrub grows above 6,500 feet and blooms from mid-June to late July.

Red Elderberry, Flor Sauco
Sambucus racemosa var. *microbotrys* •
Honeysuckle Family

Native Americans have used the red berries as food but some people find the berries to be toxic, so they should be treated with caution. The blue elderberry, which does not grow here, is the source of elderberry wine, jelly, and pies.

A common shrub, red elderberry grows up to 6 feet tall and is crowned with short, rounded clusters of small creamy-white flowers. The flowers have 5 petals and 5 stamens. The large, opposite leaves are pinnately compound with 5 to 7 lanceolate serrated leaflets.

Red elderberry is found in meadows and open woods above 8,000 feet and blooms in June. The red berries ripen in August.

Valerian

Valeriana arizonica • *Valerian Family*

Herbs in this genus have been used for sedation, bronchial spasms, and intestinal cramps.

Before the flowers open, this dainty herb has a terminal fuzzy red flower head about 1/2 inch wide. The clustered flowers open a light pink and soon mature white, with 5 flaring lobes. One style and 3 stamens protrude, continuing the fuzzy appearance. The stem leaves are opposite and pinnately compound, divided once. The few leaflets are oval and entire, with the end one larger. The long-stalked basal leaves are oval and have small teeth.

Usually found in protected places on north-facing slopes, this plant grows above 8,000 feet and blooms from April to June.

Apache Plume

Fallugia paradoxa • *Rose Family*

Cliffrose (Purshia stansburiana)*, a similar shrub also in the Rose Family, has cream-colored flowers with 5 to 10 pistils. Cliffrose leaves are shiny, more leathery, lack white-hairy undersides, and are sticky to the touch.*

The showy white flowers and the distinctive reddish plumes often are seen on this shrub at the same time. The 1-inch flowers have 5 broad petals, 20 or more pistils, and many stamens. The styles become distinctive reddish feathery tails that carry the seeds on the wind. The 1/2- to 1-inch leaves are bunched and have 3 to 7 pinnate lobes, with edges curled back. The undersides are finely white-hairy. This tangle-branched shrub grows up to 7 feet tall.

These shrubs grow up to 7,500 feet and bloom from April to October.

Chokecherry, Capulin

Prunus virginiana • *Rose Family*

Although the fresh berries are not particularly tasty to eat, the chokecherry makes excellent jelly and wine. The plant makes a purplish red dye. Chokecherry is a sacred plant to the Navajo.

You may "scent" this shrub before you see it. Blooming on elongated, many–flowered racemes, the creamy-white flowers are small with 5 petals and many stamens. This spineless shrub, or small tree, grows to 8 to 9 feet tall. The alternating 1 1/4- to 4-inch leaves are longer than wide with finely serrated edges.

Chokecherries grow along streams, in moist canyons, or on slopes. Blooming occurs from May to July followed by deep-red fruits in July through September.

Ninebark
Physocarpus monogynus • *Rose Family*

The species name monogynus *means "one pistil" but this species can have up to three pistils.*

Little clusters of tiny white or pinkish "roses" look like bouquets. They are located at the ends of the branches or in the upper leaf axils. The $1/4$- to $1/2$-inch flowers have 5 broad petals, many protruding stamens, and 1 to 5 styles. The 1- to 2-inch leaves are alternate, palmately lobed, and irregularly toothed. The leaf stalks are about the length of the leaves. This well-branched 3-foot shrub has bark that may shred as the plant matures.

Ninebark grows above 8,000 feet and flowers in June and July.

Wild Strawberry
Fragaria vesca, Fragaria americana • *Rose Family*

The two species of wild strawberries in the Sandias are difficult to differentiate. The fruits are edible but please leave them for the robins, bears, and other wildlife to eat.

Wild strawberry plants look like their domestic cousins, only smaller. Strawberry plants spread by runners (stolons). The $1/2$-inch-wide flowers, in a loose cluster at the top of a leafless stalk, have 5 white petals, and many stamens. The leaves have 3 coarsely toothed leaflets, 1 to $2^{1}/2$ inches in length. The ripe fruit is a miniature red strawberry.

Strawberries grow in shady areas above 8,000 feet and bloom from late May through June, with fruits ripening by the end of July.

Fendler's Sandwort
Arenaria fendleri • *Pink Family*

German-born Augustus Fendler (1813–1883) collected plants in New Mexico in 1846 and was the first botanist to study plants here in the American period.

Look for this low, dainty plant in the rocks around the summit. It has one or more upright stems, each with a few white flowers at the top. The $1/2$-inch flowers have 5 petals, 10 stamens with white filaments and dark anthers, and 3 white styles. The 5 green sepals are pointed and have glandular hairs. The basal leaves are long, very narrow, and entire. The stem leaves are similar but shorter, and are opposite.

This plant grows in bright sunshine on dry hills or on the mountaintop. It blooms from July to September.

Oshá
Ligusticum porteri • *Parsley Family*

*The Parsley Family includes vegetables such as carrots and parsnips, as well as flavoring herbs dill, coriander, and parsley. It also includes poison hemlock and water hemlock, which are very poisonous. Oshá has a multitude of medicinal uses, including treatment of viral infections, bronchial inflammations, and indigestion. **Misidentification and use of these plants has resulted in death.***
Large umbels of tiny white flowers crown the single, 2 to 4-foot-tall stem. Flowering stalks arising from the leaf axils give a branched appearance to the plant. The lower pinnately compound leaves may reach 2 feet in length and are divided several times, giving a lacy appearance. The leaf size decreases up the stem.

Oshá blooms in mid-July and grows above 9,000 feet.

Canada Violet
Viola canadensis • *Violet Family*

Although they have attractive flowers and nectar to attract pollinators, the violets may not be fertilized. Very small flowers, often not visible (below ground level), bloom later and are self-fertilizing.
Most violets seen in the Sandias are white. The irregular 5-petaled flowers face outward. The 1-inch flower is white with a yellow throat and purplish back. The 3 lower petals have purple lines. The middle lower petal has a spur on the rear. The heart-shaped leaves are fine-toothed. The alternate stem leaves are up to 3 inches wide. Their stalks may be as long as the plant height, 6 to 12 inches.

Violets grow in damp woods above 7,500 feet and bloom intermittently from May to October.

Baneberry
Actaea rubra • *Buttercup Family*

All parts of this plant are poisonous and can cause serious reactions, even cardiac arrest, if taken internally.
Feathery racemes of delicate white flowers are eye-catching on this plant. The flower stalks grow at the stem tips and from the upper leaf axils. The tiny petals and petal-like sepals drop off early in flowering, leaving many long white stamens to give a feathery appearance. This branched plant is 1 to 3 feet tall. The alternate leaves are large and pinnately compound. The leaflets are unevenly toothed. The fruits are shiny red or white berries.

Baneberry grows in rich, moist, shaded woods above 8,000 feet. Blooming occurs in June followed by the ripened berries in August.

Pasque Flower
Pulsatilla patens ssp. *multifida* • *Buttercup Family*

Pasque means blooming around Easter. Pulsatilla *refers to the Passion of Christ on the cross.*
This Easter delight has one upward-facing flower on an 8-inch upright hairy stem. The flower has 5 to 7 broad, pointed, white to lavender petal-like parts with hairs on the back, and many yellow stamens. The styles extend into 1-inch feathery tails that carry the seeds aloft. A ring of hairy bracts appears as a silky collar just below the flower. The flower stalk extends upward, leaving the bracts behind, as the hairy basal leaves emerge. These leaves are palmately compound and long-stalked.

This plant blooms briefly in early April at 7,500 feet and a month or more later at 10,000 feet.

Plains Larkspur
Delphinium wootonii • *Buttercup Family*

The tall larkspur found high on the mountain is Delphinium sapellonis. *Its flowers are mottled brownish-purple and not very attractive. It is found only in parts of northern New Mexico, and is listed as rare and sensitive. Larkspurs intergrade easily, making identification difficult. Treat them as poisonous.*
Lavender-mottled whitish flowers grow in a raceme on the 8- to 12-inch stem of this foothills plant. The typical 1-inch irregular larkspur flower has a rear-pointing spur. The leaves are palmately compound, with the leaflets deeply and narrowly lobed.

This plant grows up to 6,500 feet and blooms in May and June.

Blackfoot Daisy
Melampodium leucanthum • *Composite Family*

A foot-shaped bract below each ray flower turns dark when it matures. This is a very drought-resistant plant.
Rounded masses of white flowers found in desert-like environs characterize the blackfoot daisy. It is seldom taller than 6 inches. The many-branched plant has showy 1 to 1¹/₂-inch white flower heads on long naked stalks. The 8 to 10-ray flowers have 1 or 2 notches on their outer margins and are often purple veined underneath. The disk flowers are yellow. The 1- to 2-inch lanceolate leaves are opposite and have a grayish appearance. The leaves are entire or sometimes lobed.

In dry areas below 6,500 feet, the blackfoot daisy blooms intermittently from May through September.

89

Daisy, Spreading Fleabane
Erigeron divergens •
Composite Family

*Fleabanes were once believed to repel fleas.
The equal-length bracts help distinguish this
genus from other daisy-like composites.*
Lovely little flower heads with many layered white,
pink, or pale blue-lavender rays and yellow disk flowers
punctuate the landscape. One or more inch-wide
flower heads terminate on 12-inch-tall stems. The green bracts are numerous,
straight, nearly equal in length, and do not overlap. The 1-inch alternate stem
leaves are entire and wider toward the ends. The basal leaves are similar and
somewhat larger, and may drop early.

These plants grow at lower elevations and bloom from April to September.

Easter Daisy
Townsendia exscapa •
Composite Family

Look for these flowers at ground level. One to a few 1 to
2-inch-wide, stalkless flower heads are nestled among
the crowded basal leaves. The 15 to 30 white to pinkish-
purple $1/2$- to $3/4$-inch ray flowers surround the yellow
disk flowers. The flower head is held in a $3/4$-inch-deep involucre (a cup-like
arrangement of bracts that holds the flowers in the head). The very narrow, lanceolate leaves are entire and up to 2 inches long. The leaves may be sparsely soft
haired or have straight stiff hairs.

Easter daisy may be seen in bloom as early as April and is found in sandy
locations below 8,000 feet.

Yarrow
Achillea millefolium •
Composite Family

Historically, all parts of this plant have been used as medicine, insecticide, and fumigant. Achilles reportedly used it to heal his warriors' wounds. Native Americans called it "nosebleed plant," because it slows bleeding.

Looking like the yarrow you grow in your yard, the white, or occasionally pink, flat-topped 1 to 2-inch cluster of small flower heads grows on a single, fibrous stem about 1 foot tall. The flower head consists of 2 to 6 rounded $1/8$-inch ray flowers surrounding 10 to 30 small, yellow disk flowers. The 1 to 3-inch alternating leaves are divided 2 to 3 times into very fine segments that give a feathery fern-like appearance. All parts have a pleasant, herbal, woodsy smell.

This widespread plant grows in meadows and partial shade above 7,000 feet and flowers from May to August.

Baby Asters
Chaetopappa ericoides, syn. *Leucelene ericoides* •
Composite Family

Little bouquets of dainty white flowers arise from a single root. The branching stems are 4 to 6 inches tall. The terminal flower heads are small, with about 12 white, $1/4$-inch ray flowers surrounding the yellow disk flowers. The ray flowers turn pinkish with age. The hairy leaves are alternate, entire, and linear.

The plants grow on dry plains and rocky slopes up to 7,500 feet. The flowers bloom in April and May.

Plants with Yellow to Orange Flowers

Bladderpods
Physaria spp. •
Mustard Family

Some years the foothills are carpeted in spring with these bright flowers from the mustard family.

Three yellow bladderpods are found in the Sandias: *Physaria fendleri, Physaria intermedia,* and *Physaria pinetorium.* The 4-petaled flowers are in a short raceme. These plants often have several 6-inch stems that arise from a common point at the ground and tend to sprawl. The stem leaves are alternate and narrow, somewhat wider toward the outer end. The basal leaves of *Physaria fendleri* and *Physaria intermedia* are narrow and unlobed, while those of *Physaria pinetorium* are spoon-shaped and slightly lobed. The fruits are bladder-shaped pods with points on the ends. The stems and leaves are hairy, giving the plants a grayish appearance. *Physaria pinetorium* is often misidentified as *Physaria ovalifolia.*

These mustards grow in the dry foothills, but *Physaria pinetorium* also occurs on the crest. They bloom from April into the early summer.

Twistpod Draba
Draba helleriana •
Mustard Family

Many yellow mustards grow in the area. The shapes of the leaves and pods are very useful in distinguishing one mustard from another.

Flowers of the mustard family grow in a raceme and have 4 petals, usually at right angles in a "Maltese Cross." This low yellow mustard often appears slightly irregular with the petals closer together in pairs. The fruits are 1/2-inch-long green pods, starting out flat with a pointed end. They twist like a corkscrew as they age. The leaves are alternate, ovate, and somewhat hairy. They may have a few shallow teeth.

Twistpod is ubiquitous, growing from the lower slopes of the Sandias up to the crest. It blooms from late spring to early fall.

Western Wallflower
Erysimum capitatum •
Mustard Family

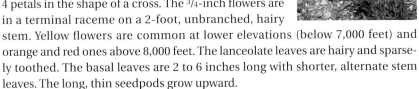

Edibles in this family include cabbage, rutabaga, cauliflower, radishes, and turnips. In other countries, flowers that grew well against walls were referred to as "wallflowers."

The western wallflower is easy to recognize with 4 petals in the shape of a cross. The 3/4-inch flowers are in a terminal raceme on a 2-foot, unbranched, hairy stem. Yellow flowers are common at lower elevations (below 7,000 feet) and orange and red ones above 8,000 feet. The lanceolate leaves are hairy and sparsely toothed. The basal leaves are 2 to 6 inches long with shorter, alternate stem leaves. The long, thin seedpods grow upward.

The western wallflower blooms from mid-May through August.

Hooker's Evening Primrose
Oenothera elati, syn. *Oenothera hookeri* •
Evening Primrose Family

Oenothera *means "wine-scented." In early summer the fragrant blooms open in the afternoon and fade by the following morning. By late summer they bloom all day.*

These bright yellow flowers are often seen blooming along the roadside. They bloom in a raceme on a 1 to 4-foot stem. The flowers are 3/4 to 1 1/2 inches wide. The 4 broad petals fade to orange. There are 8 stamens and a 4-lobed stigma. The hairy stem has alternate 2 to 8-inch-long, lanceolate leaves that are entire, wavy-margined or toothed.

This plant grows in canyon bottoms from 6,000 to 9,000 feet. It blooms from mid-June to mid-September.

Cinquefoils
Potentilla spp. •
Rose Family

Cinquefoil *means "five-leafed" in French.*
Shrubby cinquefoil is planted as an ornamental.
The herbaceous species readily hybridize,
making identification difficult.

Orange-throated flowers with many stamens and 5 broad yellow petals characterize cinquefoils. Five of the six species in the Sandias are herbs with flowers clustered atop 4 to 20-inch stems. Varileaf cinquefoil *(Potentilla gracilis* var. *pulcherrima)* and *Potentilla coccina* have palmately compound leaves with 5 to 7 toothed leaflets. Pretty cinquefoil *(Potentilla hippiana)* and *Potentilla anserina* have long stalked, pinnately compound, blue-green leaves with hairy undersurfaces. Prairie cinquefoil *(Potentilla pennsylvanica)* has pinnately compound leaves with up to 15 deeply and narrowly lobed leaflets. Shrubby cinquefoil *(Potentilla fruticosa* syn. *Pentaphylloides floribunda)* is a small shrub with pinnately compound leaves.

All species grow above 7,500 feet and bloom all summer.

Globemallows
Sphaeralcea spp. •
Mallow Family

Globemallows are used for sore throats, skin
rashes, and as a hair conditioner, appearing
in herbal stores as Yerba de Negrita.

Globemallows look like small hollyhocks with 1-inch-wide orange-red flowers in racemes topping the stems. All globemallow flowers have 5 petals and the many stamens are united into a column. Leaves help to distinguish between species. Red globemallow *(Sphaeralcea coccinea)* has sprawling upturned stems. The leaves are pinnately divided with 3 deeply lobed leaflets. Globemallow *(Sphaeralcea hastulata)* has $3/4$ to $2^1/2$-inch wedge-shaped leaves with many variations. The taller narrow-leaf globemallow *(Sphaeralcea angustifolia)* has short-stalked lanceolate leaves with smooth, wavy, or toothed leaf margins.

Globemallows bloom up to 8,000 feet, from May to frost.

Fringed Gromwell, Puccoon
Lithospermum incisium • Borage Family

*This species produces 2 types of flowers. The spring flowers
are conspicuous. The smaller summer flowers lack petals,
grow in the lower leaf axils, self-fertilize, and produce
most of the seeds.*
Five yellow fringed lobes flare from the long narrow
flower tubes that grow in the upper leaf axils of this hairy 4- to 16-inch-tall herb.
The flowers are $1/2$ to $1^1/4$ inches long and $1/2$ to $3/4$ inches wide. The 5 sepals are short
and enclose only the base of the tubes. The narrow, entire, stalkless leaves are 1 to
2 inches long and alternate on the stems, which branch at the base of the plant.

　　　This puccoon grows on dry hills up to 7,000 feet. It blooms from mid-April
through early summer.

Wayside Gromwell, Puccoon
Lithospermum multiflorum • Borage Family

*This species is also called purple gromwell after the dye
from its roots. In France it is called* plante aux perles,
*because the hard, white shiny seeds resemble pearls. The
genus name comes from the Greek, meaning "stone seed."*
Bright yellow tubular flowers are in nodding, slightly
coiled clusters at the top of the stems. The short tubes are
wide below the 5 short, flaring lobes, which are not fringed. The 5 sepals are hairy.
The leaves are linear and alternate on the stem. The plant is about 4 to 16 inches tall.

　　　Growing on dry hillsides up to about 9,000 feet, this plant blooms from June
to September.

Yellow Sky Pilot
Polemonium brandegei • Phlox Family

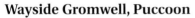

The Sandias are the southern limit of this plant.
Look for this low, densely leaved plant along the edge
of the crest and in the rocky outcroppings in early summer. The yellow flowers have 5 flaring lobes at the end
of a 1-inch tube. They grow in the outer leaf axils and at
the end of the stems. The lower leaves are 2 to 3 inches
long and pinnately compound, divided once. They
appear to have whorls of 3 to 4 tiny leaflets around the midrib. The stems, leaves,
and sepals are hairy and sticky.

Mexican Squawroot, Bear Corn
Conopholis alpina var. *mexicana* •
Broomrape Family

Squawroot is a parasite on oak tree roots.
It has no chlorophyll.
This plant looks like a corn cob standing upright in the ground. The pale yellow plant is stubby and thick, usually 4 to 6 inches high. It grows in groups. Its leaves are overlapping vertical scales on the stem. They are yellowish, turning darker with age. The irregular flowers face outward. They have short, curving tubes ending in stubby lobes, 2 upper and 3 lower. The style protrudes and has a knobby stigma.

Growing in patches under pines and oaks up to 7,500 feet, these plants bloom in May and June.

Mountain Parsley
Cymopterus lemmonii
syn. *Pseudocymopterus montanus* •
Parsley Family

Mountain Caraway
Aletes acaulis • *Parsley Family*

These are "fly flowers," which have no scent in comparison
to bee-pollinated flowers. Flies are attracted to yellow, flat-topped,
or bowl-shaped flowers with numerous, well-exposed pistils and stamens.
These two plants can easily be confused, as both have small compound umbels of tiny yellow flowers at the tops of the stems. Mountain parsley has basal and stem leaves pinnately divided 3 times; it grows as tall as 18 inches. Mountain caraway is shorter and has bare stems and basal leaves divided once. The leaflets have both deep and shallow lobes with pointed ends.

Both plants grow above 7,000 feet. Mountain parsley blooms from June to frost. Mountain caraway blooms in May and June.

Deervetch
Lotus wrightii • *Pea Family*

The common name comes from the plant being browsed by deer.

The flowers and leaves of this plant are small, but the irregular pea-type flowers will catch your eye. They are yellow, orange, or both on opening and become reddish with age. They are $1/2$ inch long, stalkless, and grow in the leaf axils. The alternate, stalkless leaves appear to be palmately compound, divided into 3 to 5 lanceolate stalkless leaflets up to $1/2$ inch long. They give the appearance of small leaves partially whorled around the stem. This hairy plant grows as tall as 18 inches and is branched at the ground.

Deervetch grows in open, dry woods up to 9,000 feet and blooms from May through September.

Golden Pea
Thermopsis rhombifolia • *Pea Family*

This plant is believed to be poisonous.

The bright (knock your eyes out) yellow flowers are in dense terminal racemes that arise from upper leaf axils. The irregular 5-petaled flower is a typical pea flower about $3/4$ to $1^1/2$ inches long, with 10 stamens. The palmately compound leaves have 3 broadly lanceolate leaflets 1 to $1^1/2$ inches long. The branching stems are 1 to 2 feet tall. The fruit pod is $1^1/2$ to 3 inches long, slender, flat, hairy, and erect.

Golden pea grows in forest openings above 7,000 feet and blooms in May or early June.

Golden Smoke, Scrambled Eggs
Corydalis aurea • *Fumitory Family*

The plant is poisonous. It can be an annual or biennial.

These unusual yellow flowers are in elongated, sparse racemes on branched stems up to 16 inches tall. The irregular 4-petaled, $1/2$- to $3/4$-inch flowers are 2-lipped. An upper petal extends into a rounded spur to the back and a hood in front. The lower petal is shaped like a scoop. The 2 side petals surround the 6 stamens and 1 pistil. The bluish-green leaves are alternate and pinnately compound with deeply lobed leaflets.

Golden smoke grows in gravel soils, disturbed areas, and damp, open woods. It is found above 6,000 feet and blooms sporadically throughout the summer.

Wooly Mullein
Verbascum thapsus • *Figwort Family*

Miners dipped the stalks in tallow to make torches; hence one common name, "miner's candle." Another, "hag taper," refers to use by witches.

The basal rosette of large, fuzzy-haired leaves grows during the first year of this biennial plant. During the second year a single, stout flowering spike 2 to 6 feet tall is produced. The dusty yellow flowers are slightly irregular and have 5 lobes and 5 protruding, orange-tipped stamens. The clasping, alternate stem leaves are like the basal leaves but smaller.

This alien species grows almost anywhere and indicates disturbed soils. It blooms all summer.

Creeping Mahonia, Oregon Grape Holly
Berberis repens • *Barberry Family*

This is considered one of the best medicinal plants. The fruit is edible and is used to make jams. Animals eat the fruit too.

This evergreen shrub grows close to the ground, usually 3 to 6 inches high and rarely over 20 inches. The cupped, $1/4$-inch, yellow flowers grow in short racemes. They have 6 petals, 6 stamens, and 1 style. The alternate $2^1/2$-inch leaves are pinnately compound. The 3 to 7 leaflets have spiny-toothed margins and resemble holly leaves. The plant spreads by a creeping underground stem. The round blue-black fruit is about $1/4$ inch in diameter.

Creeping mahonia grows above 6,500 feet and blooms in April and May.

Chocolate Flower, Green Eyes
Berlandiera lyrata • *Composite Family*

Lyrata means "lyre-shaped" and refers to the shape of the leaf of this plant. The seeds have been used for seasoning.

This flower smells like chocolate! The $1^1/2$-inch-wide flower heads have 8 red-veined yellow ray flowers surrounding maroon disk flowers. The ray flowers soon drop, leaving the green petal-like bracts that look like "green eyes." The flowers are on branched stalks. The 5-inch leaves are basal and alternating on the stem. They are pinnately compound with irregularly lobed leaflets. The end lobe is the largest. The plant grows up to 16 inches tall.

This aromatic plant grows in dry environs up to 6,500 feet and blooms from April to September.

Cut-leaf Coneflower
Rudbeckia laciniata • *Composite Family*

The roots and leaves can be made into a tea.
A tall plant with yellow droopy ray flowers catches your eye. The flower heads have 6 to 16 yellow, 1- to 2-inch-long ray flowers surrounding a cone of yellow disk flowers. Long stalked flower heads grow at the end of the stem and from upper leaf axils. Lower alternating leaves, up to 8 inches in length, are deeply cut into about 7 lobes, each variously toothed. As the leaves ascend the stem, the leaf length decreases. This unbranched plant has a stem 3 to 6 feet tall.

Cut-leaf coneflower is usually found in wet areas and along the roadsides from 6,500 to 9,000 feet. The flowers bloom from August to mid-September.

Goldenrods
Solidago spp. • *Composite Family*

Goldenrod characteristics vary widely, making specific identification difficult. Although they have been given a bad name as a cause of hay fever, the sticky pollen of goldenrods is not airborne but is carried by pollinators.
In late summer or fall, these bright yellow flowers decorate the landscape. Many 1/8- to 1/4-inch flower heads, with few to many ray flowers and many disk flowers, are densely packed in various types of clusters. The stems vary from 4 inches to 4 feet in length. The alternate leaves are stalkless, linear to ovate, entire to toothed, and up to 4 inches long and 1 1/2 inches wide.

Goldenrods grow from the foothills to the top of the mountain.

Hairy Golden Aster
Chrysopsis villosa, syn. *Heterotheca villosa* • Composite Family

Navajos used this plant for treatment of sexually transmitted diseases. Roots have been heated and used for toothaches.
This plant's common name is very apt, in the Sandias, as all parts are hairy. The 1-inch flower heads have 10 to 25 yellow ray flowers surrounding the darker yellow disk flowers. The branched 4 to 20-inch stems terminate in one flower head or a flat-topped cluster. The gray-green 1 to 2-inch leaves are alternate, entire, and lanceolate, almost stalkless, and appear to twist.

Hairy golden aster grows in dry environs at all elevations and blooms from mid-July through September.

Mexican Hat, Prairie Coneflower
Ratibida columnifera • *Composite Family*

Mexican hats are prolific seed producers and very hardy. Planted in gardens, they may dominate in the second year. Sombrero-shaped flower heads top the stems of this plant, which reaches 14 inches or more in height. Upright domes of tiny disk flowers have a lower fringe of 3 to 7 yellow or maroon rays drooping downward. The dark disk flowers open starting from the bottom of the dome, giving a bald look to the greenish buds above. The leaves are alternate and pinnately compound, with lobed leaflets.

Often found on roadsides or in dry meadows up to 7,500 feet, this species blooms through the summer.

Nodding Groundsel
Senecio bigelovii • *Composite Family*

The genus, Senecio, *contains many species, some of which contain alkaloids that are poisonous. Over 100 species occur in the West.*
It seems as though the flower buds have not opened on this odd-looking plant. The long-stalked, nodding flower heads, about 3/4 inches long, have no ray flowers and are composed of yellow disk flowers that are tightly enclosed in narrow green bracts and appear to be unopened. The alternate clasping leaves are 4 to 8 inches long, lanceolate, and toothed. The 1 to 3-foot plant is single stemmed.

Nodding groundsel is found in mountain meadows and forests above 8,000 feet and will bloom from mid-July to September.

Perky Sue
Tetraneuris argentea • *Composite Family*

Alpine Stemless Bitterweed (Tetraneuris acaulis) *could be misidentified as a dwarf perky Sue when seen growing among the rocks at the crest. This cushion plant has stemless flowers and hairy lance-shaped leaves that resemble those of perky Sue.*
One-inch flower heads on this "perky" plant are terminal or on stalks in the leaf axils. The yellow disk flowers are surrounded by 12 yellow ray flowers with 3 teeth at their ends. The few basal and alternating stem leaves are gray-green, lanceolate, entire, and densely silver-haired. The plants grow up to 12 inches tall.

Perky Sue grows in sunny locations up to 7,000 feet and blooms from May to September.

Showy Golden-eye
Viguiera multiflora •
Composite Family

*Mountain meadows glow with this plant's
bright yellow flowers.*
Loose clusters of 1-inch flower heads grow on branched
stems 1^1/$_2$ to 3 feet tall. The 10 to 14 ray flowers surround the darker yellow disk flowers. The disk becomes cone shaped as the ray
flowers fade. The finely haired leaves are opposite on the lower stem and alternate higher up. They are lanceolate, prominently veined, and entire or slightly
toothed.

This very showy plant covers meadows and roadsides with yellow from
August to October. Showy goldeneye grows at all elevations.

White Ragweed
Hymenopappus filifolius •
Composite Family

*The common name comes from the dense curly
hairs covering the stems and leaves, which give this
1 to 2-foot-tall plant a powdered white appearance.*
The rayless 1-inch flower heads grow singly on branched
stalks. The disk flowers are yellow and have long project-
ing stamens and 1 projecting style. The 5^1/$_2$-inch, mostly basal leaves are pinnately
compound and divided 2 to 3 times into linear, fleshy segments. The stem leaves
are alternate, usually 2 to 4, but sometimes are absent or reduced in size.

White ragweed grows in the foothills and is occasionally seen at higher
elevations. It blooms from May to September.

Prickly Pear
***Opuntia* spp.** • *Cactus Family*

Be careful where you sit; the barbed hairs will penetrate clothing in large numbers and require embarrassing help to remove. The fruits, called tunas, *can be made into jelly with due caution. The young edible pads, called* nopalitos, *can be found fresh or canned in some stores.*
All cacti in the genus *Opuntia* have branching, jointed stems that grow in segments. Prickly pear segments are flat and fleshy, with round or elongated pads. Areoles (pits) occur on the pad edges and in rows across the surfaces of the pads. Spines may arise from any areole, but flowers and new pads grow only from those on or near the edges. Two kinds of spines grow from the areoles. The big ones are 1 inch long on most species and up to 7 inches on some. The number of these spines varies from none at some areoles to 10 or so. They may lie close to the pad surface or point away from it. The other spines, called glocids, are tiny barbed hairs. They cluster along the pad edges and at the bases of the larger spines. The 1- to 3-inch flowers have many waxy petals, many stamens, and 1 centered style. Rounded knobby fruits with flat or depressed outer ends may turn reddish with age. *Opuntia polyacantha* has rounded pads and yellow flowers. Two to about 6 spines grow close to the pad surface at most areoles, and one longer spine grows outward from the surface. Other species in the Sandias have greenish-yellow or pinkish to red flowers.

These plants grow in arroyos and on dry hillsides up to 8,000 feet. They bloom in May and June.

To Learn More:

Carter, Jack. *Trees and Shrubs of New Mexico.* Mimbres Press, 1997.

Harrington, H. D. *Edible Native Plants of the Rocky Mountains.* Albuquerque: University of New Mexico Press, 1967.

Ivey, Robert DeWitt. *Flowering Plants of New Mexico.* 4th ed. Albuquerque, N.Mex.: published by the author, 2003.

Kershaw, Linda, Andy MacKinnon, and Jim Pojar. *Plants of the Rocky Mountains.* Lone Pine Publishing, 1998.

Jercinovic, Gene. *Wildflowers of the Manzano Mountains.* Torreon, N. Mex.: published by the author, 2003.

Moore, Michael. *Medicinal Plants of the Mountain West.* Santa Fe: Museum of New Mexico Press, 1979.

———. *Medicinal Plants of the Desert and Canyons.* Santa Fe: Museum of New Mexico Press, 1989.

Niehaus, Theodore F., Charles L. Ripper, and Virginia Savage. *Southwestern and Texas Wildflowers.* New York: Houghton Mifflin, Co., 1984.

Schreirer, Carl. *A Field Guide to Wildflowers of the Rocky Mountains.* Bel Air, Md.: Homestead Publishing, 1996.

Spellenberg, Richard. *Audubon Field Guide to North American Wildflowers: Western Region.* New York: Alfred A. Knopf, Inc., 2001.

CHAPTER 8
Coniferous Trees and Shrubs

Mary Stuever

Corkbark fir
Abies latifolia var. *arizonica*

Height: 40–60 feet; Diameter: 6–24 inches;
Needles: 1 inch; Cones: 2–4 inches; Evergreen

The inside of this tree's soft, spongy bark resembles cork, thus the common name. This fir has short needles that curve upward, and like other true firs, the needles are soft, flexible, flat, and have a whitish line on both upper and lower surfaces. Cones stand erect on the upper branches and fall apart after maturity leaving erect "candle-like" stalks. Corkbark fir is limited to the upper reaches of the mountains above 9,500 feet and reproduces in shady environments. Expect snow packs to remain late into the spring where this tree grows.

Engelmann Spruce
Picea engelmannii

Height: 80–120 feet; Diameter: 18–36 inches;
Needles: 1–1 1/8 inches long;
Cones: 1–2 1/2 inches; Evergreen

Spruce needles grow on woody pegs or pedestals. When needles fall off, a rough twig remains. The 4-sided needles are sharper than flat fir needles, although this spruce is the least spiny. When crushed, Engelmann spruce needles emit a skunkish odor. The reddish bark grows in distinctive elephant-ear-like plates. Builders favor the white wood for vigas and log homes. Engelmann spruce often grows at high elevations in association with corkbark fir. It is the only naturally occurring species of spruce in the Sandias. Blue spruce grows in nearby mountain ranges (Jemez, Sangre de Cristos, Mount Taylor) but appears to have missed migrating to the Sandias during the ice ages when today's conifer forests were established.

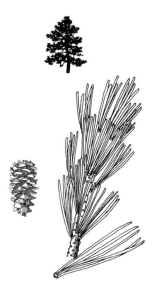

Limber Pine
Pinus flexilis

Height: 60–120 feet; Diameter: to 30 inches;
Needles: in 5's, 1¹/₂–3 inches;
Cones: 3–6 inches; Evergreen

In 1993, researchers from the Laboratory of Tree Ring Research in Tucson, Arizona, dated a live limber pine near the Sandia Crest back to A.D. 416! That makes it one of the oldest living trees in the world. The 5-needle limber pine occurs throughout mixed-conifer forests, though rarely in large numbers. On the crest, these trees are stunted from exposure to wind and cold. These deep-rooted trees are quite wind-firm. The closely related southwestern white pine *(P. strobiformis)* grows on drier sites in the Sandias. Limber pine needles clump near the end of branches and are longer and yellow-green in color. The wider spaced, southwestern white pine needles are bluer and finer.

White Fir
Abies concolor

Height: 80–100 feet; Diameter: 15–30 inches;
Needles: 2–3 inches; Cones: 3–5 inches; Evergreen

Many out-of-state nurseries come here to collect white fir seeds. They claim the Sandias produce the bluest foliage favored by Christmas-tree growers throughout the country. The flexible, flat needles of white fir are the longest of the true firs. This silvery, bluish tree has highly resinous bark, smooth when young and deeply furrowed with age. The cones fall apart upon maturity leaving a long, upright spike on the top branches in the winter. Because of this, fir cones are hard to find intact on the forest floor! Like most conifers, fir cones grow near the top of the tree. This is to avoid self-pollination from the male flowers on the lower branches.

The Singularly Blue White Firs of the Sandias

When out-of-state nurseries wish to propagate Christmas trees with the blue-tinged foliage loved by holiday buyers, they often come to the high Sandias to collect the seeds of—white fir! The white fir trees here, they say, have some of the bluest foliage found anywhere.

Douglas-Fir
Pseudotsuga menziesii **var. *glauca***

Height: to 130 feet; Diameter: to 36 inches;
Needles: 1 inch, flat, blunt;
Cones: 3 inches, blunt; Evergreen

Douglas-fir has been incorrectly called a spruce, hemlock, true fir, or pine. Actually, it is in a class of its own. Douglas-fir is most easily identified by its cone. A ribbon-like, three-pronged bract extends from each cone scale. The cones hang down from the limbs, unlike the true-fir cones that stand erect. Mature trees have thick, distinctive, multicolored bark. In the Sandias, there are several large Douglas-fir trees, but due to shady forest conditions, not nearly as many young Douglas-fir as white fir seedlings. Pueblo dancers often wear boughs of Douglas-fir during ceremonial dances.

107

The Elders of the Sandias

When dendrochronologists, scientists who study tree rings to determine ages, were examining trees near the Sandia Crest they found limber pines that had sprouted in A.D. 416—more than a thousand years before Europeans arrived in North America. They also found a Douglas-fir that had sprouted in A.D. 995, before the Normans invaded England. As the scientist who found the trees wrote, "This is a remarkable discovery as such ancient tree-ring resources are rare, not only in the Southwest but worldwide."

Ponderosa Pine
Pinus ponderosa

Height: 60–120 feet; Diameter: to 39 inches;
Needles: in 3's, 5 inches;
Cones: 3–6 inches; Evergreen

If the distinctive red, scaly mature bark doesn't immediately give this tree away, take a deep whiff of the bark and you will know the ponderosa pine by its vanilla or butterscotch odor. Although this tree does grow on the steep west slope, it is more widespread in the East Mountains, where gentler terrain allows a wider transition zone—between the high mixed-conifer forests and the woodlands—where ponderosa pine reigns. This stately pine is a major lumber tree throughout the Southwest.

Piñon Pine
Pinus edulis

Height: 15–35 feet; Diameter: to 12 inches;
Needles: in 2's, $3/4$ to $1^1/2$ inches;
Cones: 1–2 inches; Evergreen

The small, bushy, resinous piñon pine is a compact tree with an often irregular-shaped trunk. This tree is slow growing: a piñon with a 6-inch diameter can be as much as 150 years old. The piñon is known for delicious nuts from its squatty cones. The edible nuts are popular in candies and in Spanish and Puebloan cooking, as well as cuisines worldwide. Wildlife, such as deer, bear, woodrats, piñon jays, and wild turkeys are fond of the seeds. Piñon pine is prized firewood because of its dense wood and pungent odor. It is the state tree of New Mexico. Recently piñon trees throughout the state, including the Sandias, have experienced dramatic die-off due to drought-induced bark-beetle outbreaks. Also, this tree is easily damaged by high winds.

Rocky Mountain Juniper
Juniperus scopulorum

Height: to 30 feet; Diameter: to 20 inches;
Needles: droopy scales;
Cones: berry-like, 2 seeds; Evergreen

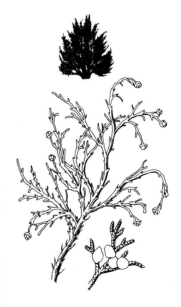

Rocky Mountain junipers can attain the oldest age of junipers—a family of trees known for longevity—with specimens commonly 250 to 300 years old, and a tree in Utah reported to be 3,000 years old. The sharp, silvery-green, scale-like leaves cluster on distinctive drooping twigs. The stringy bark of this juniper provided diaper material for native people. The straight young stems make excellent fence posts. The heartwood of the Rocky Mountain juniper is deep red with a rich aroma reminiscent of cedar. As a result, people often make the mistake of calling junipers "cedars" after a related but different tree. However, "Juniper Crest" doesn't have the same ring as "Cedar Crest."

Alligator Junipers

Throughout southern and central New Mexico the alligator juniper, with its distinctive checkered bark, is among the most common and impressive trees. Yet in the Sandias the trees abruptly become more scarce as they approach their northern limit in southern Colorado.

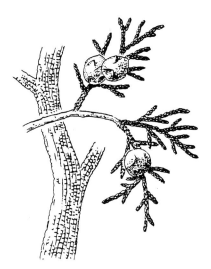

Alligator Juniper
Juniperus deppeana

Height: to 65 feet; Diameter: to 60 inches;
Needles: scales;
Cones: 1/2 inch, berry-like, 4 seeds;
Evergreen

The distinctive, checkerboard bark of this juniper reminds us landlocked desert dwellers of alligator skin. When left alone, this juniper has the capacity to develop broad, large trunks. Once cut, the root sprouts from this species multiply like the brooms of *Fantasia*. The wood generally is a light tan in the center, with light-yellow sapwood. In the Sandias, alligator juniper is not a common juniper, which is odd since it is the most prolific tree just south in the Manzanos. The largest tree of this species in New Mexico has a girth of more than 26 feet.

One-Seed Juniper
Juniperus monosperma

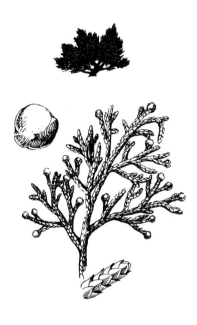

Height: to 35 feet; Diameter: to 20 inches; Needles: scales; Cones: berry-like, 1 seed; Evergreen

Like many juniper species, one-seed juniper trees are either male or female. In late winter, the male trees take on a coppery tint from the thousands of tiny pollen-emitting cones. The bane of allergy sufferers, one-seed juniper is the most widespread tree in the Sandia foothills. The berry-like cone generally has only 1 seed, thus the common name. The aromatic foliage is packaged in sachets by a Placitas business and marketed worldwide. Junipers are drought resistant and resprout after cutting, burning, or removal by other means.

CHAPTER 9
Broadleaf Trees and Shrubs

Mary Stuever

Quaking Aspen
Populus tremuloides • *Willow Family*

About the time hot-air balloons rise from the Fiesta grounds in Albuquerque, hillsides in the higher reaches of the Sandias are turning golden as coin-sized quaking-aspen leaves change to shades of yellow, orange, and red. The most dominant deciduous tree of our forest, aspens are found from Mexico to Canada. They grow in mixed-conifer stands where sunlight is abundant and thus are among the first trees to recolonize an area that has been disturbed, as by fire. A remnant of cooler times when seeding conditions were more favorable, today the white-barked aspen trees almost always grow from roots established thousands of years ago.

Willows
Salix spp. • *Willow Family*

Willows often grow in thickets along streamsides, though some species are midsize forest trees. They have narrow, lance-shaped leaves. The young bark is smooth and red, and often twigs are used in basket-making. Willows play an important role in stream ecology. The fibrous, matted roots keep erosion in check, and the trees shade the cool water. A source of salicin, which forms salicylic acid or aspirin when ingested, willow bark has been used by many indigenous peoples for pain relief.

Rocky Mountain Maple
Acer glabra • *Maple Family*

T'aa dichíí, the Apache name for maple, means "leaves turn red." This maple has many classic maple characteristics: sugary sap, 3- to 5-lobed leaves, red leaf stems, paired seeds with papery wings, and smooth bark. In the fall, the leaves can turn a reddish color, but they are generally yellow, unlike the bright red of its cousin the bigtooth maple *(Acer grandidentatum)*, which is well known from Fourth of July Canyon south of the Sandias in the Manzanos. Often Rocky Mountain maple is a small tree growing in the shade of white-fir and Douglas-fir forests. In the Sandias, the lobes of this maple are often so dissected, they look like the leaflets found in box elder.

Box Elder
Acer negundo • *Maple Family*

Box elder, with its notched leaves, sometimes has an identity crisis; it is often mistaken for poison ivy *(Toxidendron radicans)* or its cousin, Rocky Mountain maple. Box elder, with light-green leaves, is a tree or shrub while poison ivy, with darker, puffier leaves, is a vine or low shrub. The center leaflet has a leaf stem as opposed to the lack of leaf stem in Rocky Mountain maple. A common tree along waterways, box elder also grows well in poor sites, making it a popular urban planting.

Gambel Oak
Quercus gambellii • *Oak Family*

The large, deeply lobed leaves of this widespread shrub and tree make Gambel oak an easy woody plant to identify. A key habitat indicator, Gambel oak can be found from the upper-elevation piñon stands through the mixed- conifer forests. Gambel oak forms vast thickets, especially after forest fires. In shaded environments, the shrubs can become tall trees if left undisturbed for a long time. Gambel oak provides important wildlife habitat, with deer browsing leaves and stems; turkeys and squirrels favoring acorns; and bears, rabbits, and many songbirds finding shelter in its leafy branches.

Wavyleaf Oak
Quercus X paucifolia • *Oak Family*

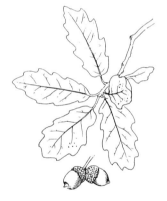

Oaks are known for their tendency to hybridize, and no other Sandia Mountain oak is more promiscuous than wavyleaf oak, which is not a true species but a category for Gambel oak–gray oak hybrids. The leaves, though highly variable, are generally smaller and less deeply lobed than those of Gambel oak but share the same thin texture. Wavyleaf oaks can tolerate drier, hotter environments and thus are generally found at lower elevations than Gambel oaks, although where both oaks' ranges overlap they can be found growing side by side. Although it occasionally attains small tree stature, wavyleaf oak generally forms copious shrub fields or forest understories.

Gray Oak

Quercus grisea • *Oak Family*

The leathery leaves of this oak are about an inch to 2 inches long and sport a dull-green color due to the star-shaped hairs that are generally thicker on the leaf's underside. Its acorns grow on stalks. A lower-elevation oak, this small tree can be extensive in the juniper woodlands of the Sandia foothills. It commonly hybridizes with other oaks. After a fire, oaks often sprout prolifically, and this oak is no exception. It often grows with Fendler buckbrush and mountain mahogany.

Shrub Live Oak

Quercus turbinella • *Oak Family*

A low-elevation oak, shrub live oak will have green foliage year-round. The lobes of the thick, leathery leaves are so spiny that one is reminded of holly. The undersides of the leaves are thick with star-shaped hairs. The acorn nuts are narrow and pointed, and although the acorns provide a seasonal food source for animals, wildlife or livestock rarely browse the leaves. Shrub live oak is clump-forming, and colonies of this long-lived species may persist from roots that are thousands of years old.

Fendlerbush

Fendlera rupicola • *Hydrangea Family*

In May and June the glorious half-dollar-size white flowers of fendlerbush catch the observer's eye. Throughout the year, the pea-sized hardened fruits remain on this lanky, bark-shredding shrub. Opposite clusters of narrow, rolled-edged leaves grow at the branch nodes. Primarily a woodland species, the name *rupicola* means "lover of rocks" and nails its likely habitat. This bush provides good forage for deer and is noted for its appeal to goats. With its deep roots, fendlerbush is quite drought-resistant and when top-killed by fire, resprouts from roots.

Little-leaf Mock Orange
Philadelphus microphyllus • *Hydrangea Family*

The citrus scent of the fragrant white flowers on this shrub inspires the common name "mock orange." The June blossoms have four broad, separate white petals, surrounding a yellow tangle of many stamens. Related to—and often confused with—fendlerbush, the leathery leaves, though still lance-shaped, are broader and the leaf's edges are only slightly rolled. The undersides of these shiny leaves are dull from downy hairs, giving the plant a slightly silvered appearance. When mashed, the leaves can be used as soap.

Cliffbush
Jamesia americana • *Hydrangea Family*

At home both in rock crevices and the forest, this graceful shrub sports round clusters of 5-petaled, waxy, white flowers. The egg-shaped leaves have even-sized teeth along the margins and are oppositely arranged on the twigs. The young twigs are white to tan, with mature bark reddish-brown and peeling. The genus is only found in western North America and was first described by Edwin James, the physician-botanist on Major Long's 1820 expedition to the Rocky Mountains. The plant, however, dates back to the Oligocene (roughly 35 million years ago) making it a very old tree genus.

Red Elderberry, Flor Sauco
Sambucus racemosa **var.** *microbotrys* •
Honeysuckle Family

Red elderberry is a hard shrub to miss. It displays short, rounded pyramids of small creamy-white flowers in June followed by clusters of ripened, shiny red berries in August. The large pinnately compound leaves have 5 to 9 long, lance-shaped, jagged-edge leaflets. Found in open meadows and woods above 8,000 feet, this shrub rarely grows more than 6 feet tall. The berries have been reported as both poisonous and edible—and one should definitely err in the direction of caution and avoid eating them.

Apache Plume, Poñil
Fallugia paradoxa • *Rose Family*

All summer, showy white flowers and clusters of red feather-like seeds grace this tangle-branched shrub. The seeds' feathery tails, designed for wind dissemination, are said to inspire the name "Apache plume" because of the resemblance to "war bonnets." Although Apaches did not don this costume of the Plains Indians, the plant grows throughout the historic range of the Apache people. The tiny leaves have 3 to 7 delicate fingers, similar in shape to the stickier leaves of cliffbush. These shrubs are often found growing with rabbitbrush in arroyos in the foothills, although they can occur elsewhere.

Chokecherry, Capulín
Prunus virginiana • *Rose Family*

Found mostly along streams or in moist canyons, the chokecherry can form extensive thickets or be represented by a solitary tree. In early summer, the small, creamy-white flowers grow in sausage-shaped clusters on the ends of new twigs. Deep-red, tart cherries form from July to September. Although the fresh berries are not particularly tasty to eat, the chokecherry makes excellent jelly and wine. Fruit and foliage are utilized by many wild animals and livestock, although large volumes of the fresh foliage can result in hydrogen cyanide poisoning. Many of the chokecherries in Las Huertas canyon are host to a black fungus that forms cankers on the stems and shortens the lifespan of the trees.

Ninebark

Physocarpus monogynus • *Rose Family*

This short shrub with delicate arching branches rarely reaches more than 3 feet high. The kidney-shaped leaves of ninebark have 3 to 5 distinctive lobes and multiple teeth along the leaf edges. In June and July the tiny whitish-pink, 5-petaled blossoms cluster at the branch tips. The seed pods are inflated and, like many other plant parts, are covered in tiny star-shaped hairs. As the stem matures, the continually shredding bark gives an appearance of having "nine" lives. Poultices of boiled roots have been used to ease pain from open sores.

Wild Rose

Rosa woodsii • *Rose Family*

Unlike the cultivated roses, wild roses only have 5 petals, but they do have prickles on the stem below where each leaf is attached. The showy pink flowers are 2 inches across and have many yellow stamens. The rose hips, a good source of vitamin C, are red when mature and can persist on the bush well into winter. The leaves are compound with 5 to 9 oval leaflets and are arranged alternately on the stem.

Mountain Spray

Holodiscus dumosus • *Rose Family*

The "sprays" of tiny, cream-colored flowers at the tips of the branches inspire many names—rock spirea, rock spray, ocean spray, and mountain spray. The single leaves are roughly oval with ragged edges. Multiple stems branch from the base of this sprawling shrub. The bark is often shredding, though young bark, such as that found on twigs, is dark red. Although frequently growing in moist environments, mountain spray is often found on rocky, unstable slopes, where its fibrous roots provide erosion control.

119

Mountain Mahogany
Cercocarpus montanus • *Rose Family*

The long, feathery seeds of this common wood-land shrub are more likely to catch the eye than the petal-less, inconspicuous flowers. Despite its lack of showy blossoms, mountain mahogany soon becomes familiar to Sandia Mountain visitors who come to recognize its evergreen wedge-shaped leaves with strong parallel veins and jagged edges toward the leaf tips. Called *palo duro* in Spanish, "hard wood," the crooked wood of this shrub has long been used by native peoples for construction of sturdy implements such as digging tools, cradleboards, and snowshoes.

Skunkbush Sumac
Rhus trilobata • *Sumac Family*

A rounded, compact shrub of the woodlands, skunkbush sumac attracts ample attention in the fall when its foliage turns a stunning red. Known also as "three-leaf sumac," the compound leaves have three variously lobed leaflets. When crushed the stems and leaves emit an evil smell—thus the common name "skunkbush." Apaches make "lemonade" from the fruits, which are a good source of vitamin A. Because these fruits remain on the bushes through the winter, they are an important food source for grouse and songbirds.

New Mexico Locust
Robinia neomexicana • *Pea Family*

In early summer along the Crest Highway and in Las Huertas Canyon, droopy, hanging clusters of rose-pink flowers advertise the New Mexico locust. This thorny small tree can form impenetrable thickets. It is clearly in the pea family, as attested by the irregular pea-flowers, the hairy pods, and the numerous oval leaflets forming pinnately compound leaves. Puebloans have used the flexible, sturdy wood for making bows.

Four-wing Saltbush
Atriplex canescens • *Chenopodiaceae Family*

If you relied on the papery, tan, 4-winged seed to identify this shrub, you would miss half of them. Each shrub only produces the flowers of one sex, male or female, and only the females produce the characteristic seed. These faded-green shrubs often grow with sagebrush, but these leaves are entire and do not have lobes. Resistant to drought, these shrubs thrive in alkali soils; in the Sandias they are found primarily in the foothills. They provide forage for wildlife and domestic livestock.

Rabbitbrush, Chamisa
***Ericameria nauseosus*,** syn.
Chrysothamnus nauseosus •
Sunflower Family

In late summer when the golden flowers of rabbitbrush line the roads, you know that fall is not far away. Navajo weavers use the dense clusters of small, yellow flowerheads to produce a rich-yellow to light-orange dye. They also use the stems and leaves to produce a drab-green color. As the name suggests, rabbits find food and shelter among these shrubs, but deer, elk, and pronghorn browse them as well.

121

Currants and Gooseberries
Ribes spp. • *Gooseberry Family*

The *Ribes* genus includes the currants and gooseberries, a group of small waist-high shrubs with simple, alternate leaves with very wavy leaf edges. Known for berries that are valued by humans, bears, birds, and other beasts, gooseberries also are distinct in having spines. One common currant, wax currant *(Ribes cereum),* has drooping pink flowers, small orange to red berries, with stems and fruit free of spines or prickles. Its leaves are not as deeply lobed as other members of the genus. At higher elevations, the trumpet gooseberry *(Ribes leptanthum)* has erect pink to white flowers and many long, sharp spines. Another common species is alpine prickly gooseberry *(Ribes montigenum)* with prickle-covered stems, fruits, and flowers.

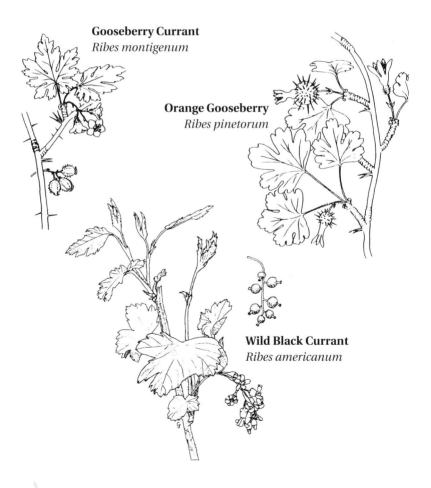

Gooseberry Currant
Ribes montigenum

Orange Gooseberry
Ribes pinetorum

Wild Black Currant
Ribes americanum

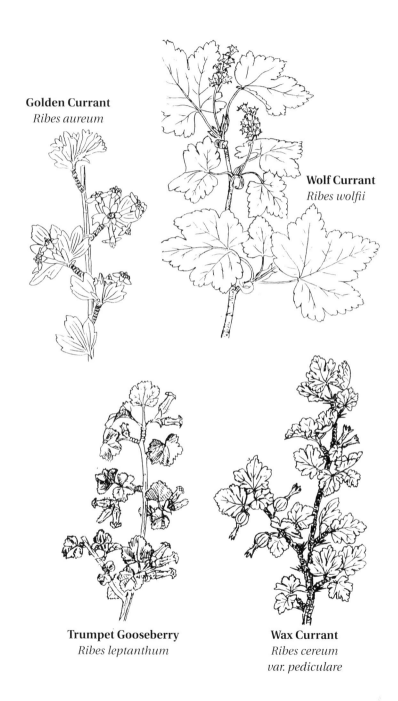

Golden Currant
Ribes aureum

Wolf Currant
Ribes wolfii

Trumpet Gooseberry
Ribes leptanthum

Wax Currant
Ribes cereum
var. pediculare

To Learn More about Conifers and Broadleaf Trees:

Carter, Jack L. *Trees and Shrubs of New Mexico.* Silver City, N.Mex.: Mimbres Publishing, 1997.

Carter, Jack L., Martha A. Carter, and Donna J. Stevens. *Common Southwestern Native Plants: An Identification Guide.* Silver City, N.Mex.: Mimbres Publishing, 2003.

Elmore, Francis H. *Shrubs and Trees of the Southwest Uplands.* Tucson, Ariz.: Southwest Parks and Monuments Association, 1976.

Ivey, Robert DeWitt. *Flowering Plants of New Mexico,* Fourth Edition. Albuquerque, N.Mex.: R. D. & V. Ivey, Publishers, 2003.

Lamb, Samuel H. *Woody Plants of the Southwest.* Santa Fe, N.Mex.: Sunstone Press, 1975.

Little, Elbert L., Jr. *Southwestern Trees: A Guide to Native Species of New Mexico and Arizona.* Agricultural Handbook No. 9. U.S.D.A. Forest Service, 1950.

Stuever, Mary and Daniel Shaw. *Philmont Fieldguide.* Cimarron, N.Mex.: Boy Scouts of America, 1985.

CHAPTER 10
Tree Diseases

Eugene Van Arsdel and David A. Conklin

The Sandia Mountains contain a rich diversity of tree diseases. Some diseases can be quite damaging, deforming and eventually killing trees. At the same time, diseases have an important role in the ecology of the forest. Like fire and insects, most diseases are natural "disturbance agents" that affect forest structure and composition. Disease-causing organisms—especially the decay fungi—also contribute to nutrient recycling. Diseases such as root rot can be a cause for concern in the heavily-used recreation sites of the Sandias, since they may result in tree failure. Among the diseases most likely to be encountered in the Sandias are broom rust and mistletoes.

Broom Rust

Broom rust, also known as yellow witches' broom, is very abundant on white fir in the Sandias. The dense masses of yellow foliage, or "brooms," are easily seen in the summer along the Crest Highway and trails between the Doc Long and Capulin Spring picnic areas. This disease is also found at higher elevations on corkbark fir.

Like most tree diseases, broom rust is caused by a fungus, *Melampsorella caryophyllacearum.* In the summer, the needles in the brooms become covered with tiny yellow to orange fruiting bodies. These produce spores that infect chickweeds, the "alternate host" of the fungus. Meadow chickweed *(Cerastium arvense)* and tuber starwort *(Pseudostellaria jamesiana),* both common wildflowers in the mountains, are alternate hosts for this disease. Spores produced on these plants cause new infections on fir trees. A unique feature of this disease is that the needles fall off the brooms in late autumn and reappear each spring.

Mistletoes

Mistletoes can also cause witches' brooms on their host trees, but they are very different from broom rust. Mistletoes are parasitic flowering plants (not fungi) and are spread by seed. Juniper mistletoe *(Phoradendron juniperinum)* is very common on junipers on both the east and west sides of the Sandias. Although this species is leafless, it is a "true" mistletoe, closely related to the species that grows on cottonwoods in the Rio Grande Bosque and other mistletoes used as Christmas decorations.

Dwarf Mistletoes

Three species of dwarf mistletoe *(Arceuthobium* spp.) infect ponderosa pine, piñon, and Douglas-fir. These plants have less chlorophyll than the true mistletoes and are typically olive to yellowish or straw-colored. Ponderosa-pine dwarf mistletoe is common in the Doc Long Picnic Area and can be found along many trails throughout the Sandias. Douglas-fir dwarf mistletoe (illustrated) is abundant along the Crest Highway above the Capulin Springs area and along portions of the Tree Spring Trail. This unique species can cause huge brooms, sometimes used as nesting platforms by birds and small mammals. Piñon dwarf mistletoe is somewhat less common but is scattered throughout the woodlands on both sides of the mountain.

The principal difference between the true and the dwarf mistletoes is their means of spread. True mistletoes produce fleshy berries relished by birds, which pass the seeds in their feces. Dwarf mistletoes are spread by small exploding fruits that shoot the sticky seeds up to 40 feet. Both types of mistletoes have persistent root systems within the bark of the tree that steals water and nutrients. Both types weaken and can eventually kill their host trees. These unique plants can only grow on living trees and, once established, usually survive until the tree dies.

Fauna of the Sandia Mountains

Introduction

Robert Julyan

Like the plants upon which they depend, the animals of the Sandias, in variety and numbers, reflect the elevational and topographic complexity of the mountains. Rosy finches from the Arctic come to Sandia Crest for the winter. In the foothills roadrunners stalk among Chihuahuan Desert cacti for lizards.

Much of this diversity results from the Sandia Mountains being located at the boundary of two ecological regions. To the south, the Manzanita and Manzano Mountains link the Sandias with the plants and animals of the Chihuahuan Desert. To the north, the Ortiz and San Pedro Mountains help connect the Sandias with the ecosystems of the Sangre de Cristo Mountains and the Southern Rocky Mountains. At the same time, the Sandia Mountains, like other mountains of the Basin and Range Physiographic Province, are isolated by basins from other mountains and thus have developed a unique and highly localized array of species. The Sandias' closest neighbors are the Manzanita Mountains to the south, an extension of the Manzano Mountains farther south. Neither range has a neighbor to the east or west.

Within this diverse array, only the species you're most likely to encounter have been included in this book. (It's for this reason that we don't deal with the fish of the Sandias, though a few fish do exist here.) Insect species number in the thousands in the Sandias, but we notice only a few. So also with plants. One goal of this book is to raise your awareness of the abundance and variety everywhere in nature. Learning just one butterfly species leads to learning many more.

If that happens, each author of this section has compiled a list of references with more complete or specific information about the subject.

CHAPTER 11
Arthropods

Ernest Giese and David Lightfoot

Introduction
This chapter deals with the insects found in the Sandias, though it also includes other organisms in the phylum Arthropoda that are related to insects. These include spiders, scorpions, ticks, mites, pill bugs, centipedes, and millipedes. (The phylum Arthropoda also includes water-dwelling creatures such as crabs, lobsters, crayfish, and other crustaceans.) Not only are members of this phylum some of the most beautiful creatures in the mountains, but also they perform essential roles in the mountains' ecosystems. Note: The arthropods below are arranged in phylogenetic order, reflecting their evolutionary sequence.

Centipedes
Order Scolopendromorpha,
Family Scolopendridae

Centipedes are large snake-like predatory arthropods with 15 to 177 pairs of legs. They live in burrows in the soil and come out at night to search for prey. Centipedes are venomous. The first pair of legs are hollow with sharp hollow claws that serve as fangs and inject venom. The last pair of legs are elongated with large claws and serve as pinchers, often used to grasp prey. Centipedes have a pair of antennae on their heads. The bites of centipedes can be painful, but they are not dangerous to humans. Several species of centipedes live in the Sandias. The largest and most frequently observed is *Scolopendra polymorpha* (illustrated). These large centipedes can be up to 5 inches long.

Millipedes
Class Diplopoda

Millipedes are elongate and wormlike animals with many legs. Most millipedes have 30 or more pairs of legs with 2 pairs for each body segment. Millipedes are usually found in damp places under leaves or bark in the soil. They are slow moving, do not bite, and have no venom. Most millipedes do produce foul-smelling fluids when disturbed. They are scavengers that feed on decaying plant material. Sometimes hikers find the white, coiled remains of their exoskeletons. The large desert millipedes *Orthoporus ornatus* (illustrated) are about 5 inches long and can be found in the Sandia foothills.

Dragonflies—Blue Dasher
Pachydiplax longipennis
Order Odonata,
Family Libelluidae

One of the most conspicuous insects is the dragonfly. Adults spend most of their time "on the wing," that is, flying around, patrolling areas and capturing prey. Immature stages (nymphs) are aquatic, and adults are usually found near water, but adults are often found far from water as well. Both immature and mature forms are predatory and consume large numbers of other insects, including mosquitoes. Several species of dragonflies occur in the Sandias. Males of the western pond hawk (*Erythemis collocata,* shown in illustration) are whitish-blue and females are green.

Damselflies—Northern Bluet
Enallagma cyathigerum
Order Odonata,
Family Coenagrionidae (4 families)

Damselflies are the dainty cousins of the dragonfly. They can appear playful, alighting on outdoor furniture, twigs, your knee, with their wings folded. Some species are blue (males) or gray (females) in color, such as the western forktail, *(Ischnura perparua,* illustrated). Immature characteristics are similar to those of the dragonfly. Damselflies are found along streams in the Sandias.

Jerusalem Crickets
Order Orthoptera,
Family Stenopelmatidae

Jerusalem crickets are large, wingless, burrowing crickets found in arid regions throughout North America. They are omnivores, feeding on plant and animal material in and on the soil. Adult males often wander at night during the summer following rain. Jerusalem crickets can be found under rocks and logs during the day. *Stenoplematus fuscus* (illustrated) occurs across an elevation range from the Rio Grande into the ponderosa-pine zone of the Sandias. Another species occurs from the ponderosa-pine zone into the mixed-conifer zone. Jerusalem crickets look ferocious, and many people believe that they are venomous, but this is not true. Jerusalem crickets have no venom, but large individuals can give a pinching bite.

Grasshoppers

Order Orthoptera, Family Acrididae

Approximately 50 species, most uncommon, of these well-known plant-feeding insects live in the Sandias, mostly in meadows but also along roadsides and trails. The Wrangler grasshopper (*Circotettix rabula*, illustrated) attracts attention on warm summer days because the males perform mating flights where they hover above the ground making loud snapping and cracking sounds. These grasshoppers prefer high-elevation open rocky areas.

Praying Mantids

Order Mantodea, Family Mantidae

Praying mantids (singular "mantis") are large predatory insects found throughout the lower Sandias below the mixed-conifer zone. *Stagmomantis limbata* (illustrated) is one of two common native large mantids of the region. Females have short wings; males are much smaller and slender with long wings. Three additional species of small short-winged mantids that live on the ground are also found here. Mantids are sit-and-wait predators. They are well camouflaged on vegetation where they sit still and grab insects and spiders with their large grasping forelegs. Adults occur in the late summer, and mantids spend the winter as eggs in hard frothy egg cases laid on branches. When threatened, these spectacular insects will rear up and spread their bright-colored hind wings in an attempt to scare predators.

Cicadas

Order Homoptera, Family Cicadidae

While walking a road or trail you may hear a rather loud shrill sound in the trees or shrubs. Finding the creature can be difficult, but the characteristic sound tells you to look for a cicada such as *Cacama valvata* (illustrated) clinging to a branch or twigs. One group of cicadas that occurs in the Sandias makes loud ticking sounds from trees instead of the familiar buzz. Most are between $1/2$ to $1 1/2$ inches long. Most species of cicadas spend many years as immature nymphs underground feeding on the sap of tree roots. The shed skins of those cicada nymphs with large grasping claws are often seen on the trunks of the trees where the cicadas emerged to become winged adults.

131

June Beetles
Order Coleoptera, Family Scarabaeidae

June beetles (or June bugs, or May beetles) are fairly large oval beetles that fly at dusk, and are often attracted to lights at night. Many species occur in the Sandias. The ten-lined June beetle, *Polyphylla decimlineata* (illustrated) is the largest and most obvious species in the Sandias. These beetles spend most of their lives as white grubs in the soil feeding on plant roots. They pupate and mature in the spring and early summer. The adults feed on plant leaves. You are likely to see these beetles around lights at night in the summer throughout the Sandias.

Ladybird Beetles
Order Coleoptera, Family Coccinellidae

Ladybird beetles are well-known, brightly colored oval insects that sometimes congregate in mass numbers in the mountains in springtime. A good place to see these masses is along the Crest Trail. Ladybird beetles spend the winter as adults and come down the mountain looking for aphids, their chief source of food. *Coccinella monticola* (illustrated) is particularly fond of aphids on conifer trees. Both adults and larvae feed on aphids and scale, which are pests on fruit trees, making ladybird beetles among the most beneficial insects to humans. Many species of ladybird beetles occur in the Sandias. Most are orange and black, but some are entirely black or gray in color.

Eleodes Stink Beetles, Pinacate Beetles
Eleodes obscurus
Order Coleoptera, Family Tenebrionidae

Eleodes obscurus (illustrated) is in the darkling beetle family, sometimes mistaken for ground beetles *(Carabidae)*. In New Mexico, where they are common, they usually are referred to as pinacate beetles. They are large, shiny black beetles that walk slowly and are plentiful during dusk along trails and open ground. When disturbed some species will raise their abdomen and secrete a malodorous black fluid. Many other species mimic this behavior, but do not produce the fluid or odor. These beetles spend most of their several-year lives as larval worms in the soil. Many species of *Eleodes* and other darkling beetles occur in the Sandias.

Velvet Ants
Order Hymenoptera, Family Mutillidae

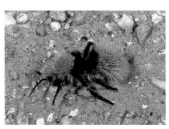

Despite the name, velvet ants actually are wasps. The females are wingless and pack a powerful sting when disturbed. The males are larger and have wings; they do not sting. Both are charac-terized by having dense red or cream-colored hair, resembling velvet, on their bodies. Female velvet ants such as *Dasymutilla* (illustrated) are found along trails in hot, dry areas. Many species of velvet ants occur in the Sandias. These wasps are nest parasitoids of ground-nesting solitary wasps and bees, including the tarantula hawk wasps. An especially large red velvet ant parasitizes tarantula hawk wasp nests.

Ants
Order Hymenoptera, Family Formicidae

Many species of ants are common throughout the Sandias. Most ants are scavengers, but some specialize on harvesting plant seeds, and others specialize on sugar secretions from plants and plant-sap-feeding insects such as aphids. The large carpenter ants (*Camponotus* sp., illustrated) nest in the dead wood of fallen and standing trees. Ants live in colonies like bees, with a fertile queen that lays all of the eggs and produces all of the individuals in the colony. Worker ants are sterile females that have no wings. Only the few fertile queens and males possess wings and can fly. Mating swarms of winged ants are common after summer rains. Some ants, such as the western seed harvester ant, build large conical mounds for nests. Most ants protect themselves by squirting formic acid at intruders, but some, like the western harvester ant, have stingers like wasps, and can sting.

Tarantula Hawk Wasps

Pepsis formosa
Order Hymenoptera, Family Pompilidae

The tarantula hawk wasp *(Pepsis formosa,* illustrated) is the New Mexico State Insect. Tarantula hawk wasps are members of the spider wasp family. The females will capture a tarantula, sting and paralyze it, and drag it to a cell underground. It then lays an egg, and the developing larva feeds on the paralyzed tarantula while it is still alive. These wasps are not true parasites but rather parasitoids, because they kill their host. Some tarantula hawk wasps will attack the tarantula in its own burrow. Most have bright blue-black bodies with orange wings. The female has a very efficient sting. Several genera and species of similar-looking tarantula hawk wasps occur in the Sandias.

Bumblebees

Order Hymenoptera, Family Apidae

Bumblebees are very common on flowers in meadows of the Sandias during the mid and late summer months. These native bees are important pollinators of many species of flowers. Like the related but exotic European honeybee, our native bumblebees collect nectar and make honey for the larvae in their nests. Bumblebees live in small colony hives in the ground, often in old rodent burrows. Many species of bumblebees and other native bees occur in the Sandias. The orange, yellow, and black *Bombus lapponicus* (illustrated) is especially common at high elevations.

Western Tiger Swallowtail
Papilio rutulus
Order Lepidoptera, Family Papilionidae

One of 2 large yellow butterflies that look like a kite flying in canyons and streambeds is the western tiger swallowtail (illustrated). Both males and females are attracted to thistle flowers and wild mountain lilac. Swallowtails emerge in the spring at lower elevations but in midsummer at higher elevations. Larval food plants include willows, cotton-woods, and alders. The other large yellow swallowtail common in the Sandias is the two-tailed swallowtail, *Papilio multicaudata,* which is larger than the western tiger swallowtail. Another common swallowtail butterfly of the Sandias is the mostly black with yellow Baird's swallowtail, *Papilio machaon bairdi.*

Orange Sulphur
Colias eurytheme
Order Lepidoptera, Family Pieridae

The orange sulphur (also called the alfalfa butterfly) is a common medium-sized white or yellow butterfly in the Sandias. The orange sulphur was introduced from Europe when immigrants came to North America in the 1880s. Orange sulfur larvae feed on alfalfa and many other herbaceous legumes. Other common pierid butterflies of the Sandias include the checkered white, dainty sulphur, and Sara orange tip.

Western Pygmy Blue
Brephidium exile
Order Lepidoptera, Family Lycaenidae

This is the smallest butterfly in North America, with a wingspan of only 1¹/₂ to 1³/₄ inches. It is found in dry, disturbed areas along the base of the Sandias and flies to September. Saltbush, pigweed, and lamb's quarters are among its larval food plants.

135

Sandia Hairstreak
Callophrys macfarlandi
Order Lepidoptera,
Family Lycaenidae

The Sandia hairstreak (illustrated) is the New Mexico State Butterfly. It is found only in scattered colonies from the Sandia Mountains to the Chisos Mountains in Texas, where it flies rapidly around junipers and other trees and shrubs in the spring. Another brood flies from mid to late June. Larvae feed on flower heads and seed capsules of beargrass *(Nolina)*. The type specimen of the Sandia hairstreak butterfly was found in the Sandias by Paul Ehrlich, the famous population biologist. The very similar-looking and closely related juniper hairstreak *(Callophrys gryneus siva)* is common in the Sandias, and their caterpillars feed on juniper.

Atlantis Fritillary
Speyeria atlantis
Order Lepidoptera,
Family Nymphalidae

The Atlantis fritillary (illustrated) is very common even at the highest elevations of the Sandias, especially in meadows with flowers where the caterpillars feed on violets. Other similar looking Fritillaries, such as the variegated fritillary *(Euptoieta claudia)*, also occur in the Sandias at lower elevations.

Hoary Comma—Zephyr
Polygonia gracilis zephyrus
Order Lepidoptera,
Family Nymphalidae

The zephyr is strictly a mountain butterfly. Preferring elevations 5,000 feet or higher, it can be found along trails and wooded areas throughout the Sandias, from May through July, often resembling a dead leaf. It likes to stop and sun itself in open areas on bare soil along trails and roads. Larvae feed only on squaw currant. A darker-colored late-season brood occurs in August and September.

Mourning Cloak
Nymphalis antiopa
Order Lepidoptera,
Family Nymphalidae

The mourning cloak is one of the first
butterflies you will see in the spring. The adults
hibernate during the winter and become active
as soon as temperatures become warm enough
for the butterflies to fly—March in the foothills
and April in the mountains. This very common butterfly is found worldwide.
Larval food plants include willows, cottonwoods, elms, and hackberries.

Painted Lady
Vanessa cardui
Order Lepidoptera,
Family Nymphalidae

The painted lady is considered to be the most
widely distributed and abundant butterfly in
the world. It is present in the Sandias from the
foothills to the mountaintops and from March
to October. It is most common on roadsides wherever flowers are present. In some
years the painted lady will travel in mass migrations from Mexico northward.
Larval food plants include thistles and many other composites.

Weidermeyer's Admiral
Limenitis weidermeyerii
Order Lepidoptera,
Family Nymphalidae

Sometimes known as the "white admiral," this
butterfly can be found along roads and canyons
at low to mid elevations in the Sandias. It flies
between May and mid-August. Its larvae feed on
willows and aspens.

California Sister

Adelphia bredowii
Order Lepidoptera,
Family Nymphalidae

This is one of the most common butterflies in the lower canyons of the Sandias. It is closely related to the California sister of the West Coast. Sisters are very territorial and like dragonflies patrol their areas. They have been known to chase bats and dragonflies. Its larval food plant is oak.

Monarch

Danaus plexippus
Order Lepidoptera,
Family Nymphalidae

Monarchs are the famous bright orange butterflies that migrate between Canada and overwintering grounds a few hundred miles north of Mexico City. They pass through our area from mid-August to the end of September and are the most abundant butterflies during that time. Monarchs may reproduce many times during their long migration. The larvae feed on milk-weeds.

Noctuid Moths

Order Lepidoptera,
Family Noctuidae

The army cutworm moth (*Euxoa auxiliaris,* illustrated) is one of the more common of many species of noctuid moths that occur in the Sandias. These moths are medium-sized insects ($1/2$–1 inch) and are usually mottled brown and gray. The caterpillars live on the ground and feed on many types of plants that they encounter, mostly feeding at night. Many other types of moths occur in the Sandias, including inch-worm or looper moths, brightly colored tiger moths, hummingbird-like hawk moths, and the large and striking giant silk moths such as the polyphemus and the Columbian silk moths.

Tachinid Flies
Order Diptera, Family Tachinidae

Several species of large bristly orange and black tachinid flies are common on flowers in the Sandias. They are bee mimics, and often mistaken by people for bumblebees. The mimicry protects them from predators, which also mistake them for bees. Tachinid flies are parasitoids (parasites that kill their hosts) of other insects. Many are host specific to only certain types of insects, and many are considered beneficial to humans. The adults of these flies are harmless and do not bite. They feed on flower nectar like bees. Many species of tachinid flies occur in the Sandias, and most are small gray or black flies that look very similar to house flies.

Scorpions
Vaejovis coahuilae

Class Arachnida, Order Scorpiones, Family Vaejovidae

Scorpions are well-known Arachnids of the American Southwest. They are characterized by having a curved tail with a stinger. They are nocturnal; during the day scorpions can be found under stones and bark. If disturbed scorpions can inflict a painful sting. Of the 40 species in the United States only one has a potentially fatal sting, and it lives in Arizona and southwestern New Mexico. Because scorpions are nocturnal and hide beneath bark and objects, humans rarely see them. Only a couple of species of scorpions occur in the Sandias, including *Vaejovis coahuilae,* seen here.

Tarantula
Aphonopelma spp.

Order Araneae, Family Theraphosidae

Tarantulas are very large hairy spiders that are often greatly feared, but in the United States they are less venomous than the black widow. Nonetheless, tarantulas do bite, sometimes causing infection, and some species have hairs on the abdomen that can cause skin irritation when handled. Tarantulas construct burrows in the ground and can be found among low-lying vegetation. At least two species of tarantulas occur in the Sandias.

Western Black Widow
Latrodectus hesperus
Order Araneae, Family Theridiidae

The body of the black widow spider is about 12 mm ($\frac{1}{2}$ inch) long and has a characteristic red hourglass design on the bottom of a rather large, round abdomen. Immature black widow spiders are white and brown, and females gradually become black with a bright-red hourglass on the underside of the abdomen as they grow older. The bite of the female black widow can be fatal, caused by a neurotoxin injected into the nervous system. The male black widow does not bite and is white and brown, and less than half the size of the female. Only the female can spin a web. Black widow spiders are found under stones, around stumps, in woodpiles, around buildings, and in similar places.

Wolf Spiders
Order Araneae, Family Lycosidae

Wolf spiders live on the ground and run about in search of insect and spider prey. They do not build snare webs like other spiders, but hunt and chase insects, or live in burrows in the soil, from which they pursue prey. Wolf spiders have excellent vision. Many species of wolf spiders live in the Sandias; the largest is the Carolina wolf spider, *Hogna carolinensis,* seen here. You are likely to see wolf spiders running across the ground during the daytime hours. Burrowing species are more active on the soil surface at night.

Ticks
Order Acari, Suborder Ixodida

Ticks are parasitic and can be a serious health hazard by transferring diseases between humans and animals. Fortunately, ticks are not common in the Sandias, and no tick species dangerous to humans lives here. If you are concerned about ticks, here are some tips: Check your body carefully for them every few hours. Ticks are small and easy to miss. They attach to any part of the body head to toe. Other tips include: stay on trails outdoors, and avoid areas of overgrown brush and tall grasses; wear light-colored clothes to easily spot ticks; wear a hat, long-sleeved shirt, and long pants tucked into boots or socks; and use insect repellent containing DEET or permethrin (follow package directions), or safe and effective natural repellents containing catnip or lemongrass.

To Learn More:

Insects: A good general guide for insect identification to the family level.

Borror, Donald J. and Richard E. White. *A Field Guide to the Insects of America North of Mexico.* Peterson Field Guides. Boston: Houghton Mifflin, 1970.

Butterflies: Good field guides for butterfly identifications to the species level.

Brock, J. P. and K. Kaufman, with the collaboration of Rick and Nora Bowers and Lynn Hassler Kaufman. *Butterflies of North America.* Kaufman Focus Guides. New York: Houghton Mifflin, 2003.

Glassburg, J. *Butterflies through Binoculars: The West: A Field Guide to the Butterflies of Western North America.* Oxford and New York: Oxford University Press, 2001.

Spiders and Other Non-Insect Arthropods: A good field guide for spiders and other non-insect arthropods to the family level.

Levi, H. W. and L. R. Levi, under the editorship of Herbert S. Zim. *A Guide to Spiders and their Kin.* St. Martin's Press, 2002.

Southwest Insects and Other Arthropods: A useful reference book for Southwest insects and other arthropods.

Werner, F. and C. Olson. *Learning about & Living with Insects of the Southwest: How to Identify Helpful, Harmful, and Venomous Insects.* Tucson, Ariz.: Fisher Books, 1994.

CHAPTER 12
Reptiles and Amphibians

Rich Anderson

Introduction

The species accounts in this section include the reptiles most likely to be seen in the Sandia Mountains. (A reference list of all the species that exist in the region is included in appendix 3 of this book.) Although it is possible to encounter any of the local reptiles and amphibians in these beautiful mountains, it will be most instructive for the layperson to become familiar with the species in these accounts first. Field observations can be compared with the description of the common species in this book. Similar species are also described in the species accounts for those animals that do not fit the description ideally.

Western Diamondback Rattlesnake
Crotalus atrox

Venomous; Length: 6 inches to 6 feet;
Scales: Keeled (having a central ridge);
Activity: Crepuscular (most active at dawn and
dusk)/nocturnal; Habitat: Desert grassland;
low-elevation open piñon-juniper woodland;
Prey: rodents, birds.

Occurring in its highest densities along the western foothills, the diamondback rattlesnake can be observed in and around the many rock outcrops there. As an ambush predator, it spends most of its time in areas frequented by rodents, its primary prey. Its diamond-shaped markings and substrate-similar coloration make it very cryptic. Rattlesnakes are by their nature reclusive but will rattle if surprised or threatened. "Don't Tread On Me!" is the implicit and universal message of a rattlesnake's warning sound. It is prudent when encountering any venomous snake to carefully move away from it. From a safe distance (about 15 feet), you may take the time to appreciate the rarity of the encounter, as well as the complexity and specialization of such a highly evolved animal. In addition to relatively acute eyesight, rattlesnakes have extremely sensitive pits between their eyes and nostrils that are capable of detecting the heat of their mammalian prey. The contrasting black-and-white tail bands give the western diamondback rattlesnake the nickname "coontail rattler." Diamondbacks, and all other rattlesnakes, are beneficial to humans because they consume rodents—including those carrying diseases such as plague and Hantavirus. It is well documented that people who attempt to handle or kill rattlesnakes are much more likely to be bitten than those who leave them alone.

Similar species: *All other blotched snakes such as gopher snakes, glossy snakes, and hognose snakes lack the rattle at the end of their tail. Non-venomous snakes can mimic a rattlesnake's behavior, some flattening their head in an effort to make it appear more triangular and viper-like. Also, many snakes rattle their tails when disturbed, which in dry leaves and debris can mimic the sound of a rattle. The other two species of rattlesnakes in the Sandias lack the black and white banding on the tail.*

Prairie Rattlesnake
Crotalus viridis

Venomous; Length: 6 inches to 3¹/₂ feet; Scales: Keeled; Activity: Crepuscular/nocturnal; Habitat: Open or slightly wooded flat grassland; Prey: rodents, birds.
Encounters with this species are most likely in the lower elevations, but unlike western dia-
mondback rattlesnakes, which are concentrated mostly in the western foothills, prairie rattlesnakes occur throughout the Sandias. The bold white or cream-colored lines on the sides of the face and the small amount of black at the base of the rattle are two distinguishing characteristics of this species.

Blacktail Rattlesnake
Crotalus molossus

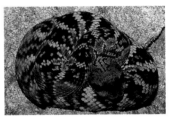

Venomous; Length: 6 inches to 6 feet; Scales: Keeled; Activity: Crepuscular/nocturnal; Habitat: Piñon and ponderosa–Gambel oak forest from 3,000–10,000 feet; Prey: Rodents, lizards
This species is one of the treasures of the Sandia
Mountains. Blacktail rattlesnakes are beautiful animals, arguably one of New Mexico's prettiest rattlesnakes. They tend to occur at higher elevations and on south-ern exposures. They have a dark mask and as their name indicates, a black tail. Each individual scale is uniform in color and the colors range from grays and browns to creams and yellows.

Bullsnake, Gopher Snake
Pituophis melanoleucus

Non-venomous; Length: 8 inches to 6¹/₂ feet; Scales: Keeled; Activity: All times of day or night; Habitat: Desert grassland, piñon-juniper woodland, ponderosa pine–Gambel oak forest; Prey: Rodents, birds, lizards, insects
Gopher snakes are fairly common in the Sandias, often seen basking outstretched on a road or beside a trail. The tan background with darker brown blotches run-ning along the body helps distinguish this species. They have pointed snouts, which are adapted for digging in loose sand for rodent prey. These heavy-bodied snakes are generally slow and easily observed, but when startled they often retract into a threatening strike coil, inflating their bodies with air in order to appear larg-er and more intimidating. Once inflated, the snake opens its mouth slightly and lets out a loud, prolonged "HISSSSSSSS." Because of this behavior, and a general similarity in coloration, gopher snakes often are confused with rattlesnakes.
Similar species: *glossy snake, hognose snake, rattlesnake.*

145

Striped Whipsnake
Masticophis taeniatus

Non-venomous; Length: 8 inches to 5 feet;
Scales: Smooth; Activity: Diurnal;
Habitat: Desert grassland, open piñon-juniper
woodland, ponderosa pine–Gambel oak;
Prey: Small reptiles, rodents, birds, insects

Walk in the foothills long enough, and you will eventually encounter one of the range's most common snakes. Look for the striped whipsnake's dorsal (back) coloration of charcoal black or deep brown with two thin pale yellow "racing" stripes along both sides of the body. The underside of the animal is pale yellow, transitioning to bright pink toward the tail. In cooler weather the whipsnake often basks on warm ground and, like the coachwhip, retreats into thick brush or a burrow during the heat of the day. Striped whipsnakes are commonly seen draped across the surface of oak bushes in the western foothills. Sometimes these snakes lie still hoping that potential predators mistake them for a stick. Among the fastest snakes in North America, striped whipsnakes and coachwhips are effective foraging predators, pursuing their prey with lightning speed and accuracy.

Similar species: Striped whipsnakes are sometimes confused with garter snakes, with which they share a similar color pattern. All garter-snake species in central New Mexico have three stripes running the length of their body: one down the middle of the back and one down each side of the body. The striped whipsnake, by comparison, does not have a stripe on the center of the back, only on the sides. Patchnose snakes are easily differentiated from whipsnakes by their light background color, dark stripes, and enlarged rostral scale.

Wandering Garter Snake
Thamnophis elegans

Non-venomous; Length: 6 inches to 3 feet;
Scales: Keeled; Activity: Diurnal and crepuscular;
Habitat: Riparian zones in piñon-juniper,
ponderosa–Gambel oak, and mixed-conifer
forests; Prey: Fish, amphibians, and invertebrates

These water lovers are generally found along perennial streams on the north and east sides of the Sandia Mountains. Wandering garter snakes are characterized by a drab gray or brown background color with three stripes running the length of the body. One stripe runs down the midline of the back; the others run down each side of the body. When surprised, garter snakes are quick to seek protective cover or water. Many do this before being noticed.

Similar species: whipsnakes, patchnose snakes, other garter snakes.

Prairie Lizard
Sceloporus undulatus

Total length: 1 1/2 to 7 inches; Scales: Keeled; Activity: Diurnal; Habitat: Desert grassland, open piñon-juniper woodland, ponderosa–Gambel oak forest, mixed conifer, mountain meadow; Prey: Insects

The most common and widespread reptile in the Sandia Mountains, prairie lizards can be found during the warmer months in almost any habitat with sun exposure. Their dorsal pattern is made up of grays, browns, and tans arranged in an intricate pattern of crossbands and spots. Perched atop rocks or logs, they interact with nearby individuals and engage in social displays. Excited males climb to a conspicuous location and compress their bodies and throats in order to expose a bright blue underside that acts as a signal to competing males and receptive females. They also perform push-ups to declare intentions and stake territory.

Similar species: *The tree lizard is similar to the prairie lizard, although not as common. Tree lizards are smaller, flatter, thinner, and more gray.*

Short-horned Lizard
Phrynosoma douglasii

Total Length: 1 to 5 inches; Scales: Keeled with extensive spiny projections; Activity: Diurnal, crepuscular; Habitat: Desert grassland, open piñon-juniper woodland, ponderosa–Gambel oak, mixed conifer, mountain meadow; Prey: Insects, mostly ants

Often called "horny toads," horned lizards are truly lizards despite their stout toad-like build. They are relatively flat, their skin is very spiny, and a crown of spikes projects from the backs of their heads. They are found in almost all areas of the Sandia Mountains but especially in the ponderosa–Gambel oak vegetation zone. Horned lizards have a prodigious appetite for ants. They are often found on or around ant mounds using their short and sticky tongues to lap up their preferred prey. Horned lizards are also known for a very startling defense behavior–squirting blood from a specialized pocket behind the eyes. The blood is noxious when sprayed into a potential predator's mouth and eyes, and although natural predators more commonly elicit the defensive response, it can also be provoked by humans.

Chihuahuan spotted whiptail

Whiptail Lizards, Bluetails, Racerunners
Various species of the genus Cnemidophorus

Total length: 1¹/₂ to 12 inches; Scales: Granular and smooth; Activity: Diurnal; Habitat: Desert grassland, open piñon-juniper woodland, ponderosa–Gambel oak; Prey: Insects

As their name implies, whiptail lizards possess long, slender tails that resemble a whip in shape. The tail is designed to break off when struck by a pursuing predator. The severed tail writhes emphatically and attracts the attention of a would-be predator while the lizard makes a hasty retreat. Whiptail lizards are active foragers and probably the most entertaining and easily encountered of the local herpetofauna. They move around in the dappled sunlight under bushes and trees and probe the leaf litter for insect prey. Between feeding forays, whiptails thermoregulate by resting their bellies in sun-warmed soil. Acutely aware of their surroundings, whiptails are wary of movement, but the motionless observer is often treated to a series of humorous antics.

The three most common whiptail lizards in the Sandias are the New Mexico whiptail *(Cnemidophorus neomexicanus)*, the Chihuahuan spotted whiptail *(C. exsanguis)*, and the checkered whiptail *(C. grahamii)*. The table below will help in identification:

	Adult Size (Approx. Total Length)	Preferred Habitat	Characteristics
New Mexico whiptail	8 inches	Desert grassland	Turquoise tail, striped dorsum
Chihuahuan spotted whiptail	10 inches	Piñon-juniper	Pale yellow spots on brown background
Checkered whiptail	12 inches	Piñon-juniper	Yellow and black checkered pattern

Collared Lizard
Crotaphytus collaris

Total length: 2¹/₂ to 14 inches; Scales: Smooth, granular; Activity: Diurnal; Habitat: Desert grassland, open piñon-juniper woodland; Prey: Insects, small lizards, small snakes
One of the more impressive reptilian experiences in the Sandias is seeing a bright green collared lizard perched atop a rock on the side of the trail. These awesome lizards are fairly common along the foothill trails during the hot summer months. So named for the conspicuous black and white collar around their necks, their pale off-white background color and ochre-green reticulated pattern often render them invisible in their rocky and grassy habitat. During the hottest part of the day, when most other animals retreat to shadows and burrows, collared lizards still bask in the sun. They elongate their legs with toes pointed skyward in order to keep as little skin as possible in contact with the hot ground. They also gape their mouths to evaporatively cool themselves. Collared lizards have large, muscular heads that produce a formidable bite. They also have the impressive ability to run on their hind legs.

Great Plains Skink
Eumeces obsoletus

Total length: 2 to 8 inches; Scales: Smooth; Activity: Usually crepuscular (evening and early morning); Habitat: Desert grassland, open piñon-juniper woodland, ponderosa–Gambel oak forest; Prey: Insects
Great Plains skinks are fairly common but not often seen. In warmer months, they are active only during cooler daylight hours. Skinks prefer

Note: Photo is of juvenile form.

thicket-like cover and are very good at slipping away undetected. Occasionally they forage for insects in the open. Adult Great Plains skinks are easy to recognize: they are fairly large, stout-bodied, and beige in color with black spotting in the middle of each scale and orange spotting on the sides. Hatchling Great Plains skinks emerge August through September and do not resemble the adults at all. Their bodies are black, and their tails are bright indigo blue. They also have white spots on their face—a gorgeous lizard indeed!
Similar species: *The many-lined skink* (Eumeces multivirgatus) *is also found in the Sandias. Adults are smaller than Great Plains skinks and about 5 or 6 inches long. Many-lined skinks are either dark brown or pale tan with dark stripes running the length of their bodies.*

149

Tiger Salamander
Ambystoma tigrinum

Total length: 4–7 inches (adult), 1–5 inches (larvae); Activity: Nocturnal, crepuscular following periods of precipitation; Habitat: areas surrounding sources of still water; Prey: Insects

Tiger salamanders are the only salamanders to be found in the Sandia Mountains. They are brilliant black and yellow animals. Tiger salamander populations tend to be concentrated near permanent or semi-permanent sources of still water. Adults spend most of their lives underground, but can usually be seen during periods following rainfall when they migrate to breeding ponds. Tiger salamanders typically breed during the monsoons of summer and lay their eggs in ponds where the eggs hatch into larvae. The larval salamanders spend several years in their home pond before metamorphosing into the terrestrial adult form. The larvae are most commonly seen in stock tanks, small lakes, and ponds.

To Learn More:

For more detailed descriptions of the reptile and amphibian species of New Mexico there are two great sources:

The one most specific to New Mexico, and a must for the serious reptile and amphibian enthusiast, is *The Amphibians and Reptiles of New Mexico* by William Degenhardt, Charles Painter, and Andrew Price. Published in 1996, by the University of New Mexico Press in Albuquerque, this book is packed with detailed range maps and scientific information about the natural history of these fascinating creatures.

A more general guide for the western United States is the *Field Guide to Western Amphibian and Reptiles* (Peterson Field Guide Series) by Robert C. Stebbins. A good general field identification guide, the Peterson's guide includes the herps from all the western states and Baja California.

CHAPTER 13
Birds

Art Arenholz

Introduction

In this chapter, we feature thirty birds you are most likely to see when you visit the mountain. Each bird description provides tips to help you identify the bird, to know when the bird is here, and where to look. We included birds from various families, seasons, and elevations. The birds are listed by families, such as hawks, warblers, sparrows, etc. The order of these families follows the Forest Service's *Birds of the Sandia and Manzano Mountains* bird list, and almost every bird book. Ornithologists place birds in their orders based on perceived evolutionary development, with the oldest birds listed first and the more recently evolved birds in the end.

We know you will see many other species, especially once you start looking for them. The bird list of almost 250 species for the Sandia Mountains is available at no cost at the local Forest Service visitor centers. It was compiled by expert birder Hart Schwarz. Below are listed several excellent field guides to further your study of birds. If you see a bird that resembles one of these thirty, try looking in bird books under the same family (for example, woodpeckers) to narrow your search.

Turkey Vulture
Cathartes aura

Length: 27 inches
The turkey vulture is a large, dark, soaring bird that can easily be mistaken for an eagle. Two good clues that it is not an eagle are that it rocks unsteadily from side to side as it soars and that it holds its wings up in a moderate "V."

Given good light, the vulture shows contrasting, 2-toned underwings: black in front and silver-gray in back. It has a tiny, red head, a long tail, and rarely flaps as it flies.

Turkey vultures are an important part of nature's clean-up crew; they sometimes find food by smell, which is unusual for birds. This sense of smell was discovered when a flock of vultures soared repeatedly over a gas pipeline, which helped engineers locate an elusive leak.

Vultures migrate south in fall and return in spring. A good place to see them is along the Crest Spur Trail, which runs from the upper La Luz Trail to the crest.

Red-tailed Hawk
Buteo jamaicensis

Length: 22 inches
This is our most common large soaring hawk. Very visible because of its hunting styles, it often chooses a conspicuous perch from which it scans for prey, or it soars in wide circles, using thermals as an invisible elevator.

Only the adult has the brick-red tail; the juvenile's tail is brown and striped. The best identification mark for both ages is a narrow, dark bar on the leading edge of the underwing. When seeing a perched hawk, look for the pattern of dark-light-dark-light: dark head, light breast, dark belly band, and light abdomen.

Look for red-tailed hawks soaring over the foothills to the west from the upper tram deck or from the Sandia Crest cliffs. Also, as you drive, look on the roadside poles and trees for perched hawks. Some red-tails migrate, but others are here year-round.

In March and April, visit the Sandia Hawk Watch site to see migrating hawks. Take the Three Gun Springs Trail 194 to the wilderness fence, then follow the marked Hawk Watch Trail 215 to the site (about 2 miles long and 900 feet up.)

Golden Eagle
Aquila chrysaetos

Length: 36 inches
The golden eagle is a huge, dark, soaring bird with a 7-foot wingspread. Its courtship dives in spring are visible for several miles. Usually, the male climbs high in the sky, folds his wings, dives, and pulls up just above the ground.

To identify this eagle, look for extra-long wings, a steady flight (unlike the teetering flight of a turkey vulture), and a golden wash on the back of the head and neck.

Sometimes, the golden eagle uses deception while hunting. When it finds its prey, it flies away and slowly loses altitude. Then it turns back, flies low and fast, and surprises its prey.

The best time and place to see golden eagles is late February to mid-April at the Sandia Hawk Watch site as they migrate north. Take the Three Gun Spring Trail to the wilderness fence, then go right on the Hawk Watch Trail 215 to the site (about 2 miles and 900 feet vertical).

American Kestrel
Falco sparverius

Length: 11 inches
The American kestrel is the smallest and most common of the falcons in the Sandias. The kestrel hunts in open areas, and it is often seen hovering over an open field. It also perches on wires and branches, where it frequently bobs its tail as it scans below for small prey.

It is easy to identify. The boldly patterned head has two vertical stripes of black on a white cheek. The back and tail are a bright, rusty color (the only falcon to show this color). Males have bluish wings while females have the same rusty color on the wings. Like all falcons, the kestrel has pointed wings.

To find American kestrels in the Sandias, look on the lower half of the mountain in open areas with grass; also look on power and phone lines anywhere. Two good places are along the Crest Highway, especially near open meadows and along the Foothills Trail 365, on the western slopes of the mountains. A few kestrels do not migrate but stay here even in winter.

Scaled Quail
Callipepla squamata

Length: 10 inches
To find this year-round resident, look in desert grasslands or arid, brushy areas. These quail feed on the ground and usually, when surprised, run away rather than fly. When they do fly, they explode from the grass and fly only a short distance.

This plump, gray bird is sometimes called "cotton-top" for its bushy, white crest. Feathers on the upper back and breast look shingled or scaly, hence the name.

In spring and early summer, the males call repeatedly from a rock, shrub, or fence post. Breeding usually occurs after summer monsoon rains begin in July or August. Population numbers vary between wet and dry years.

Good places to look for scaled quail are along the trails in the western foothills. Try the lower part of the Embudo Trail 193, which starts at the eastern end of Indian School Road in Albuquerque.

153

Wild Turkeys in the Sandias

In February 2004, New Mexico Game and Fish trapped 21 wild turkeys—3 toms (also called gobblers) and 18 hens—near Chama and released them near Balsam Glade in the Sandias. Wild turkeys once were abundant in the Sandias, but in the late1800s when more and more settlers were moving to New Mexico, wagon loads of turkeys were hauled off to market—and eventually turkeys disappeared from the Sandia Mountains. Now, wildlife biologists are optimistic that the turkeys will thrive on good habitat here and return to being an important part of the mountains' fauna.

Band-tailed Pigeon
Columba fasciata

Length: 15 inches

The band-tailed pigeon is a bit of a contradiction. It is very sociable in small flocks, but it is shy and wary with people. Unlike most doves (small) and pigeons (large), these birds feed in trees and live in dense forests.

To visualize a band-tailed pigeon, picture a city pigeon on steroids, living in the woods. The band-tail's body is gray; the head is purplish with a dark-tipped, yellow bill, and a white, half-collar on the back of the neck.

The voice is a hollow, owl-like hooting. Many visitors mistake this "song" for an owl's call. Most band-tails migrate, but a few stay here some winters.

A reliable place to find them is the lower area of Capulin Springs Picnic Area, just uphill from the ski area along the Crest Highway. Listen for their loud wingbeats as they fly from tree to tree.

Greater Roadrunner
Geococcyx californianus

Length: 23 inches

Although the roadrunner is the state bird of New Mexico, it is probably better known from being in cartoons with Wiley Coyote. The distinctive but comical appearance of this bird belies its predatory behavior. Much of its diet consists of mice, lizards, birds, insects, birds' eggs, and snakes.

This large, slender, very long-tailed, brown-and-white-streaked bird can fly and glide, but it prefers to run. After searching for food by walking fast, it then runs toward a food item, at speeds up to 15 mph. It does not migrate and has a fascinating way to keep warm in winter. It exposes to the sun a patch of black skin on its back, which acts as a solar collector.

Roadrunners live in dry, open country, perhaps with a few shrubs, as well as in neighborhoods. A good place to look for this bird is just east of Tramway Boulevard and along Forest Road 333 (the road to the Juan Tabo Picnic Area).

Broad-tailed Hummingbird
Selasphorus platycercus

Length: 4 inches

The male of this midsized hummer produces a sound with his wings that, for many people, defines summer in these mountains. This shrill, trilling sound helps the male let other hummers know his territorial boundaries. He is audible to a distance of about 100 yards and is often heard before he is seen.

The male is green above and white below with an iridescent, rosy-red throat when viewed straight on or in certain light conditions. The female looks a lot like the female rufous hummingbird: green above and white below with rusty sides and rust at the base of the tail. Broad-tails are here from April through September, nest throughout the Sandias, and are the Sandias' most common hummingbird.

Look for them near masses of red or purple tubular flowers. Try Capulin Spring Picnic Area, lower area, just off the Crest Highway. As you hike, wear something red—you might get to see a hummer up close.

155

Rufous Hummingbird
Selasphorus rufus

Length: 3³/₄ inches
The rufous hummingbird is a tiny, feisty, bully bird that drives other hummingbirds away from "its" feeder or patch of flowers. The male is the color (and weight) of a bright copper penny. In good light, his throat is an iridescent orange-red; his chest is white, washed with rust. The female has a green back, white front, with rufous on the flanks and the base of her tail.

This hummer, who winters in Mexico and nests as far north as Alaska, has the longest migration (as much as 3,000 miles) of any North American hummingbird. Some people suggest that this long migration explains the aggressive disposition. This bird visits the Sandias only during fall migration (July to October), and takes an alternate route along the Pacific Coast north in the spring.

Good places to look for them are the meadows above and below the parking lots for the 10K Trail 200, on the Crest Highway. They favor mountain figwort, a shrub with many tiny dull flowers, which are found in these meadows.

Hairy Woodpecker
Picoides villosus

Length: 9¹/₂ inches
As you hike throughout the year, you can often locate a woodpecker nearby by the "tap-tap-tap" sound as it searches for hidden food in a tree. Sometimes you will see or hear a piece of bark fall, loosened as the bird searches the trunk for food.

The hairy woodpecker is a black-and-white bird with a large, sharp bill. It is dark above, white below, with a white patch in the center of the back. Only the male has a red patch on the back of the head. Woodpeckers move *up* the tree trunk, using their stiff tail feathers to prop themselves.

Listen and look for this bird along the North 10K Trail 200, the Crest Trail 130, north or south of Sandia Crest, and at any of the picnic areas along the Crest Highway.

Say's Phoebe
Sayornis saya

Length: 7 inches

Say's phoebe is a flycatcher. It eats little else but insects, which it hunts by hovering over an open field or by watching from a low, prominent perch. When it sees an insect, it darts out, catches it in midair, and returns to a nearby perch.

In addition to this distinctive "fly-catching" behavior, look for a small bird with a blackish tail and head, a sandy-colored body, and a peach-colored belly and undertail. Say's phoebes often pump their black tails up and down while perched.

Nests can be found in low, sheltered locations, such as under the eaves of a picnic shelter or similar structure. Say's phoebes do not need a nearby water source because they obtain all the moisture they need from their diet.

Even during winter, look for this small, busy flycatcher in the Sandias' western foothills, such as along the long, north-south Foothills Trail 365.

Steller's Jay
Cyanocitta stelleri

Length: 12 inches

This large, dark, crested jay is the western cousin of the eastern blue jay and was named for a German naturalist, George Steller. It is the only crested jay in the Sandias.

Steller's jay is black on its head, crest, and neck; the rest of the bird is a beautiful, deep blue. The Steller's jay often lowers its crest when it flies and can look like an uncrested jay. Its raucous call, often a repeated series of "shack," signals its presence.

This jay is usually found from the mid-mountain ponderosa forest to the top of the Sandias. In winter, especially in poor food years, Steller's jays move to lower altitudes.

Look for this handsome, noisy bird at most of the eastern picnic areas along the Crest Highway, such as the Doc Long, Capulin Spring, and Ninemile Picnic Areas.

Western Scrub Jay
Aphelocoma californica

Length: 11 inches
This jay is usually the easiest jay to find at lower elevations. It is noisy and conspicuous, often perching in a prominent place and calling repeatedly. Then it flies in a long, swooping arc to another visible perch.

This crestless jay has gray underparts, with blue on the head, wings, and tail. The back is brownish-gray, which helps distinguish it from other jays. It also has a light throat bordered below by a dark necklace.

The western scrub jay lives from the brushy Sandia foothills to the neighborhoods of Albuquerque. It prefers scrub oak areas, because acorns are a favorite food. But unlike the flocking piñon jays, the scrub jay is usually found alone or in pairs.

Its call is a harsh, angry sound, usually repeated three or more times, and rising as if asking a question.

Easy places to find scrub jays, throughout the year, are trails in the western Sandia foothills. Popular trails are the Three Gun Springs Trail 194 (north of I-40 in Tijeras Canyon) or the Piedra Lisa Trail 135 (north of the lower tram terminal near the Juan Tabo Picnic Area).

Piñon Jay
Gymnorhinus cyanocephalus

Length: 10¹/₂ inches
If you want to see a piñon jay, it is unlikely that you will see just one. Forming noisy social flocks, even while nesting, these jays wander the piñon-juniper area searching for their favorite food, piñon pine seeds.

The piñon jay is fairly easy to identify: a uniform dull-blue color overall; a short, squared-off tail; and a sharp, spike-like bill. The tail and bill are quite unlike those of other jays.

But its flocking tendency and piercing calls often are enough to identify a flock. You often will hear piñon jays before you see them.

Look and listen for piñon jays in the lower parts of the west side of the Sandias. The Elena Gallegos Picnic Area (east off Tramway Boulevard and south of the tram) is often productive. Be patient and listen for the piñon jay ruckus as you look at other birds.

Clark's Nutcracker
Nucifraga columbiana

Length: 12 inches
This large, noisy bird often prefers the tallest tree at the top of the mountain. Once it is heard, the call is easy to remember: harsh, grating, drawn-out, and loud.

"Clark's crow," as it was called in the 1800s, is a chunky bird. Body and head are light gray, but the flashing wings and tail are black and white. The bill is long and sharp, adapted to opening pinecones to extract pine seeds.

This fearless, noisy bird buries up to 30,000 seeds each year, mostly on south-facing slopes when the snow melts quickly. This behavior and the fact that it does not migrate enables the Clark's nutcracker to nest in late winter, thus obtaining the choice nest sites. And like his cousins, the jays, Clark's nutcracker does not find all the buried seeds and adds new trees to the forest.

The best place to see and hear Clark's nutcracker is along trails near the top ridge of the mountain. Good choices are the Crest Spur Trail and the South Crest Trail 130, between Sandia Crest and the upper tram terminal.

Violet-green Swallow
Tachycineta thalassina

White-throated Swift
Aeronautes saxatalis

Length: 5 inches
If you are along the cliffs of the Sandia Mountains between March and October, you might see swifts and swallows gracefully flying and catching insects. The most common swallow in the Sandias is the violet-green; any swift you identify can safely be called the white-throated.

Violet-green Swallow

Two good identification marks exist for a violet-green in flight. One is white flank patches that almost meet on top and contrast with dark upper parts, which only show green or purple sheens when the sun hits them just right. The other is snow-white underparts. The swift shows dark and light underneath, not pure white. The wings of the swallow are shorter and wider than the swift; in a long glide, the wings of the swift are sickle-shaped—curved, long, and thin. In a pinch, when asked to identify what you are observing, you can just say you are watching the swallows and the swifts.

In clear weather, these graceful, fast birds fly very high; in poorer weather, they fly closer to the mountain. Swallows catch insects, their sole food, along cliffs and near water, so you should look for them there. Try the area near Sandia Park Pond, south of the Crest Highway just east of Tinkertown Museum, for both swallows and swifts. Also look as you hike the Crest Trail 130.

Mountain Chickadee
Parus gambeli

Length: 5 inches
This is a small, plump, active bird of the western coniferous forest. Any flock of small songbirds is likely to contain several mountain chickadees. Listen as they call their name huskily: "Chick-a-dee-dee-dee."

Easily seen because they are bold and inquisitive, their field marks are equally bold: a black cap and throat, white line over the eye and underparts, and dark-gray back, wings, and tail.

Feeding mostly on insects, they often hang upside-down on a thin branch and even hover to extract a juicy morsel. Also fond of seeds, they store a cache of seeds to help get through the cold winter.

If an owl, snake, raccoon, or other predator appears, chickadees lead the "mobbing" effort by flying at and sometimes striking the predator.

Look for this energetic acrobat in any eastside picnic area, and listen for their calls as you hike the Crest Trail, or other trails in the upper half of the Sandia Mountains.

Red-breasted Nuthatch
Sitta Canadensis

Length: 4¹/₂ inches
The dry forests of the Sandia Mountains are only rarely dense with birds. One such occasion is when one finds a mixed flock of small birds actively feeding as they move through the trees. Your best clue that a mixed flock is nearby is the frequent call of the red-breasted nuthatch. Sounding like a toy tin horn, this call tells you to stop and scan nearby trees for chickadees, nuthatches, kinglets, and other small birds, including warblers in season.

The red-breasted nuthatch is easy to identify. This small bird is dramatically marked with a black cap, black eye line, and a bright white eyebrow between the cap and eye line. The back is blue-gray, and the underparts are rusty-red. Behavior also helps in identification. Nuthatches often climb head-first *down* the tree trunk, while looking for choice morsels overlooked by woodpeckers and creepers, who climb *up* the tree trunk.

While there is an area of overlap, the red-breasted nuthatch favors the higher spruce-fir forest, while the white-breasted nuthatch prefers the lower parts of the mountain.

An excellent place to look for red-breasted nuthatch at any time of the year is the lower Capulin Spring Picnic Area.

White-breasted Nuthatch
Sitta carolinensis

Length: 6 inches
This common and conspicuous bird usually leaves the upper mountain to his cousin the red-breasted nuthatch and lives year-round in the more open woods of the lower mountain. When searching for it, listen for a faint "tap-tap-tap" and a louder, nasal, urgent "Ank! Ank! Ank!" and look for a stubby-tailed, large-headed bird climbing head-first *down* the tree or limb.

The white-breasted nuthatch has a black cap and nape with a dark eye on an all-white face. Do not be fooled by the rusty thighs and lower belly on the white underparts; this is not the smaller red-breasted nuthatch. These sparrow-sized acrobats, like all nuthatches, hang upside-down from large limbs and call often.

The best places to look for the white-breasted are the lower picnic areas along the Crest Highway, such as Cienega Canyon, Doc Long, and Capulin Spring.

Western Bluebird
Sialia mexicana

Length: 7 inches
A flock of western bluebirds is a favorite find of many birders. They are often found perched together on fences, wires, or small trees near open fields. Their deep-blue color is especially beautiful when the birds fly in good light.

The western bluebird is purple-blue on the head, wings, and tail; the breast and part of the back are rusty red. Female bluebirds are similar, but their colors are more subdued. Juveniles have a speckled breast, but all show some blue in the wings and tail.

Because these birds prefer scattered, medium-sized trees, you can find them in piñon-juniper areas all year. Try the Foothills Trail 365 on the west side of the Sandias or the lower part of the road to Sandia Crest on the east side of the mountain.

161

Yellow-rumped Warbler
Dendroica coronata

Length: 5 1/2 inches

The yellow-rumped warbler is one of the best-known warblers for two reasons. First, it is one of the most visible since it often sits on a prominent perch, showing its yellow rump and flying out to catch insects in midair. Second, a few stay all winter at lower elevations, because unlike most other warblers they can subsist on berries when insects are scarce.

This small bird is the only warbler here with a yellow throat, bright yellow rump, yellow sides, and white patches both on the wings and the tail that contrast with a dark head, back, and tail, as well as white underparts.

Affectionately known as "Butter Butt," this active bird can often be found at the hollow log at the Lower Capulin Spring Picnic Area. They nest along the Tree Spring Trail 194, south of the Crest Highway. In winter, you might find them almost anywhere at low elevations.

Western Tanager
Piranga ludoviciana

Length: 7 inches

In the arid, often brown Southwest, the male western tanager looks like a tropical bird. He is yellow and black with a red face and head—very striking!

While the brightly colored male is easy to identify, the female is more subdued. She is dull yellow with dark wings that have yellow wing bars. The tanager bill is heavier, almost stubby, compared to the sharp bill of similar orioles.

Tanagers visit us just for the summer, and fly back to the tropics early each fall. They nest in open woodlands and feed on insects, fruit, and berries.

Their raspy song sounds like a robin with a sore throat.

The best time to look for western tanagers is the morning when they sing from the tops of conifers. Good places to look are the picnic areas at lower elevations along the Crest Highway: Cienega Canyon, Sulfur Canyon, and Doc Long. Take time to walk around and listen for the hoarse song in spring and early summer, often coming from high in a tall tree.

Spotted Towhee
Pipilo maculates

Length: 8 inches
The spotted towhee is a large, long-tailed sparrow that forages noisily on the ground in the
underbrush, often causing it to be heard before
it is seen. Using a jump/shuffle motion, they
scratch in the leaf litter to find insects and seeds.

You will discover that this bird has a dark hood, red eye, robin-red sides, and a
white belly. The dark back is spotted with white, and the dark tail has white corners.

In spring, the male sings from a high perch on a shrub and is easily seen. In
other seasons, you have to listen and search for these birds, though they are
here all year.

Spotted towhees nest throughout the mountain, either in brushy meadows or
shrubby forest clearings. Good places to look are the picnic area roads along the
Crest Highway, from Doc Long to Ninemile.

Canyon Towhee
Pipilo fuscus

Length: 9 inches
The canyon towhee is quite common year-
round in the foothills, but its plain color and
secretive habits keep it from being well known.
Predominantly brown, it likes to feed under
bushes and cars.

Understated perhaps but still handsome, this large sparrow has a rusty-col-
ored undertail and crown. Its pale throat is bordered by a necklace of dark streaks.
The canyon towhee is mostly a ground-dwelling bird, but in spring males will sing
from a low but easily seen perch.

Look for these solitary or paired birds in piñon-juniper areas or stands of
cholla ("stick") cactus. Try the Three Gun Spring Trail 194, north of I-40 near
Monticello subdivision. Or try the cactus area near Tramway Boulevard and Forest
Road 333, the road to the Juan Tabo Picnic Area. But don't be surprised if a canyon
towhee is feeding under your car when you return.

Dark-eye Junco
Junco hyemalis

Length: 6 inches

If you hike in the Sandias and see and identify only one bird, it is likely to be the junco. This handsome, gray sparrow can be found year-round, often in small flocks along the trails. Your key identification mark is the flash of white along the outer tail feathers as the bird flies.

The formerly separate species of junco were recently combined into one species, the dark-eyed junco. Many people call them "snow-birds," because they arrive at feeders at the start of winter. My non-birding neighbor calls the wintering Oregon junco the "executioner" bird for its coal-black hood. Our summer nesting junco is the gray-headed race, with a light-gray hood and body and a bright rusty back.

Look for juncos as you walk anywhere in the mountains but only at higher elevations in summer, such as along the Crest Trail.

Black-headed Grosbeak
Pheucticus melanocephalus

Length: 8 inches

When we hear the very long, melodic song of the black-headed grosbeak, we can be sure that winter has gone. Arriving in late April, the male (and surprisingly, sometimes the female) sings persistently from near the top of a tall tree.

Both the male and female have a large head and an outsized, heavy, triangular bill. He has a black head (of course), wings, back, and tail, and dull orange-brown on the breast, collar, and rump. She has a strongly brown-and-buff-striped head with a body streaked like a big sparrow. Both have yellow on the underwings. They can nest in a surprisingly wide variety of habitats, from lowland riparian areas to the top of the Sandias.

Promising places to find these summer residents include the roads through Doc Long and Ninemile picnic areas, and the hollow log at the Lower Capulin Spring Picnic Area, all off the Crest Highway. On the west side of the Sandias, Piedra Lisa Trail 135, north of the tram, is a good bet.

Western Meadowlark
Sturnella neglecta

Length: 9½ inches
As you walk across a grassland, a stocky bird
flushes and flies away. Its flight is weak and
fluttering, and it stays close to the ground. You
notice the back of the bird is brown and the
short tail has white edges.

Shortly thereafter, the bird hops onto a
weed stalk, puts its head back, and sings a long,
loud, bubbling song. You notice the bright yellow breast is crossed with a black
"V," and you recognize the western meadowlark from the flight, the tail, the song,
the colors, and the bill.

Meadowlarks like open grassy areas, perhaps with scattered shrubs, at lower
elevations in the Sandias any time of the year. Try the lower part of the Three Gun
Springs Trail 194 (off I-40) or the Foothills Trail 365, perhaps starting at the Elena
Gallegos Picnic Area (east off Tramway and south of the tram).

Hermit Thrush
Catharus guttatus

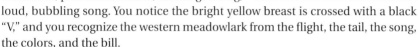

Length: 7 inches
The hermit thrush has one of the most beautiful songs on the mountain. It begins with a
long, clearly whistled introductory note followed by a variable phrase. Each successive
song begins with the long, flute-like note, but
successive phrases are at different pitches. Sometimes, the clarion call sounds far
away but is quite close.

The hermit thrush has the bill, body, and upright posture of an American robin
but is noticeably smaller. The thrush has a complete whitish eye-ring, dark-brown
spots on a light breast, gray-brown upperparts, and a contrasting reddish tail.

Like its cousin the robin, the hermit thrush often hunts for food on or near
the forest floor. If you scare one, it will often fly only a short distance and then
perch and look at you.

Hermit thrushes nest from Cienega Picnic Area (on the Crest Highway just
below the ski area) to the top of the mountain. Their song is heard all day but more
often in the morning and evening. A morning walk on the Crest Trail 130, between
the crest and the tram, is often productive.

165

Rosy Finches at the Crest

The three species of rosy finches are exceptionally hardy little birds that spend summers in separate ranges in the far north. Then, from November to March, at least some members of each species arrive at the Sandia Crest to spend the winter amid the wind and cold of the ten-thousand-foot mountain. Because this is among the few places where all three species can be seen together, the crest has become a magnet for serious birders wishing to add rosy finches to their life lists.

Rosy Finches (Black, Brown-capped, and Gray-crowned)
Leucosticte sp.

Length: 6 inches

From late November to March, birders from around the world come to Sandia Crest to see the elusive rosy finches. Currently declared to be three species, these "winter finches" or "refrigerator birds" are usually easy to find here.

Some of these birds breed in the far north, some on Arctic tundra, while others breed above timberline in the Intermountain West. Thus they consider the cold, snowy top of the Sandias to be a mild winter resort. They forage and fly in tight flocks, sometimes 50 birds or more, and are easy to see at the seed feeders near the Crest House Restaurant at the top of the Crest Highway.

Rosy finches are medium-sized brown or black birds, with pink on the belly, wings, and rump. The three species are brown-capped, gray-crowned, and black rosy finch. If you need help sorting them out, ask at the gift shop and restaurant near the feeders.

Red Crossbill
Loxia curvirostra

Length: 6 inches
Red crossbills are the only birds in this area that
have bill tips that cross. With this adaptation
they can pry open the cones of evergreen trees
and extract the seeds using their long tongue.
The cracking sound this makes can lead you to
a flock. Another important sound is the loud flight calls, "Jip-Jip-Jip."

Red crossbills are small, but their calls and their colors help identify them.
Males are dull red, females are dull yellow, both have dark wings and tail. Rarely
alone, they roam the forest in small flocks looking for an area with a good cone
crop at any time of the year.

Good places to look for crossbills are in the tops of trees near the 10K Trail
200 parking lot on the Crest Highway, and at the Ninemile Picnic Area, just off the
Crest Highway.

To Learn More:

Coulter, Catherine, et al. *Winging It: A Beginner's Guide to Birds of the Southwest.* Albuquerque: University of New Mexico Press, 2004.

Dunn, Jon L., et al. *Field Guide to the Birds of North America.* 3rd ed. Washington, D.C.: National Geographic Society, 1999.

Farrand, John Jr. *Western Birds.* New York: McGraw-Hill, 1988.

Kaufman, Kenn. *Lives of North American Birds.* New York: Houghton Mifflin Co., 1996.

Peterson, Roger Tory. *Western Birds.* Peterson Field Guides. Boston, Mass.: Houghton Mifflin Co., 1990.

Raynes, Bert. *Birds of Grand Teton National Park and the Surrounding Area.* Jackson Hole, Wyo.: Grand Teton Natural History Association, 1984.

Sibley, David Allen. *The Sibley Guide to Birds.* New York: Alfred A. Knopf, 2000.

———. *The Sibley Guide to Bird Life and Behavior.* New York: Alfred A. Knopf, 2001.

True, Dan. *Hummingbirds of North America.* Albuquerque: University of New Mexico Press, 1993.

U.S. Forest Service—Southwest Region. *Birds of the Sandia and Manzano Mountains.*

Waldon, Bob. *A Guide to Feeding Winter Birds in British Columbia.* Seattle, Wash.: The Mountaineers Books, 1994.

CHAPTER 14

Mammals

Paul J. Polechla, Jr.

The mammals of the Sandia Mountains and neighboring areas have attracted the attention of humans for roughly ten thousand years. At places such as Sandia Cave Archaeological Site, Pleistocene megafauna such as woolly mammoths, mastodons, and giant sloths are associated with Sandia projectile points made by early humans. Since the Pleistocene, the mammals of the Sandias have changed to reflect the changing climate and human impact. From my own observations and other sources, I have tallied a total of 83 native or naturalized species of modern mammals living or that have lived in the area. The list includes 1 marsupial (pouched mammal), 4 shrews, 14 bats, 1 bear, 3 skunks, 4 mustelids (weasels and allies), 5 canids (dogs), 2 felids (cats), 10 squirrels, 2 geomyids (pocket gophers), 5 heteromyids (kangaroo rats and pocket mice), 1 beaver, 16 cricetids (deer mice and allies), 3 murids (Old World mice and rats), 1 porcupine, 4 hares and rabbits, 4 artiodactyls (cloven-hoofed mammals), and 1 perisodactyl (horse). The mammals section is not comprehensive but rather a good representation of the most common species found in the Sandia Mountains.

Right hind foot measurements given are from the back of the heel to the tip of the longest claw.

Montane Shrew
Sorex monticolus

Total length: 3.5–4.9 inches; Tail length: 1.4–2 inches; Right-hind-foot length: 0.5 inch
The montane shrew is a stout-bodied brown shrew with a long tail. It occurs in moist areas around aspen groves, riparian areas such as willow thickets, and subalpine forest openings. It eats insects, earthworms, other invertebrates, and some plant material. Montane shrew population numbers run in cycles with extreme highs and lows. The shrew constructs a nest of grass and leaves about 10 cm (approximately 4 inches) in diameter but does not tunnel or burrow. Pregnant females have a gestation period from 20 to 22 days, bearing 2 to 9 offspring and averaging 6 per litter.

Desert Shrew
Notiosorex crawfordii

Total length: 3.3 inches; Tail length: 1 inch;
Right-hind-foot length: 0.4 inch

The desert shrew is one of 4 species of shrews living near the Sandias. Generally, shrews are small, night-active insect-eaters with pointed noses and tiny beady eyes. They have a very high metabolism rate necessitating eating almost constantly. Cats sometimes bring them back to their owners instead of eating them when they discover that they have a disagreeable taste. Their skulls and other bones can be found in regurgitated barn- or great-horned-owl pellets, since most birds don't have a discriminating sense of smell. Scientists capture them by sinking large tin cans into the ground. This tiny shrew, weighing only 5.4 grams (2/10 of an ounce), is the only one near the Sandias with a total of 28 teeth; all others have 32. This gray shrew has been collected on the tablelands below Placitas on the hot-dry west slope of the Sandias in the Lower Sonoran life zone. It eats insects and freshly killed mammals, birds, and reptiles. It is often associated with wood-rat nests and beehives.

Silver-haired Bat
Lasionycteris noctivagans

Total length: 3.9 inches; Tail length: 1.7 inches;
Right-hind-foot length: 0.4 inch

The silver-haired bat is one of 14 species of insect-eating nocturnal bats found in the Sandias. Bats are the only mammals capable of self-propelled flight. They have a tail membrane that extends from the trailing edge of their hind legs to their tail. They use the tail membrane in flight to catch insects like a pocket in a baseball glove. They scoop up water with their mouth on the wing. They also have a thin membrane from their hind legs' leading edge to the trailing edge of their front legs. They also have a membrane between their elongate fingers. Their thumb is free and is used as a hook to hang upside down. All bats use echolocation (like radar), emitting high-frequency clicks that bounce off their environment, enabling them to detect moving and stationary objects. This is how they are able to distinguish, in a split second and in total darkness, a moth from a tree. Silver-haired bats are readily identified by their unique characteristics: black hairs with white tips, partly furred tail membrane, and short ears. At Sandia Park, these bats inhabit open mountain meadows surrounded by a mixture of conifers. At Tijeras Canyon and San Pedro Creek, they occur along riparian stands. In summer in our area these "frosted" bats roost in rocks, tree cavities, and buildings but winter and breed out of state.

Hoary Bat
Lasiurus cinereus

Total length: 5.4 inches; Tail length: 2.2 inches;
Right-hind-foot length: 0.5 inch
This tree-roosting bat is the only New Mexico
bat with back fur having 4 color bands: a dark-
brown basal band, yellow band, chocolate-
brown band, and white terminal band. It is the
largest of the hairy-tailed bats with a large skull
and long forearm. Its ears are concealed by the
long fur but are still longer than its hind feet. This bat chatters a lot in flight while
it catches moths and other insects. Although bats such as the hoary bat will not
attack people willfully, they will defend themselves by spreading their wings, gap-
ing their mouth, and clicking and hissing if disturbed. The female hoary bat is a
particularly careful mother, cradling her young in her wing membranes, shifting
them from side to side while suckling, and licking them clean. Despite this, if a
newborn falls, it uses its mother's bright pink umbilical cord as a "safety line" to
break its fall.

Brazilian Free-tailed Bat
Tadarida brasiliensis

Total length: 3.7–3.9 inches;
Tail length: 1.4–1.5 inches;
Right-hind-foot length: 0.4 inch
The Brazilian free-tailed bat is aptly named, as
it has a tail that extends beyond its tail membrane. The ears of this insect-eater almost join
in the center of their forehead like a Star Trek
character. These Neotropical bats are much
more common in the Rio Grande Valley than in
the Sandias. They occur in an area up to and
including the piñon-juniper woodland (on the East Mesa and Tijeras Canyon)
plus Hell and Cedro canyons in the nearby Manzanita Mountains. This is the
species that makes the "Bat Flight" in Carlsbad Caverns National Park so famous.
They roost in caves, rocks, and under bridges and are known to be migratory.

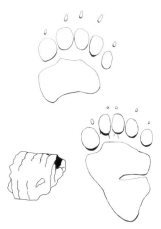

Black Bear
Ursus americanus

Total length: 59.1 inches;
Tail length: 4.9 inches;
Right-hind-foot length: 6.9 inches

Actually, in the Sandia Mountains, as in other areas in New Mexico, black bears are not often black. Their color ranges from blond and cinnamon to brown, dark-chocolate, and liver-colored, depending on the effects of molting, sun-bleaching, and ambient lighting. Unlike the grizzly bear, which has been extirpated from New Mexico, the black bear has a Roman nose, rounded back, and shorter claws rather than a dished face, humped back, and long claws.

Imagine a football lineman sleeping for five months and then trying to make up for the rest of the year by eating for seven months, and one can get a sense of what a bear's life is like. A mature boar, or male bear, can tip the scale at 500 pounds, while a sow, or female bear, can weigh 400 pounds. A bear's "diet," if you can call it that, is legendary for this mostly vegetarian member of the order Carnivora. It starts off in the spring grazing on grass, then switches to insects when the anthills, termite mounds, wasp hives, and rotten logs infested with beetle grubs warm with the longer day length. With summer, the bear begins to feed on ripening fruit; look for various native plant seeds in their scat, including prickly-pear cactus fruit or tunas, bear-corn, New Mexico elderberry, chokecherry, and wild plum. As the summer passes into fall, look in bear scat for pieces of acorns from the Gambel, gray, and shrub live oaks, as well as piñon fragments. These two food sources are high in lipids and help bears store fat to overwinter. Good reproduction the following year is dependent on the oak or piñon crop. The "berries" of the one-seed, Rocky Mountain, alligator, and common juniper are an annual staple in their diet since they produce every year, unlike oaks and piñons. When there is a normal or a wet El Niño year then everything is fine because bears eat the wild foods. When there is a dry La Niña winter and spring, the bears travel down the mountain and forage in humans' rich garbage dumpsters and watered gardens and orchards. Here they scarf down plums, peaches, pears, apples, and even pumpkins, as well as refuse. If they come across a beehive that is not encircled by a hot wire they might rip it apart for the honeycomb. Pet food carelessly left outside also is fair game. Unclean barbecue grills, birdseed, hummingbird feeders, and compost piles with melon rinds and fruit peelings are all too enticing for bears. The habituated bears learn to associate food with people and lose their fear and respect of people. With more and more housing developments around the mountains, bear-human encounters have become so frequent in the Sandia Mountains that concerned citizens and legislators have made it a state law to "bear-proof" garbage containers. Wildlife officers, mandated to look after public safety, are forced to trap "offending" bears and release them in remote wild locations. One "two strikes and you're out" bear was exiled to Mount Taylor, only to return to the Sandias—a straight-line distance of sixty-eight miles! Wildlife officials and citizen groups alike try to educate people regarding responsible human behavior in bear country. You can help too by paying attention to the following:

1. Never feed bears or wildlife either purposefully or accidentally.
2. Pick apples, other fruit, and berries, especially those on the ground. Do not plant fruit trees near homes if you live in the mountains.
3. Keep garbage in a locked garage or shed and take it out the morning of pickup. Put mothballs (poison) in a sock and hang it near the garbage to disguise the smell and ward off bears.
4. Don't feed pets outdoors. Don't leave food dishes outside or store pet food near doorways leading outside.
5. Hang bird feeders between trees or poles at a height of seven feet off the ground.
6. Bring in hummingbird feeders at night or hang them high from a wire.
7. Don't feed suet in spring, summer, or fall.
8. Store birdseed in a closed container.
9. Clean barbeque grills after use and store indoors.
10. Don't place melon rinds or fruit in a compost pile except in winter.
11. Don't leave groceries in your car overnight.
12. Keep poisons and garbage bags locked inside a shed.
13. Keep woodpiles away from your house.

"Remember: a fed bear is a dead bear."
Protect humans and Sandia black bears!

Northern Raccoon
Procyon lotor

Total length: 34.6–40.1 inches; Tail length: 12.9–19.4 inches;
Right-hind-foot length: 3.9–5.1 inches

The raccoon is one of the more northern species of the Procyonid family, which includes ringtails, coatis, kinkajous, olingos, and six West Indies and Latin American raccoons. New Mexico, Arizona, and Texas are the only U.S. states with three procyonids: the Northern raccoon, ringtail, and coati. The Sandias have the first two species. The raccoon is much more stocky than the agile ringtail. In central New Mexico, the northern raccoon is simply called raccoon (English from an Indian word) or "coon" for short; Spanish-speakers call the animal *mapache,* from the Nahuatl. The raccoon has a black mask and bushy tail with black-and-tan rings. Our coons tend to be more reddish brown than the dark-gray ones of the Midwestern and Rocky Mountain populations. Raccoons are plantigrade, that is, they walk on the bare soles of their five-long-toed feet like a bear or a human. They commonly patrol the banks of the Rio Grande, but they also live in the Sandias. Look for their tracks and quarter-sized scat filled with berries, seeds, or invertebrates near springs and riparian areas.

Ringtail
Bassariscus astutus

Total length: 28.6–30.1 inches; Tail length: 14.5–15.2 inches;
Right-hind-foot length: 2.6–2.7 inches

The ringtail, or *cacomixtle,* has roots in the New World tropics. Related to the raccoon, the ringtail is more agile since it can rotate its hind feet half a circle and climb down a tree trunk or rock face as fast as up—head first! These charismatic critters have a white mask instead of a black one like the raccoon, extra-large pink ears, and a tail with eight conspicuous black and white rings. They bound from boulder to boulder effortlessly. They can shinny up two adjacent walls like a chimney sweep, or they can "ricochet" off one rocky ledge to another with equal finesse. They dine on rodents and insects, as well as on succulent fruits.

Once thought to occur only in the desert, they are now found in many life zones, from the Lower Sonoran to the Hudsonian. The highest elevation recorded for the species relative to the latitude is at the Crest House Restaurant at 10,678 feet.Ringtails have lived in the Sandias since the Pleistocene, when the habitat was predominantly spruce and Douglas-fir, and their remains have been found in Sandia Cave. They were recorded there again nearly fifty years ago, in piñon-juniper habitat. And recently the ringtails' characteristic pencil-thin twisted scat and five-toed dainty catlike track have been seen on the dusty ledge leading to the cave. These nocturnal mammals are most often seen at night.

Striped Skunk
Mephitis mephitis

Total length: 24.5–25.5 inches; Tail length: 11.2–12.2 inches;
Right-hind-foot length: 2.4–2.7 inches

The striped skunk is one of three skunks known in the Sandias. The striped skunk is a generalist, while the western spotted skunk is a rock specialist. The hog-nosed skunk, with longer claws and a prehensile snout, is adapted for rooting in decaying vegetation for ground-dwelling insects and their allies. A hog-nosed skunk was trapped at the base of a ponderosa pine at 7,000 feet in Domingo Baca Canyon in 1901. Efforts to find others have not been fruitful. The striped skunk is much more common than the other species; it is found in the Rio Grande Valley and around the base of the Sandias. The striped skunk usually has a white "V" extending backward from the tip of its nose to the tail. This striking pattern serves as a warning to its "business end," armed with two anal glands ready to fumigate anything trying to hassle it. If you have skunks in your area, the best way to deal with them is to remove any garbage.

Long-tailed Weasel
Mustela frenata

Total length: 15.7–16.5 inches; Tail length: 5.6–6.5 inches;
Right-hind-foot length: 1.5 inches

The subspecies of long-tailed weasel that occurs in the Sandias is unique. It has a black mask and is sometimes called the bridled weasel *(M. f. neomexicana)* and also has a black eye ring, muzzle, ears, forehead, and tail tip. The rest of its strikingly colored face is white. Its back is a rich fawn, and its belly is a buffy orange. Weasels have elongated bodies with short legs: an ideal shape for entering rodent burrows or crevices in log and rock piles, searching for rodents and rabbits. Weasels frequent a variety of habitats throughout the Sandias. People often mistake the bridled weasel for the black-footed ferret, but the long-tailed weasel has brown and not black feet and is half the size of the black-footed ferret. A black-footed ferret was found at the base plain of the mountain in Albuquerque on Twelfth Street in 1925.

The Eurasian ferret or polecat of pet-store fame lacks a mask and is two to three times the size of the black-footed ferret. The fur on the polecat's back is black-tipped, giving it a "soiled" appearance. Several incidences of escaped pet polecats have been noted near Albuquerque. Pet owners should act ethically and legally responsible by keeping their pets indoors. Release of exotics has been proved to be a detriment to the native wildlife.

Ermines, a small mustelid more common farther north, also inhabit the Sandias, but this is their southernmost limit. Their chocolate-brown back and sulphur-white belly are diagnostic colors in the summer. They and some northern populations of long-tailed weasels molt into an all-white body and face with a black-tipped tail in the winter, an adaptation for winter camouflage.

American Badger
Taxidea taxus

Total length: 28.1 inches;
Tail length: 4.8 inches;
Right-hind-foot length: 4.2 inches

The badger is a solitary member of the mustelid family with a white forehead and a white stripe down its grizzly-gray back. Like other mustelids the badger has a potent pair of anal glands but not as foul-smelling as those of skunks. It has long claws and a robust upper body adapted for digging kangaroo rats, ground squirrels, and prairie dogs out of their burrows. Like most animals it does not attack humans but will steadfastly defend itself with its stout canines, sharp carnassials (shearing teeth), and claws—a force better left alone than reckoned with. Look for the animals, their diggings, and characteristic tracks in grasslands and clearings in the forest.

Gray Fox   Red Fox

Gray Fox
Urocyon cinereoargenteus
Total length: 36.3–37.2 inches; Tail length 14.6 inches; Right-hind-foot: 5.0–5.3 inches

Red Fox
Vulpes vulpes
Total length: 38.3 inches; Tail length: 14.6 inches; Right-hind-foot length: 6.4 inches
There are three fox species on and around the mountains: the red, kit, and gray fox. The red fox in all coloration patterns has a white-tipped tail, whereas the kit and the gray have a black-tipped tail. In addition, the gray fox has a black stripe running the length of the backside of its tail. In New Mexico the red fox varies in general color from a foxfire red to a strawberry blond or grayish red but it always has black feet and ears. The gray fox has a grizzly gray back but has rufous ears, throat, legs, flank, and underside of tail. Plus they have a white throat patch and belly. Of all the canids in the Americas the gray fox is the most arboreal. It has semi-retractile claws, or nails that can partially be drawn into a sheath at rest to retain sharpness. When climbing up a sloping oak or juniper trunk, it extrudes its claws and digs into the bark, getting the necessary traction for the ascent. This is the canid of forested areas and broken country that seeks rodents and rabbits. Besides hair and bones their scat often contains juniper berries, insects, and bear corn and is the diameter of a nickel. Its tracks and scats are smaller than those of the coyote.

The red fox is rarely seen in the Sandias, more typically observed in sagebrush grasslands and agricultural regions. They are known to occur in the Upper Sonoran, Transition, and especially the Canadian Zones above Cedar Crest, at Capulin Spring Picnic Area, and Sandia Crest, as well as in the Manzanos.

179

Coyote
Canis latrans

Total length: 60.5–61.9 inches;
Tail length: 16.0–16.3 inches;
Right-hind-foot length: 2.6 inches

The name *coyote* comes from the Nahuatl word *coyotl* and is on the Aztec codices. The Tiwa Puebloan people know the animal as *too-wha-na*. Known for being wily, the coyote figures in many Native American stories and fables. The "song dog" of the West, cousin of the wolf, has its howl in the soundtrack of many Hollywood westerns and even more campfire serenades than any other animal. Rusty legs, feet, and ears with a nose pad less than one inch wide also characterize the coyote. Coyotes usually have a black-tipped bottlebrush tail carried down when running. Wolves carry their tails straight out while running, while running dogs' tails usually have a dip in the middle. Coyotes occur in any habitat, including urban, and at any elevation. In New Mexico they devour rabbits, rodents, fruit, insects, birds, reptiles, grass, and carrion. The bitch feeds her pups the food she regurgitates. With practice one can distinguish the sign of coyotes from the domestic dog where both canids occur. A coyote's trail is more linear compared to the wandering trail of a dog, fed by its owner. A coyote track has toes and claws directed parallel to the line of travel whereas a dog's toes and claws are more splayed.

Puma, Mountain Lion
Puma concolor

Total length: 84.5–88.0 inches; Tail length: 26.0–28.5 inches; Right-hind-foot: 9 inches
The puma (a name from the Quechua language of Peru) is known by a host of other names: mountain lion and cougar (English), *león* (Spanish), *tham-mena* (Tiwa Puebloan), and *le tigre* (French-American). This is one of two native cats of the Sandia Mountains but the only one with a long tail, large body size, and lack of spots as an adult. (The blue-eyed kittens have spots that break up their outline when their mother is hunting.) Male desert pumas in New Mexico average 113 punds; females average 69 pounds. The male lion, or tom, leaves the female after copulation, and toms will kill unrelated kittens or juveniles. I often find cactus and mesquite thorns and juniper splinters under their skin, presumably from falls. Occasionally one will have porcupine quills in its paws. They are known to place their paws under the porcupine's quill-less belly and flip them. Before the porcupine can right itself the puma gives a killing bite to the underbelly. Sometimes pumas will smell "skunky" after an encounter with a striped skunk. Pumas feed primarily on mule deer, pouncing on them from ambush after a stalk and wait. The cats then eat some, cache the remainder by scraping leaves, sticks, and soil over the remains, and return nightly to feed on the carcass until it begins to decay. Pumas formerly were common at all altitudes, but now they are restricted to mountains with an occasional foray into unoccupied areas of the cottonwood bosque. Look for four-toed tracks, with no claws showing in the track, and two lobes on the front side of the footpads and three lobes on the back. The scat is silver-dollar size in diameter and contains primarily hair.

Safety Tips
To avoid a dangerous encounter with these big cats, remember the following three things: 1) supervise your children, 2) never approach the animal, and 3) always leave it an escape route. If you do encounter a mountain lion then: 1) stop (or back away slowly), 2) stay calm, 3) hold small children in your arms, 4) face the lion and "look big," 5) carry a walking stick, using it to ward off the animal, and 6) if attacked fight back with any object or your bare hands if necessary. Don't play dead.

Bobcat
Lynx rufus

Total length: 29.9–30.5 inches; Tail length: 4.9–5.3 inches; Right-hind-foot: 6.4 inches
The bobcat is the only native short-tailed spotted member of the cat family in the Sandias. Bobcats are often tawny to reddish on their backs and white on the belly, suffused with spots. Unlike the house cat, they have black-and-white markings on their ears. They occur at all elevations in the Sandias and in all habitats. Rabbits, rodents, birds, reptiles, and occasionally insects are common prey. Apparently, so long as there remains wilderness in the Sandias, the bobcat will continue to persist in adjacent urban and semi-rural areas, including Cedar Crest, Sandia Park, Tijeras, Carnuel, Placitas, and Sandia Heights, where homeowners often report sightings.

Rock Squirrel
Spermophilus variegatus

Total length: 8.8–17.9 inches;
Tail length: 3.0–7.4 inches;
Right-hind-foot length: 1.2–2.2 inches
The rock squirrel has no ear tufts, is large for a ground squirrel, and has a salt-and-pepper back, gray belly, and long, narrow gray tail. When it is molting it has a brown coat. The rock squirrel is sometimes arboreal, climbing a good height into a juniper tree. One can find them on both sides of the mountains wherever rocks are clustered together or cut banks occur, from the Rio Grande bosque to the white-fir forest of the Sandias. They are active during the day.

Texas Antelope Squirrel
Ammospermophilus interpres

Total length: 8.9 inches; Tail length: 2.9 inches;
Right-hind-foot length: 1.5 inches
The Texas antelope squirrel is a striped, ground-dwelling species with a distinctive behavior; it makes its northernmost home in New Mexico on the west flank of the Sandias. The Rio Grande serves as a barrier between the Texas antelope occurring east of the river and the white-tailed *(A. leucurus)* and Harris' antelope squirrels *(A. harrisii)* occurring west. Its habitat is the rocky foothills and arroyos in the juniper grassland and juniper-piñon woodland at elevations between 5,900 and 6,350 feet. Listen for its sharp whistle, and look for its bushy, grayish-white tail held above its head as it scurries from shade to shade. On warm days, it cools itself by retreating to its moist underground burrows. It has a white stripe on the side of its grayish back and light belly but lacks eye stripes. It is larger than a chipmunk. It does not hibernate, as we have observed these squirrels year-round in Placitas.

Gunnison's Prairie Dog
Cynomys gunnisoni

Total length: 13.1 inches;
Tail length: 2 inches;
Right-hind-foot length: 2.2 inches
Historically the Gunnison's prairie dog enjoyed a wide distribution in the foothills and the plains around the Sandias. Small remnant colonies persist sporadically in Albuquerque. As Albuquerque grew into the foothills, the Kirtland Air Force base population was the only known surviving healthy population in Bernalillo County until I discovered a couple of populations between Sandia Park and San Antonito, in juniper–blue grama grassland habitat. I saw several individuals on the south end of the San Pedro Valley and the intersection of NM 556 and NM 14. Later a road-killed specimen was found and salvaged from a nearby locality. The Gunnison's prairie dog differs from the black-tailed prairie dog in that the former has a white-tipped tail and is more solitary than the latter. Due to a previous eradication program, a 1950s study of the Sandias found no known black-tailed prairie dog populations. Prairie dogs had been devastated by rodent-control programs and development atop their colonies. Now the closest black-tailed prairie dog colony (a reintroduced one) is at Wildlife West near Edgewood where the Gunnison's is native as well.

Colorado Chipmunk
Tamias quadrivitattus

Total length: 8.7–8.9 inches;
Tail length: 3.7 inches;
Right-hind-foot length: 1.3 inches
The Colorado and the least chipmunks are
the only chipmunks documented to be in
the Sandia Mountains and the only members of the squirrel family with eye stripes.
When startled they make a "chip" call and
scamper across the log-laden forest floor holding their tails vertically like a flag at
full mast. Look for the least chipmunk at Sandia Crest, Capulin Spring, and
Kiwanis Cabin at high altitudes above 8,800 feet in the Canadian Zone. Look for
the Colorado chipmunk from the piñon-juniper zone to the mountaintop. The
least and Colorado chipmunks' ranges overlap in the Canadian zone. The
Colorado chipmunk is the largest with a larger skull and longer foot than the least.
It also has buff-colored hind feet and a gray rump. The least chipmunk has a buff-
colored lip, whereas the Colorado has a gray lip.

Red Squirrel
Tamiasciurus hudsonicus

Total length: 13.0–13.3 inches;
Tail length: 5.0–5.3 inches;
Right-hind-foot length: 2.0–2.1 inches
Oftentimes you may hear the "ch-r-r-r-r-r"
of a red squirrel echoing through the brisk
air of a cool, dark forest before you actually
see the animal. Listen for them as you hike
along the Faulty or Oso Corredor trails, in Bear Canyon, along Sandia Crest, or
near Osha, Capulin, or Cole springs. At elevations from 7,600 to 10,600 feet, the
observant person will also find their telltale middens or cut fir or spruce cones,
their favorite food, heaped up to two feet tall at the base of a tree. As the name
implies, this squirrel has a reddish-brown back with a white belly. It arches its reddish-brown, bushy tail over its back, flicking it nervously. A closer look at its head
reveals a white eye ring circling its shiny black eyes and a lack of ear tufts as on
the Abert's squirrel. Some call it the "chickaree" or the Spanish *ardilla;* the Tiwa
Pueblo people call it *tsu-wa-la-ah-na*. It fashions its year-round nest of soft moss,
grass, leaves, and small twigs high in a spruce tree several feet from the trunk.
Here the mother raises her four young during the spring and fall.

Abert's Squirrel
Sciurus aberti

Total length: 18.9–19.4 inches;
Tail length: 8.3–8.8 inches;
Right-hind-foot length: 2.8–2.9 inches
Named after U.S. Army Lieutenant James William Abert, who led a military-scientific expedition through New Mexico Territory in the 1840s, Abert's squirrel is a large, strikingly colored, arboreal rodent with hairy ears and a fluffy tail.

Now a common mammal in the Sandias, surprisingly the Abert's squirrel might not have been part of the mountains' native fauna. Homer Pickens, a former New Mexico Game and Fish Director, translocated Abert's squirrels into the Sandias (and Manzanos) in 1940. (They also were translocated into the nearby Manzanos in 1929 and may have spread northward.)

The Abert's squirrel is larger than the related eastern gray or fox squirrel and is one of three native species of tree squirrels recorded in New Mexico. It has a long, bushy, black-and-white tail, which it pumps when calling. Its back is salt-and-pepper, and its ears have long-haired tufts, hence the colloquial name "tassel-eared." The Sandia Mountains Abert's squirrel's belly typically is black instead of white as in other mountains. Many of these squirrels have a rusty red stripe down the middle of their backs. They weigh about one and a half to two pounds, a nice meal for a predator like a red-tailed hawk. They do not put on fat and do not hibernate but instead remain active all year.

The ponderosa-pine zone is the favorite habitat of Abert's squirrels, but they also venture into the edges of the piñon-juniper woodland or the Douglas-fir–spruce zone. Recently, an Abert's squirrel was photographed even on Sandia Crest. Ponderosas are the staple in their diet. I have observed them eating male and female cones, buds, needles, and the inner bark of small branches, and they often reveal their presence by littering the forest floor with branches—seventy-three under one ponderosa pine tree at Doc Long Picnic Area. Their behavior of burying seeds and returning to uncover them aids in planting trees. Abert's squirrels take refuge in holes in ponderosa pines and Gambel oaks and make nests of pine needles or oak leaves.

If you cannot locate them by their cut pine branches or showy colors, listen for their alarm call, "Cha-cha-cha-cha-cha-dweettt-dweett-dweet-cha-cha-cha," echoing through the pines. Other tell-tale signs are their hopping trail in the snow, distinctive track in the mud, and ponderosa pine cones stripped of seeds and scales.

Botta's Pocket Gopher
Thomomys bottae

Total length: 10.5 inches;
Tail length: 3.2 inches;
Right-hind-foot length: 1.3 inches

Scientists know this rodent with the large incisors, strong claws, double fur-lined cheek
pouches as a member of the Geomyidae, the
so-called "earth mouse" family. Unlike other
"earth mice" or pocket gophers, except the northern pocket gopher, Botta's pocket gophers have smooth or ungrooved upper incisors or buckteeth. The Botta's
pocket gopher's back color varies among yellow, brown, and black rather than
gray and it has a different-shaped skull than the northern pocket gopher, which
does not occur on the Sandias. Pocket gophers dig extensive underground tunnels and push out the dirt through exit holes. When done they plug these holes.
Although the bulk of their diet is roots, shoots, and tubers of broad-leaved plants,
dispersing young gophers eat aboveground snacks. Pocket gophers, falsely regarded by some people as the "bane" of gardeners, actually provide services. They promote vegetation by mixing nutrient-rich mineral soil with organically rich surface
soil, while their holes further the exchange of oxygen and carbon dioxide and the
percolation of water deep into the soil.

Silky Pocket Mouse
Perognathus flavus

Total length: 4.0 inches;
Tail length: 1.9 inches;
Right-hind-foot length: 0.6 inch

Pocket mice are smaller relatives of kangaroo
rats with a "fit in your little pocket" size, tan
color, and smaller ear cases. They are common
inhabitants of the grassland and juniper savannah of the Sandia foothills. The
hairs on their backs are tan with black tips, and they have light tan patches behind
their ears. They collect small seeds in their cheek pouches at night, carry them
back to their burrows, and plug the holes at the entrances, then spend the daytime resting and eating their cache of seeds.

Ord's Kangaroo Rat
Dipodomys ordii

Total length: 10 inches;
Tail length: 6.3 inches;
Right-hind-foot length: 1.6 inches
Although it does not have a pouch
for its young like the kangaroo, the
Ord's kangaroo rat has huge hind legs adapted for bounding like one. (The Sandias
have only one marsupial, an occasional Virginia opossum.) The Ord's kangaroo rat
was named after the early-nineteenth-century naturalist George Ord (1781–1866),
an opinionated mammal and bird scientist. The Ord's kangaroo rat is the only one
in the Sandias with five toes instead of four, like the Merriam's *(D. merriami)* and
the banner-tailed *(D. spectabilis)* kangaroo rats. Like most other kangaroo rats, Ord's
kangaroo rats have fur-lined cheek pouches, short front feet, a white "racing" stripe
on their flank of grayish-tan fur, and a black-and-white-striped tail. They have huge
ear cases adapted for listening for predators in the night and efficient kidneys
adapted for living in an arid environment. They hop around at night collecting grass
and forb seeds with their front paws and stuffing them in their cheek pouches. Then
they return to their sandy, humid burrows and deposit the food to eat at their
leisure. Look for their side-by-side tracks and tail drag in the sand, as well as for a
small depression where they have taken a sand bath.

Northern Grasshopper Mouse
Onychomys leucogaster

Total length: 6.0 inches;
Tail length: 1.7 inches;
Right-hind-foot length: 0.9 inch
Since it eats animal matter and howls, the
northern grasshopper mouse is regarded as the
"wolf" of the rodent world. Although it has incisors, a gap, and cheek teeth as other rodents, it
eats more than its share of crickets, grasshoppers, and other insects. Sometimes
it hunts other rodents for their protein, eating their heads first. Its howl is more
like a high-pitched dog whistle that you can hear and is emitted at night from an
open mouth. If its nip does not cause a potential predator to drop it, its acrid odor
might. It has velvety cinnamon-colored fur on its back and white on its belly, with
a short, stubby tail. The related Southern grasshopper mouse has a longer tail. Its
northernmost distribution is near Carnuel in the southern Sandias.

Piñon Mouse
Peromyscus truei

Total length: 7.4 inches;
Tail length: 3.5 inches;
Right-hind-foot length: 0.9 inch

Piñon mice, like many other common rodents in the Sandias, are relatively small, nocturnal, and seldom seen. Scientists studying small mammals find piñon mice readily using baited box-like live traps placed in piñon-juniper habitat. The Hantavirus crew routinely captures them at Placitas. Piñon mice have ears that are huge in proportion to their bodies, like the Disney character Dumbo, and have tufts of hair on the tips of their bicolored tails. They are excellent tree climbers. They eat piñon nuts when available, as well as juniper berries, oak acorns, mistletoe, and insects. They nest in holes in piñon trees and other natural cavities.

Deer Mouse
Peromyscus maniculatus

Total length: 6.3 inches;
Tail length: 2.7 inches;
Right-hind-foot length: 0.9 inch

The deer mouse has one of the largest distributions of any small mammal in New Mexico and North America. It occurs in all habitats in the Sandias from foothill grasslands through the forests to the windswept crest. It can be recognized by its bicolored tail, which looks as if an artist drew a black line down an otherwise white tail with a lead pencil. It has normal-sized ears fringed with white, short hind feet relative to other related mice, and a bright, tawny brown back. Its populations can go through remarkably high peaks and tremendous valleys in response to food abundance. A small percentage of these mice are infamous carriers of Hantavirus. It sheds the virus through its feces (small, black, oblong pellets) and urine. Normally, the ultraviolet rays of the sun kill the virus. Care should be exercised if these feces and nests are found inside an enclosed space like a cabin, house, or outhouse. People should use rubber gloves and a 10-percent bleach solution to clean up after mice droppings. Consult the Centers for Disease Control and Prevention website or the New Mexico Department of Health for more information prior to attempted clean-ups.

White-throated Woodrat
Neotoma albigula

Total length: 12.0–12.6 inches;
Tail length: 5.0–5.7 inches;
Right-hind-foot length: 1.3 inches
From the grasslands at the base of the Sandias
to the crest dwell three woodrat species: the
Southern Plains woodrat of the cholla-yucca
grasslands; the white-throated woodrat of the piñon-juniper woodland; and the
Mexican woodrat of the mixed-conifer habitat. The Southern Plains woodrat has
a steel-gray back, while the other two species have a brownish-gray back. With
one in hand, a biologist can distinguish the white-throated from the Mexican by
the fact that the hair on the neck of the former is white to the base while the latter has neck hairs that are gray at the base and white at the tip. Pioneers called
them pack rats for their curious behaviors. The white-throated woodrats collect
juniper and piñon sticks, prickly-pear and cholla pads and joints, and other
objects and then pile them on their nests. Woodrats have a habit of dropping the
article they are carrying to their nest for a brighter or more colorful item. My
friends and I found one in Placitas with a beer can and a shiny socket packed in
its nest. Woodrats are different from the more urban brown and house rats since
they have a furred instead of a scaly tail. They have separate chambers in the nest
for sleeping, storing food, defecating, and urinating. Juniper forms the mainstay
of their diet, as well as piñons when they come into season. The Tiwa and Spanish
people learned that they could easily raid a few of the woodrat nests and collect
their bounty of stored pine nuts.

Long-tailed Vole
Microtus longicaudis

Total length: 6.7–7.3 inches;
Tail length: 2.2–2.4 inches;
Right-hind-foot length: 0.8 inch
If you look in mountain meadows and near
springs and creeks, by parting the grass you
may find vole runways, well-worn pathways
clipped of growing vegetation, along with vole
droppings. A vole's fur nearly covers its ears, and this vole has an especially long
tail, more than a third of its body length, unlike the related Mexican vole. The
long-tailed vole can be found at elevations from 7,800 to 10,600 feet in moist environments. The Mexican vole occurs at lower drier elevations, and was found for
the first time in the Sandias thirty years ago.

189

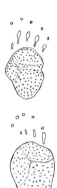

North American Porcupine
Erethizon dorsatum

Total length: 26.2–29.7 inches;
Tail length: 7.4–9.4 inches;
Right-hind-foot length: 3.6–4.5 inches

The North American porcupine is a close relative of eleven Latin American porcupines and a distant relative of eleven species of Old World porcupines. The only larger rodent in New Mexico is the beaver. Our porcupine is found from the cottonwoods of the Rio Grande bosque to Sandia Crest and toward Edgewood on the east side. Like the skunk the porcupine has an even temperament—backed up by an excellent defense. It has a battery of barbed quills that it can erect when disturbed and excited, similar to when the hair on the back of a person's neck "stands" on end while watching a horror film. The quill is coated with squalene, a fatty-like chemical that is antibacterial, preventing infection when the porcupine accidentally impales itself after a fall. It chews on the cambium, or inner bark, of trees with its powerful incisors, jaws, and jaw muscles. Technically, a "porky" cannot throw its quills. However, they are easily dislodged when a porcupine is really "ticked-off" and whips its tail. When naïve, overzealous dogs encounter them, they often wind up with a muzzle full of quills, looking like a jackass eating cactus. The owner should pull them immediately with a pair of pliers lest the muscular action of the dog pull the one-way barbs through the dog's soft tissue. Native Americans dyed the quills different colors and sewed them to leather to make attractive designs.

Black-tailed Jackrabbit
Lepus californicus

Total length: 22.8 inches;
Tail length: 3.5 inches;
Right-hind-foot length: 5.6 inches

If you are a child of the "Route 66 generation," you may remember the jackrabbit silhouette on roadside signs advertising a western curio shop. Their characteristic long black-tipped ears are great for losing heat, as well as for hearing in a warm arid environment. The black-tailed jackrabbit's tail on the back surface is black, but the under side is white. The jackrabbit is actually a hare with long legs modified for rapid running in open country. A pursued black-tailed jackrabbit is like a football halfback—weaving, bobbing, and faking its defenders. The jackrabbit will graze on grass and forbs in grasslands and piñon-juniper habitat. During droughts and winter it will switch to nibbling on mesquite, yucca, prickly pear, and cholla, carefully avoiding the spines. Baby jackrabbits are precocial, being born fully haired, open-eyed, and already able to hop and follow their mother.

Desert Cottontail
Sylvilagus audubonii

Total length: 14.2 inches;
Tail length: 1.5 inches;
Right-hind-foot length: 3.6 inches

Desert cottontails are true rabbits, unlike jackrabbits, which have longer ears and legs. They have a cottony white tail with a rufous red nape. They are born in a nest, naked, blind, and unable to hop until weeks later. When pursued they will use the ploy of doubling back and hiding in dense cover. Cottontails require this evasive behavior to survive since they are known to fall prey to reptilian (western diamondback rattlesnake), avian (ferruginous hawk), and mammalian (coyote) predators in the Sandias. Their other defense is a high reproduction rate. They eat a wide variety of grasses, herbs, and shrubs in the Lower and Upper Sonoran life zones. Their telltale sign is the cut stems of plants. If there is a diagonal cut with several ridges it was severed by a cottontail; a ridgeless diagonal cut is sign of a jackrabbit; and if it appears pinched it was eaten by a mule deer. Cottontails are coprophagous, that is, they reingest their own "M & M–shaped" feces to derive full nutritional benefit from their food.

Mule Deer
Odocoileus hemionus

Total length: 69.1 inches;
Tail length: 6 inches;
Right-hind-foot length: 21.9 inches

The mule deer is so named because its ears are large in proportion to its head, like its namesake. Another characteristic is that its antlers branch and rebranch, with the branches of nearly equal length. (The related white-tailed deer, not found in the Sandias, has antlers with a main beam and shorter tines branching off.) The tail of the "muley" is brown at the base, white in the middle, and black on the tip. These deer occur at all elevations and are commonly seen on the Crest Highway. They are browsers rather than grazers, nipping the twigs and leaves off shrubs and trees. One of their favorite foods is mountain mahogany. The mule deer is one of four artiodactyls, or hoofed animals, historically or presently in the Sandias. Like the elk, or wapiti, it is a cervid that grows velvet-covered antlers. Elk, with their large tines over their brows, were reintroduced into the Jemez Mountains and occasionally travel southeast through Las Huertas Creek. They have also been reintroduced into the Manzano Mountains to the south. Bighorn sheep are bovids with horns with a bony core and sheath. Rocky Mountain bighorn sheep, with their massive curled horns, were introduced into the Sandias by the New Mexico Department of Game and Fish in the 1930s but died out in the 1970s due to poaching, disturbance by people, and limited habitat. The last sighting was reported to the U.S. Forest Service in 1992. The fleet-footed pronghorns, whose horns have a deciduous sheath over a permanent core, have been sighted in the East Mountain area. Pronghorns have a split horn that is annually shed in both sexes.

Wild Horse
Equus caballus

The horse family had its beginning on the plains of New Mexico and western North America. Remains of ancient Eocene equids have been found in our area. The evolution of the equids is most accurately described as a many-branched shrub with only a few branches reaching the top. Fossils of Western *(E. occidentalis)* and Niobrara *(E. laurentius)* horses of the Pleistocene were found in Tijeras Arroyo and Sandia Cave. Only seven equid species remain today. At the end of the Pleistocene extinction the horse remained only in Europe, Asia, and Africa. Then in 1598 Don Juan de Oñate reintroduced horses into present-day New Mexico and the United States from Spain via Mexico and the Camino Real. Remains of these Spanish horses have been found at Pa'ako Ruins from the 1600s. The opening of the Santa Fe Trail brought the onslaught of the northern draft horses, "diluting" the gene pool of the Spanish horse. The advent of the car, pick-up truck, and tractor were almost the "last nails in the coffin" for the Spanish horse. Then, just in the nick of time, Carlos LoPopolo, the late Cindy Rogers LoPopolo, and the New Mexican Horse Project began protecting these horses by rounding up and genetically testing wild horses from other localities in New Mexico, Montana, and South Dakota. The qualifiers have been granted lifetime grazing rights on the Campbell Ranch to roam wild and free.

To Learn More:

Bailey, V. *Mammals of New Mexico.* North American Fauna. Washington, D.C.: U.S. Government Printing Office, 1931.

Clothier, R. R. *"Distribution of the Mammals of the Sandia and Manzano Mountains, New Mexico."* Ph.D. dissertation. Albuquerque: University of New Mexico, 1957.

Dobie, J. F. *The Mustangs.* Boston: Little, Brown and Company, 1952.

Findley, J. S. *The Natural History of New Mexico Mammals.* Albuquerque: University of New Mexico Press, 1986.

Findley, J. S., A. H. Harris, D. E. Wilson, and C. Jones. *Mammals of New Mexico.* Albuquerque: University of New Mexico Press, 1975.

Gotch, A. F. *Mammals, Their Latin Names Explained: A Guide to Animal Classification.* Poole, UK: Blandford Press, 1979.

Hall, E. R. *Mammals of North America. Volumes 1 and 2.* New York: John Wiley and Sons, 1981.

Hayes, J. *A Guide for Wildlife Stewards: How to Coexist with Our Wildlife.* Tijeras, N.Mex.: Sandia Mountain Bearwatch.

Ivey, R. D. *"Ecological Notes on the Mammals of Bernalillo County, New Mexico."* Journal of Mammalogy 38 (4) (1957):490–502.

Logan, K. A. and L. L. Sweanor. *Desert Puma: Evolutionary Ecology and Conservation of an Enduring Carnivore.* Washington, D.C.: Island Press, 2001.

Murie, O. J. *A Field Guide to Animal Tracks.* Boston: Houghton Mifflin Company, 1974.

Nowak, R. M. *Walker's Mammals of the World.* Volumes 1 and 2. Baltimore: Johns Hopkins Press, 1999.

Polechla, P. J. *"Food Habits of the Coyote (Canis latrans Say) in East-Central New Mexico with Special Reference to Size and Sex Differences."* Master's. Thesis. Portales, N.Mex.: Eastern New Mexico University, 1980.

U.S. Forest Service. *A Guide to the Mammals of the Sandia Mountains.* Sandia Ranger District, Cibola National Forest.

CHAPTER 15

Human Presence in the Sandia Mountains

John S. Hayden and Robert Julyan

The landscape of the dramatic, up-thrust, and broken Sandia Mountains bears the marks of millennia of past human use and habitation. The impacts tease us with brief and incomplete glimpses at several thousand years of human history. This evidence is in several forms: changes made principally to the land's surface, including road cuts and mine shafts; changes in vegetative patterns; introduction of non-native plant species; and a variety of human developments with historic documentation—all of which provide means and material to interpret the rich natural and human history of the Sandia Mountains.

Native Americans in the Sandias

Marks of the earliest human use are scarce and subtle, often amounting to little more than an isolated projectile point or a scatter of stone flakes, the byproducts of lithic tool manufacture. The earliest humans probably arrived from the Asian continent at the time of the last ice age, at least twelve thousand years ago, having traveled either coastal or inland routes or perhaps even making oceanic crossings. This is the beginning of the so-called Paleo-Indian Period. During this period, climatic fluctuations and local climates were very different from those of today. Continental ice sheets to the north produced a wetter, cooler climate-controlled landscape on which large numbers of Pleistocene animals thrived. Now-extinct species such as mammoth, giant sloth, camelops, and forms of large bison were the major prey for Paleo-Indian hunters. Dr. Linda Cordell, in *Tijeras Canyon: Analyses of the Past*, describes the situation generally thus: "Paleo-Indians were hunters and gatherers, exercising highly mobile strategies and manufacturing sophisticated hunting tools and a diversity of items appropriate for butchering game and processing hides, wood, and bone."

The earliest undisputed period for early human presence in our area is called the Clovis complex. It dates to about 11,500 years ago. Again, Dr. Cordell points out that the "artifacts from the lowest levels of Sandia Cave are sometimes cited as predating Clovis; however, the evidence is ambiguous and disputed, and the Sandia materials are treated as contemporary with Clovis."

A time of drying and warming of the climate and perhaps the added hunting pressure from humans spelled the end of the mega-fauna of the Pleistocene era. Thus, around 7,500 years ago a significant shift occurred in the technology and subsistence strategies of ancient Indians. This period, which extended to about A.D. 100, is called the Archaic Period. Hunting of medium and small game animals

Model of Tijeras Pueblo when it was occupied.

and intensive use of wild plant foods characterize this period. Stone tool assemblages are less specialized and less distinctive than in the former period. In the Sandias, surface scatters of broken stone tools and debris from their manufacture mark a few sites from the Archaic Period. Because just a few stone chips may be the only evidence remaining, it is important not to disturb or remove any object from such sites.

Then, around A.D. 100, another important shift occurred. People began to rely less on hunting and gathering and to rely more on agriculture to offset the effects of local climatic variability. Modest resources, especially water, apparently attracted people to the Tijeras Canyon area over many years. Archaic hunter-gatherer peoples used the area only seasonally. Then early in the 1300s, people who had been living in small scattered farming communities in the Tijeras Canyon area came together to build and live at locations such as Carnuel, Pa'ako, San Antonio, and Tijeras. Ancestral Puebloans also existed around the northern Sandias. This aggregation into larger villages was greatly influenced by other farmers emigrating from the Four Corners area and seems to have been a general trend over much of the Southwest.

At **Tijeras Pueblo** a dendrochronology (tree ring) date of A.D. 1313 marked the pueblo's beginning. The pueblo builders lived here for about one hundred years.

Tijeras Pueblo

Be sure to visit the Tijeras Pueblo interpretive site at Sandia Ranger Station in Tijeras, just south of the village on NM 337. There interpretive exhibits and a self-guided trail introduce you to the site. Notice the large earthen mounds under which lie the remnants of an Ancestral Puebloan village. How do the mounds differ in appearance and vegetation from that of the surrounding land? If a visit to Tijeras Pueblo excited your curiosity, join the Tijeras Pueblo Volunteer Program and get hands-on experience, or consider becoming a member of the Friends of Tijeras Pueblo and support their education programs.

During this time, the main pueblo room block grew to about two hundred rooms and was associated with several smaller outlying room blocks. This complex surrounded an open space called a plaza in which a large circular subterranean kiva (center for ceremonial and social activities) was centrally located.

For reasons not clearly understood, Tijeras Pueblo's population diminished greatly in the late 1360s and by 1370, the pueblo appears to have been abandoned. In the 1390s, approximately one hundred rooms of the main room block were reconstructed and reoccupied for another thirty-five years. Tijeras Pueblo was abandoned for good about A.D. 1425. We believe that any remaining people migrated to one of the large Tiwa pueblos along the Rio Grande.

There are other pueblo ruins nearby: **Pa'ako Pueblo ruin** is located about 3.3 miles north of the junction of NM 14 and the Crest Highway. Look for the bare weed-covered mounds just west of the highway. It was probably established in the thirteenth century and was contemporaneous with Tijeras and San Antonio Pueblos. Pa'ako was abandoned about A.D. 1425 and then was reoccupied and resettled into early historic times. It was finally abandoned in about 1670, ten years prior to the Pueblo Revolt.

Also along NM 14, the mound of the Catholic Church at San Antonio is the site of **San Antonio Pueblo ruin.** This pueblo was not only a contemporary of Tijeras but also may have been continuously occupied into the historic times.

Sandia and Other Pueblos

In addition to the pueblos in and near the mountains themselves, the people of the pueblos along the Rio Grande considered the Sandia Mountains important for game, medicinal and edible plants, timber, and other resources. Perhaps even more importantly, the mountains held numerous sites of cultural and religious significance to these peoples. Though many of these pueblos did not survive the arrival of Europeans, the people of Sandia Pueblo have maintained an unbroken spiritual and cultural connection to the mountains that continues to this day.

Prehistoric rock art in the northern Sandias.

Ancient Trails and Rock Art

Trails have provided access to and through the Sandias for thousands of years. Portions of such trails can be found in the deeper recesses of some of the larger canyons leading into the Sandia Mountains. The strategic location of such canyons offered travel routes as well as water and diverse plant and animal resources. Travelers from the Archaic period (5500 B.C. to A.D. 100) and later residents (A.D. 1200 to present) have left signs of their passing, either as debris (litter) or rock art and, unfortunately, graffiti. Careful inspection of vertical canyon walls or occasional isolated boulders may reveal rock art sites. The oldest and rarest are likely to be pictographs (rock paintings). By far, the most common form of rock art is the petroglyph. The glyphs or images are permanently scratched, pecked, abraded, or otherwise carved into the rock face rather than added to it. Only a few known rock art sites exist in the Sandias, so it is always a pleasant surprise to encounter one of them.

Widely scattered throughout the Sandia Mountains are other telltale indicators of prehistoric human activities. Sometimes past human presence is revealed through a concentration of plants that differs from the surrounding vegetation, or the presence of an exotic plant species in association with a mound or depression, the remains of human-made structures or activity sites. Sometimes, only the slight remains of an event or activity are present, such as a clearing line, berm, scar, or the remains of the actual human-made feature itself.

All prehistoric sites and artifacts are irreplaceable, and many have cultural significance. If you are fortunate enough to encounter such remains, please leave them as you found them.

The Spanish and Mexican Periods

The arrival of European explorers during the 1500s significantly changed the Native American world. With the Francisco Vasquez de Coronado Expedition of 1540–1542, the Tiwa Pueblo world and way of life felt the immediate effects as the intruders made increasing demands for labor, food, resources, and space. Treatment of residents of Kuaua Pueblo and other riverside pueblos by Coronado's men may have been sufficiently harsh to cause the Tiwas to seek refuge in the nearby mountains. Perhaps, the ruins of one or more small pueblos along the western foothills of the Sandias are "refugee pueblos."

Locally, the Spanish colonization and settlement during the seventeenth and eighteenth centuries is most evident in the land-ownership patterns in and around the Sandias. Sandia Pueblo was originally settled in the 1300s, abandoned after the Pueblo Revolt, and then resettled in 1748. Isleta Pueblo was settled before 1540, abandoned after the Pueblo Revolt, and resettled in 1718. The King of Spain officially awarded Pueblo Grants to each. More recently, mediation and Congressional action have extended to Sandia Pueblo use of public lands (Cibola National Forest) east of their present-day pueblo to the crest.

By granting lands to establish Albuquerque in 1706, Spanish authorities initiated formal settlement. Also, settlements in several critical areas near the growing ranchos, villas, and pueblos in the Rio Grande Valley were needed as "buffers" against marauders. As further inducement, lands were granted to settlers who would agree to farm and raise livestock as a precondition for the land grant. Two such land grants were the San Antonio de Las Huertas Grant and the Cañon de Carnue Grant.

San Antonio de Las Huertas Grant

Las Huertas settlers included Spanish and Native American farmers and ranchers who moved to the Placitas area from Algodones, Bernalillo, and San Felipe. The original settlement of 1765, called San José de las Huertas, was established in lower Las Huertas Canyon. The mostly undisturbed ruins of this Spanish colonial village are still visible today. Twenty-one families built their homes within the walled compound. An extensive irrigation system was constructed to water their fields outside.

According to Tony Lucero, president of the Las Huertas Grant, "From 1765 the people farmed, fed their families, and paid their taxes. There were occasional attacks by marauding tribes, but with a little help from the nearby Spanish garrison the settlers were able to defend themselves." In the 1820s, however, persistent raiding caused the settlers to abandon the site.

San Antonio de Padua Church in San Antonio.

By 1840, the raiding had subsided, and the settlers returned. There were greater numbers and many new areas within the land grant were opened up to accommodate the growing families. So it was that sometime around 1840 the present Village of Placitas was established with its own spring-fed acequia system, which still supplies irrigation and domestic water to the village. Here, as in Old Las Huertas, arroyos were filled in and sloping land was terraced to provide new fields to cultivate. Springs as far away as Tunnel Spring were accessed for village area irrigation. The ditches and pipelines of the acequia system are still in their original location.

Cañon de Carnue Grant
In 1763, settlers of mixed ethnicities, including Españoles and *genízaros,* or detribalized Indians, moved to a land grant along Tijeras Canyon. The Cañon de Carnue Grant extended north of Tijeras Canyon to include what is now Cañoncito. The village they formed, near present-day Carnuel, was called San Miguel de Laredo. Following an Apache attack in 1770, the survivors fled back to Albuquerque. But in 1819, two village clusters, built around enclosed plazas, were

established—San Miguel de Laredo, near the old San Miguel, and San Antonio de Padua, about a mile north of the present intersection of NM 14 and I-40.

San Lorenzo Church in **Cañoncito** was built in the 1870s. Gypsum was mined nearby, and flagstone was gathered for the floors of the old Albuquerque airport building and several UNM buildings. Throughout the nineteenth and twentieth centuries, San Antonio was the population and religious center of the Cañon de Carnue Grant. Early development of a water system encouraged settlement. Carnue was resettled beginning about 1816 at San Miguel and by 1819 had been granted lands extending almost to Sedillo and San Antonito.

In 1880, with fifteen families, the **Tijeras** area was the second-most densely populated of the Cañon de Carnue (now Tijeras Canyon) communities, settled shortly after the village of San Antonio.

From the mid-1830s until 1880, the only church serving the Cañon de Carnue area stood at San Antonio. It was built at the site of a third San Antonio plaza and over the ruins of an Indian pueblo. The church burned down in the 1950s and was replaced by a larger one.

Elena Gallegos Grant

The Elena Gallegos Grant, along the Sandias' western foothills, has its roots deep in New Mexico history. As Robert Julyan explains in *The Places Names of New Mexico*:

> *Elena Gallegos was a member of a family that returned to NM in 1692 with the reconquest, and in 1699 she married one Santiago Gurulé. A dozen years later New Mexico Governor Marqués de Peñuela granted to Captain Diego Montoya lands between Sandia Pueblo's southern boundary and the northern boundary of the Villa de Albuquerque, including the hamlet known as Ranchos de Albuquerque; the grant extended east to the crest of the Sandia Mountains. In the meantime, Gurulé died, and soon afterward Montoya conveyed his lands to Gurulé's widow, who according to custom had returned to using her maiden name. Subsequently, the lands became known as the* Elena Gallegos Grant *and included seventy thousand acres. Elena Gallegos died in 1731, after asking in her will that she be interred in Albuquerque's parish church and that her lands be transferred to her son, Antonio Gurulé. Eventually, much of the land was acquired by Albert Simms and given to Albuquerque Academy. In the 1980s, acting under the possibility that the mountainous portion of the grant might be sold to developers, Albuquerque voters approved a quarter-cent sales tax to purchase the land.*

That part of the grant now is administered by the City of Albuquerque. The U.S. Forest Service also aquired portions of the former Elena Gallegos Grant to augment the Sandia Mountain Wilderness.

The American Era

With the 1846 proclamation by U.S. Army General Stephen Watts Kearny assert-
ing U.S. sovereignty over New Mexico, and the lowering of the Mexican flag in the
Plaza of Santa Fe, a new era dawned in the human history of the Sandias, and
most of what we see today in the Sandias dates from this period. Following are
features from that era.

Mining *(See also chapter 5, "Geology of the Sandia Mountains.")*
From the earliest times, people have poked into every conceivable corner of the
Sandia Mountains searching for the valuable and useful materials from the variety of rocks and minerals found here. The first mines were scratched out by
ancient peoples, and the last mine on Sandia Mountain was being worked in the
mid-1970s. Early peoples obtained pigments, material for ceramics, common
building stones, stone-cutting and grinding tools, and other implements.
Spaniards came looking for gold and silver. Evidence of these activities remains
in the form of prospects or actual mine workings. The miners hoped to extract
gold, silver, copper, barite, fluorite, quartz, limestone, and building rock. Of the
more than seven thousand mines in New Mexico, the Sandias have their share of
shafts, adits, tunnels, pits, and waste piles. So, mines can be found in all ages and
stages. *Approach all with extreme caution, and avoid any with a tunnel, wood
shoring or bracing, or with steep sides.*

Have you noticed that almost every locale has its "lost gold mines"? The
Sandias have them too: the five lost mines of Montezuma. Old Spanish records
dating from 1667 relate details of mines near Placitas with names like *La mina de
la ventana* ("Window"), *La mina de la escalera* ("Ladder"), *La mina de Coloa, La
mina de Nepumeseño,* and *La mina Montezuma.* One story told of a man named
Antonio Jimenez working the Montezuma Mine; one day he set out for Old
Mexico with twelve mules laden with bullion—and never returned.

It is fairly well known that local Native Americans were forced to work these
mines. Their opinion of having to serve under horrendous conditions was clearly demonstrated. After the Pueblo Revolt of 1680, all the mines were filled in and
hidden so effectively that only the location of the Montezuma is known today.
La Madera mine, high on a ridge about two miles south of the old site of La
Madera village, consisted of several tunnels one above another. Veins therein contain barite, fluorite, quartz, and some galena.

La Luz Mine is the best-known "hard rock" mine in the Sandias. Its location
just under the vertical rim on the mountain's west face at an elevation of 10,040
feet possibly makes it among the highest mines in New Mexico. Juan Nieto discovered it in 1887. All supplies and tools were transported from Albuquerque up
along a narrow winding trail to the mine. All ore to be processed was transported
down, retracing the same route. Men and mules accomplished these arduous
tasks. Remains of the miner's log cabin are still visible. Fluorite and minor
amounts of galena comprised the mineralization, with the ore consisting mostly

of lead and silver along with small amounts of gold and copper. As Eldred Harrington told geologists Vincent C. Kelley and Stuart A. Northrop in their *Geology of the Sandia Mountain and Vicinity,* "The mine was first known as the Ruppe mine, and the term La Luz was not used until after the La Luz trail was built." Colonel Bernard Ruppe and others purchased the claim in 1907. However, a story says the mine was first known as La Luz ('the light'). It is said that on certain nights, if one is standing in the right location in Albuquerque, peering toward the mountain, the dim light from the miner's cabin can be seen—thus, the name.

SMELTERS, KILNS, AND QUARRIES
Tunnel Spring: On the northwest side of the Sandias is the Arroyo del Ojo del Orno (Spanish *horno*), "the drainage of the Spring of the Smelter." A Placitas resident once told me a Spanish gold mine was at the site of what is now known as Tunnel Spring. Several smelter ovens, or *hornos,* were located along the arroyo below the mine. Eventually, miners struck an underground stream that produced so much water that the miners were forced to abandon it. The site was developed into a fish hatchery in the 1900s and was reported to have doubled as a party house and brothel. The land ultimately was exchanged to the Forest Service. The mine tunnel from which the stream vigorously flowed was dynamited and collapsed around a collection pipe, and thus was developed into the Tunnel Spring Recreation Site. Except for the two earthen dams below the spring, little evidence remains of the hatchery or mine and smelter.

Smelter sites, mostly small and in ruins, are located in a few widely scattered locations in the Sandias and surrounding foothills. They are most often identified by the presence of the burned fuel and mineral residues called slag and are often located near the mines from which the ore was produced. At the base of the ridge in Tecolote Canyon, on private property, are ruins of an old smelter. The smelter was probably somewhat important locally for the processing of metallic ores from other sources. In the Tijeras and San Antonito areas are the remains of circular pits that are accompanied by burned rock and slag. These are kilns in which crushed limestone was "cooked" using wood fires to produce slaked lime, the main constituent of lime mortar and plaster.

Today, mining of limestone is an important industry, with Rio Grande Portland Cement Corporation's major quarries and production plant in the Manzanita Mountains near Tijeras and visible to hikers on the southeast side of the Sandias.

BUILDING STONE
This important resource has been obtained in the Sandias by local people for centuries. The depressions and rubble of rock quarry sites are fairly numerous. One such site can be found trailside less than a quarter-mile up the arroyo route of Cañoncito Trail. In the 1930s the Civilian Conservation Corps and residents of the Cienega Canyon removed tons of light-colored sandstone from a site just west of the horse trailer parking area in that canyon.

Timber

Wood products have been harvested from the Sandias for as long as people have occupied the region. Products from firewood to construction beams *(vigas)* and fence posts to lumber made this timber resource valuable to many. Timber also was taken for construction of railroads near the mountains, such as the line that went to the coal-mining camp of Hagan.

Signs of former harvesting, such as traces of wagon roads, timber skid roads, and rotting stumps, are visible over much of the mountains' lower slopes. Once, portable sawmills came to the timber. Later the timber was carried to the mills. One such early operation was the Skinner Sawmill in Tejano Canyon. The designation of the National Forest in 1908 brought to an end the unregulated cutting of timber. It would be difficult to estimate the amount of material removed over the many years. Forest Service records show that approximately five million board feet of timber was harvested during the period from 1958 to 1969. More recently small-scale timber sales resumed to promote aspen growth and improve wildlife habitat.

Range

Prior to the National Forest's administration, the Sandias were considered "commons," or lands held in common by the various land grants surrounding the mountain. They were heavily grazed by cattle, horses, sheep, and especially goats. According to Paul Ellis, who arrived in the 1880s to homestead in Las Huertas Canyon, the underbrush had been so heavily grazed by goats that even the canyon bottoms looked like open parks. Today the underbrush is so dense in many places that one can see only a few feet into the vegetation.

With the designation of the Cibola National Forest, livestock grazing was regulated. Eventually, the Sandias were divided into six range allotments. Recognizing that overuse of the range was impacting the overall condition of the Sandias' watershed, a grazing reduction program was instituted, and by 1951 all grazing was removed from the mountain. Two probable outcomes were the spread of dense underbrush over much of the mountain and loss of some valuable meadows. Overall, however, the condition of the watershed improved greatly.

Bernalillo Watershed

Visible stripes along the foothills at the northwest corner of the Sandias are rather uniform contour ditches, constructed to provide protection to the grassy slopes and rolling alluvial terrain below. Beginning in 1953, several thousand acres were treated with the construction of contour furrows, disking, and pitting, a flood retention dam (outside the Forest boundary), and reseeding of grass to protect the Bernalillo Watershed and to help prevent flooding in Bernalillo. Part of the area also became a fire-impact study area for UNM researchers.

The combined land-treatment measures and grazing protection have shown substantial improvement in vegetative cover and the watershed's ability to hold and absorb runoff. Bernalillo has not suffered flooding from the treated area runoff since.

Sightseers at Sandia Crest.

The U.S. Forest Service

By the dawn of the twentieth century, Americans had begun to awaken to the knowledge that their natural resources, once deemed inexhaustible, were finite and had degraded significantly through misuse and mismanagement. In New Mexico wildlife especially had undergone a holocaust of market hunting. By the 1900s, black bears, wolves, pronghorns, elk, mountain lions, and Rocky Mountain bighorn sheep all had been exterminated in the Sandias. To address these resource issues, Forest Reserves were created throughout the nation, including the Territory of New Mexico, and when the U.S. Forest Service was created in 1905 these became the basis for the National Forests.

The Manzano National Forest was established in 1908 and included the Sandia Mountains. The name was changed to Cibola National Forest in 1931, and the lands for which it was responsible included not only the Sandia Mountains but also the Manzano Mountains, Mount Taylor, the Magdalena Mountains, and grasslands as far away as Oklahoma, among others. The Sandia Ranger District, based in Tijeras, was given responsibility for the Sandia and Manzanita Mountains.

For almost a century, the history of the Sandia Mountains has been inextricably linked to the National Forest; the lands for which it is responsible total 100,555 acres, including more than 37,000 acres of wilderness. When the U.S. Forest Service was established, its first director, Gifford Pinchot (1905–1910), said, "Our responsibility to the nation is to be more than careful stewards of the land, we must be catalysts for positive change." Few would argue that the Cibola National Forest and the Sandia Ranger District have not fulfilled that responsibility.

Kiwanis Hut.

The Civilian Conservation Corps (CCC) in the Sandias

Throughout the Sandias are significant structures built by the Civilian Conservation Corps (CCC), monuments to peoples' struggle to overcome the economic hard-
ships of the Depression Era. Beginning in 1933, the federal relief program provided
salaries, training, and disciplined work to thousands of unemployed men while carrying out a wide range of much-needed conservation work in our nation's cities,
farmlands, lakes, and forests. CCC leaders and planners strove to ensure that constructed features fit the context of their surroundings. Special attention was given to
design, position on the landscape, choice of materials, and construction tech-
niques. To the degree possible, each structure was to be a natural extension of its
setting. As you visit the shelters at Juan Tabo or La Cueva Recreation Areas or
Kiwanis Point, judge for yourself their effectiveness.

CCC camps were located throughout New Mexico. Some camps were permanent, some were used seasonally every year, while other so-called "side camps"
existed only long enough to accomplish a particular project. Sandia Park Camp
F-8-N, one of the first in New Mexico, was established in 1933 and was usually
occupied from May through November until 1941. Side camps were set up at Juan
Tabo, Cañoncito, Sandia Ranger Station, Capulin Spring, and Las Huertas. Sandia
Park Camp was on private land north of Tinkertown Museum. Efforts are in
progress to have that site set aside as a public memorial to the CCC. Little physical evidence exists for the side camps. The best clues are to be found near Juan
Tabo Canyon. Have you ever wondered about the old stone building walls in the
arroyo above the turn-off to La Cueva Recreation Area? This was the site of the
Juan Tabo side camp. In addition to the old headquarters, you might discern the
parade ground, parts of a water system, and the sites of the warehouse and forge.

The effective working force for these projects was muscle made tough by hard

Stone ruins of a CCC camp with the west face of the Sandias in the background.

work and applied to basic, often primitive tools. Stone, wood, metal, and concrete were the materials. Under skilled and disciplined supervision, CCC enrollees from these camps built or improved administrative facilities and public recreation areas around the mountain from 1933 to 1941, including:

- Juan Tabo and La Cueva Recreational Areas, circa 1936; the entry gate and large rock shelters demonstrate the elegant stonework characteristic of CCC projects.
- 3 miles of Loop Drive (to Juan Tabo) and maintained an additional 9 miles.
- Doc Long, Upper and Lower Sulphur, and Cienega recreation areas and a pipeline in Cienega Canyon.
- Las Huertas, Crest, Cole Spring, and Cedro Peak recreation areas.
- the Kiwanis Hut on Sandia Crest as a recreational structure.
- Capulin Recreation Area.
- La Madera Ski Area lodge, toilet, water supply line, and parking area.
- many miles of hiking trails.
- the Ellis Loop road from the forest boundary at Sandia Park to Las Huertas Recreation Area.
- concrete bridges in Las Huertas Canyon.

While some of the hundreds of CCC-built structures are readily visible, many very subtle features persist to be discovered and admired by the observant hiker.

Tinkertown

Perhaps the most well-known long-term residents of the Sandias are the approximately 1,100 whittled wooden characters and critters living in the whimsical miniature frontier community of Tinkertown. They were carved by Ross Ward,  artist, sign painter, and woodcarver. Ward became fascinated by roadside attractions when his parents took him to Knotts Berry Farm in California when he was nine years old; returning home he began creating his own "town." The present Tinkertown was begun around 1962 and now is maintained as a museum and roadside attraction by Ward's wife, Carla. Ross died in 2001.

Recreation

For centuries, people in Albuquerque and surrounding villages along the Rio Grande had seen the Sandias as a jagged line on the distant eastern horizon; to them, the mountains were primarily a source of grazing land and game; recreation emerged as a major use with the arrival of Americans and mechanization, especially after 1900. Soon after 1920, a crude road was hacked to the crest; other roads followed. In the 1950s, Albuquerque's population began the mushrooming growth that continues today. No longer were the Sandias distant; they were literally in people's back yards. Since then, recreation has been the dominant activity in the Sandias, dwarfing previous uses.

Though the Sandia Mountains became part of the Cibola National Forest in 1908, perhaps the watershed year for recreation was 1928 when the Sandia Loop Road was constructed around the mountains' east side and through Las Huertas Canyon, linking all the communities surrounding the mountains. Soon after, the Forest Service constructed campgrounds and picnic areas along the route, and opened a road to the crest.

Since then, recreational use of the Sandia Mountains has continued to parallel the explosive growth of Albuquerque itself, not only in numbers of recreationists but also in types of recreation: hiking, climbing, downhill skiing, cross-country skiing, snowboarding, snowshoeing, mountain-biking, horseback riding, birding, running, picnicking, hunting, hang-gliding, and many more.

The Fathers of Downhill Skiing in New Mexico
On January 23, 2003, Robert Nordhaus, Ernie Blake, and Ben Abruzzo became the first inductees into the newly created New Mexico Ski Hall of Fame. Nordhaus led the creation of what became the Sandia Ski Area; Ernie Blake established Taos Ski Valley; and Abruzzo was owner and operator of the Sandia Ski Area and Santa Fe Ski Basin. Also a major figure in the history of New Mexico dowhill skiing was Pete Totemoff.

The hall of fame project was spearheaded by Robert Parker, among the founders of the Vail Ski Resort in Colorado. It will be located in the Sandia Peak Tram building in Albuquerque and will include skiing memorabilia, historic photos, and exhibits and information about New Mexico's downhill ski industry.

Downhill Skiing
From the Doc Long Picnic Area, a few skiers hiked upward then skied down trails. But downhill skiing in the Sandias—and New Mexico—really dates from when Robert Nordhaus opened the first ski operation at La Madera, now Sandia Peak Ski Area. In 1936 the Albuquerque Ski Club was organized and worked with the Forest Service to clear a ski slope at the present Tree Spring Trailhead. In 1937, they cleared another slope, at La Madera, and installed a rope tow. La Madera, as the area was called at the time, continued to develop and had its greatest boost in 1959 when the State Highway Department improved and paved the road from Sandia Park.

Sandia Peak Tram
In 1964 the Sandia Peak Tram Company obtained a permit from the Forest Service that would lead to the nation's longest aerial tram. Bell Engineering, Ltd., of Lucerne, Switzerland, provided engineering and machinery, while Martin and Luther, General Contractors, undertook construction. When the project was completed two years later, six million pounds of concrete and steel had gone into securing terminal and tower foundations. A helicopter was needed to bring materials to Tower 2, making approximately five thousand trips. A winch weighing forty tons hauled four cables upward, each weighing a hundred thousand pounds. The total distance between the terminals is 2.7 miles, and the elevation change is more than 3,800 feet.

The tram carries skiers to the top of the Sandia Peak Ski Area, but it is used primarily by visitors and sightseers year-round, as well as diners at the High Finance Restaurant. Hikers and runners use the tram for loop trips. A classic Sandia Mountains adventure is to park at the lower terminal, hike the connecting trail to the La Luz Trail, hike the La Luz Trail to the upper terminal and refreshments at the restaurant, then take the tram back to the car.

The "Ghost of the Sandias"
Myron Carson, who joined the YMCA in 1935 as a youngster, has fond memories of his years at Balsam Glade. He later became a counselor for the younger boys and was known as the "Ghost of Sandias," when he slid across a high wire over the campfire.

Cross-country Skiing
See chapter 18 in this guide, "Cross-country Skiing and Winter Recreation.")

Hiking
People have traveled the Sandias on foot for thousands of years, but only in the last century or so has the purpose been recreation. The Forest Service's Sandia Ranger District maintains more than 140 miles of trails, but many more miles of unmaintained trails also exist. Most use is by day hikers, though backpackers who accept the steep terrain and paucity of water feel rewarded. Perhaps the greatest enchantment worked by the Sandias, one experienced by all hikers, is that once you're in the mountains, Albuquerque vanishes.

Since its formation in 1952, the New Mexico Mountain Club has been important in the history of hiking in the Sandias, introducing thousands of people to the trails through its outings. In cooperation with the U.S. Forest Service, ts members also have built and helped maintain trails in the mountains and assisted with environmental improvement projects.

See chapter 17 of this guide, "Hiking Trails," for information about general trails information and specific hiking routes.

The Electronic Site
A shining, mechanically bristling collection of towers makes up the antenna farm near the Sandias' highest point. The array began in 1945 when the New Mexico State Police selected Sandia Crest from a study of potential transmitter sites on various mountaintops in the state. That year, a small building was constructed and is still present. A generator operated by college students on the site provided electric power to the transmitter. The following year, mostly muscle power built a power line. Trucks hauled poles and wire up the mountain. Men and mules then dragged the materials downhill, setting poles and stringing wire as they went. Military and federal installations soon followed. By the early 1950s the first of the high-power television and radio broadcast facilities was in operation. Other electronic communications applications appeared, and small two-way repeater users proliferated. The electronic site, for all its unnatural appearance, performs a tremendous service to the state. Services from high-tech communication to personal entertainment emanate from here.

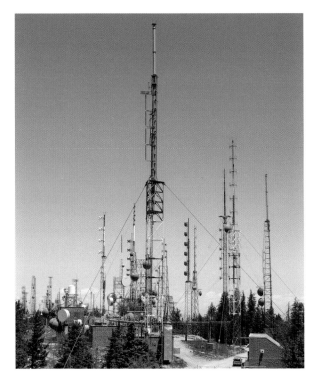

Electronic towers at Sandia Crest.

Hang-gliding

Weather conditions permitting, you are likely to see one or more brightly colored, stiff, human-bearing wings of fabric circling high above the Sandias. Hang-gliding was introduced to the Sandias in November 1973, when Terry Fitzsimmons made the first flight from near the Crest Observation Deck. A mass fly-off occurred in 1974, the same year the New Mexico Hang Glider Association was founded.

The first launching sites were from Sandia Crest itself and various sites along the crest zone from just short of North Peak to south of the Upper Tram Terminal. After testing many sites, the agreed-upon best were within the electronic site and near the High Finance Restaurant. Locally, the Sandia Soaring Association (SSA) formed. Following lengthy negotiations and a revision of the Crest Electronic Site Plan, the SSA in 1981 received a lot within the electronic site. At this writing, SSA has a permit for two launching areas—the electronic site and just north of the restaurant—as well as a landing zone north of the Elena Gallegos Picnic Area.

Today, hang-glider enthusiasts consider our mountain "World Class," a premier launching/flying/soaring site where they can enjoy the mountains' tremendous vertical relief and favorable wind currents for normal flying. Local and national competitive events are held annually, as are attempts to establish record flights for distance and time aloft.

Hang-gliding off the Crest.

Wilderness Protection

Responding to the need for formal protection of America's remaining wilderness areas, Congress in 1969 passed the Environmental Policy Act. In 1975 the Forest Service issued a Land Use Plan that identified potential wilderness. Then in 1976, U.S. Senators Frank Church of Idaho and Henry Jackson of Washington State introduced a wilderness bill that included the Sandias. Congress adjourned before its enactment, but a similar bill was introduced the next year, and in 1978 President Jimmy Carter signed the Endangered American Wilderness Act, which set aside as wilderness 30,981 acres of the Sandia Ranger District's total 100,555 acres. As Robert Julyan's *New Mexico Wilderness: The Complete Guide* explains: "Appropriately, Senator Church, supporter of the Sandia Mountain Wilderness, also was among the drafters of the 1964 Wilderness Act; in 1972, at a hearing of his Subcommittee on Public Lands, he stated: 'Sights and sounds from outside the boundary do not invalidate a Wilderness designation or make buffer and threshold exclusions necessary, as a matter of law . . .' a remarkably prescient statement regarding the Sandias."

In 1981 Albuquerque purchased portions of the former Elena Gallegos Grant in the mountains' western foothills, while the U.S. Forest Service added 6,251 acres to the Sandia Mountain Wilderness, bringing the wilderness acreage to 37,232 acres; today's total is 37,877 acres. Much of the rest was preserved as open space, providing some buffer between city and wilderness. In 1997, open-space advocates finally succeeded in keeping Three Gun Spring Canyon, on the mountains' south side, out of development. Today, the Sandia Mountain Wilderness includes about 45 percent of the mountains' total area.

See chapter 17 in this book, "Hiking Trails," for wilderness restrictions.

Doc Long

In 1910 only three forest pathologists existed in the entire United States, and one of them was in the Sandia Mountains. William Henry "Doc" Long lived in a cabin at the site of the present Doc Long Picnic Area, where he conducted pioneering research into tree diseases. Some of the older trees around the picnic area may have been planted by Long himself. In fact, foresters believe that at least one Austrian pine (*Pinus negra*) still exists within a mile radius of the picnic area—though they haven't found it.

Respect Private and Sandia Pueblo Land

Though most of the Sandias are in public ownership, private in-holdings exist, such as Ellis Ranch. Much of the northwestern Sandias are part of Sandia Pueblo Indian Reservation, and Albuquerque Academy owns land around Bear Canyon in the western Sandias. The present enjoyment we have of the mountains results from cooperation among all these groups, so it is **important** to respect boundaries and fences. If you desire access to one of these areas, get the landowner's permission first.

A Note to Friends and Visitors to the Sandias

I have long wished to publish a THANK YOU to each one of you who has spent time in the Sandias, who has enjoyed some aspect of its vast resources and treasures, and has returned the favor in some manner. Did you realize that just by observing courtesy to others and respect for the forest and its natural members you made a positive contribution to its proper use and management? If you did not leave litter, or better yet if you were one of the many who picked up litter left by someone else, you deserve an extra measure of gratitude. It would not be possible to manage the Sandias and most of our National Forest resources without the able help and assistance of our force of Volunteers—those actually enrolled and those who just "get it done" anonymously; so, thank you folks, you are the most valuable resource in the forest!

—*John S. Hayden, Sandia District*
Resource Forester, retired

215

To Learn More:

Bachen, Lou Sage. *Las Placitas: Historical Facts and Legends.* The Friends of Placitas, Inc., 2000.

Cordell, Linda S. *Prehistory of the Southwest.* A School of American Research Book. Orlando, Fla.: Academic Press, Inc., 1984.

————, ed. *Tijeras Canyon: Analyses of the Past.* Albuquerque: Maxwell Museum of Anthropology and the University of New Mexico Press, 1980.

Julyan, Robert. *The Place Names of New Mexico.* Albuquerque: University of New Mexico Press, 1998.

————. *New Mexico Wilderness Areas: The Complete Guide.* Englewood, Colo.: Westcliffe Publishers, 1998.

Melzer, Richard. *Coming of Age in the Great Depression: The Civilian Conservation Corps in New Mexico, 1933–1942.* Las Cruces, N.Mex.: Yucca Tree Press, 2000.

Schaafsma, Polly. *Indian Rock Art of the Southwest.* Albuquerque, N.Mex.: University of New Mexico Press, 2001.

Sturtevant, William C., and Alfonso Ortiz, eds. *Handbook of North American Indians, Vol. 9, Southwest.* Washington, D.C.: Smithsonian Institution, 1979.

CHAPTER 16
Place Names of the Sandias

Robert Julyan

The following is intended to include almost all the names found on the Forest Service's *Sandia Mountain Wilderness Map* and Mike Coltrin's *Sandia Mountain Hiking Guide*. Look there for locations of features.

Agua Sarca Canyon/Cañon Agua Sarca. Spanish, "blue water," a common New Mexico name for springs, including the one in this canyon.

Albert G. Simms City Park. Simms, a lawyer, came to Albuquerque around 1930 and soon became a prominent local figure financially and politically, serving as a member of Congress. He acquired the Elena Gallegos Grant (see below) and later donated most of it to Albuquerque Academy, of which he was a founder and financial backer.

Apache Canyon. Origin unknown.

Armijo Canyon/Arroyo Armijo. A Spanish personal name, specific origin unknown.

Arroyo Seco. Spanish, "dry gulch."

Balsam Glade. One of the early American settlers of the eastern Sandias mistook the white fir that grows here for balsam fir, similar in appearance but growing in the northeastern United States. He always called this area "Balsam Glade," and the name stuck.

Barro Canyon. Spanish, "clay," possibly for clay deposits here.

Barts Trail. Named for Bart Barton of Albuquerque, longtime member of the New Mexico Mountain Club, who on his own initiative built the original trail, which has since been rerouted.

Bear Canyon. Such names come either from numerous bears, or more likely, a specific incident involving a bear.

Bill Spring. Like Doc Long Picnic Area, near which it is located, Bill Spring likely was named for William Henry "Doc" Long, the early Forest Service plant pathologist who lived and conducted experiments here.

CCC Route. This route to the South Peak area was built and used by the Civilian Conservation Corps in the 1930s.

Capulin Peak. Spanish, "chokecherry."

Cañoncito Spring, Trail. Spanish, "little canyon," for its location in a small canyon.

Carlito Spring. Named by Carl Magee Sr., founder and editor of the *Albuquerque Tribune,* who lived here, to honor his son, Carl Magee Jr., who had been killed. Formerly called Whitcomb Springs, for a Union veteran of the Civil War who homesteaded here. Magee ultimately moved to Oklahoma City, where he invented the parking meter.

Carnuel Peak/Pico de Carnuel. Named for its proximity to the village of Carnuel just to the south, whose name is a corruption of a Tiwa Indian word meaning "badger."

Chimney Canyon. This precipitous canyon was named for a chimney-shaped rock formation near the top.

China Wall/Peñasco Blanco Trail. Both the English name and the Spanish name, meaning "white bluff," refer to prominent limestone cliffs near the junction of the Peñasco Blanco Trail and the Crest Trail.

Cibola National Forest. This name, derived from a word in Spanish referring to "bison," is appropriate because this National Forest includes not only mountains such as the Sandias but also the High Plains stretching into Oklahoma—inhabited by millions of bison when Spaniards arrived in the Southwest. The name also was used by early Spanish speakers to refer to the realm within which the fabulous seven golden cities sought by Coronado and later *conquistadores* were thought to exist.

Cienega Canyon. Spanish, "swamp, marsh, wetland."

Cole Spring. Chauncey Cole and his family moved to New Mexico around 1920 and bought land in this area. He was fond of this spring, and when the U.S. Forest Service established a picnic area here they named it for him.

Cueva. Spanish, "cave." Two canyons in the Sandias, one on the east side and one on the west, are named La Cueva, both because they contain caves.

Davis Cave. Named for Ken Davis, associated with the better-known Sandia Cave nearby.

Deer Pass. Specific origin unknown.

Del Agua Canyon. Spanish, "of the water," because of the canyon's springs and tiny creek.

Doc Long Picnic Area. William Henry "Doc" Long was a U.S. Forest Service forest pathologist—one of three in the United States at the time— who worked in New Mexico from 1910 to the mid-1930s. He set up an experimental area where the picnic ground was built and lived in a cabin at the site. See *Bill Spring.*

Domingo Baca Canyon. The identity of this person has been lost.

Echo Canyon. Its concave configuration is conducive to echoes.

The Eye of the Sandias

Years ago, no one knows exactly when, someone painted a large eye on a rock face in a remote part of the Sandias. Nearby and perhaps much older were three green crosses. Since then, the eye has been repainted at least once and now appears with a Zia sign and tears falling down. A faint, unmarked trail leads to the eye from the trailhead at the end of Copper Ave.

Elena Gallegos Picnic Area. Elena Gallegos was a member of a family that returned to New Mexico in 1692 with the Reconquest; in 1699 she married one Santiago Gurule. A dozen years later Governor Peñuela granted to Captain Diego Montoya lands between Sandia Pueblo's southern boundary and the northern boundary of the Villa de Albuquerque. In the meantime, Gurule died, and soon after Montoya conveyed his lands to Gurule's widow, who according to custom had reverted to her maiden name. Subsequently, the lands became known as the Elena Gallegos Grant and included seventy thousand acres. Eventually, the lands were acquired by Albuquerque Academy (see *Albert G. Simms City Park*), and in the 1980s some of the lands were acquired by the City of Albuquerque and the U.S. Forest Service, to be managed as wilderness and open space.

Ellis Ranch. George Ellis arrived in the Sandias in the 1880s and during the 1890s lived here with his family. He died in 1912 and is buried at his ranch. Upper Las Huertas Creek once was called Ellis Creek.

Embudo Canyon. Spanish, "funnel," describing a broad drainage area that becomes constricted downstream to flow through a narrow, rocky gorge, like a funnel.

Embudito Canyon. Spanish, "little funnel," similar to Embudo Canyon but smaller.

Escondido Spring. Spanish, "hidden."

Eye of the Sandias. No one knows who first painted an eye on a rock face here in the southern Sandias, but it continues to be repainted and to intrigue hikers.

Faulty Trail. Built along the route of an old wagon road, this also has been called the Diamond Trail and the Mystery Trail, because the mysterious trail-builder used diamond-shaped blazes. The name Faulty Trail was adopted by the Forest Service because the southern part of the route is along the Flatirons fault zone.

Public Nature Walks

Throughout the year Sandia Ranger District staff and volunteers conduct walks and tours introducing visitors to such topics as wildflowers, birds, ecology, archaeology, and much more. Contact the Ranger District offices in Tijeras to find out about upcoming events.

Fletcher Trail. Named for Royce Fletcher, longtime New Mexico Mountain Club member who created the trail around 1980.

Gonzales Canyon. Origin unknown.

Hawk Watch Trail. Created in 1988 as a joint project between the U.S. Forest Service and the Western Foundation for Raptor Conservation, this leads to an outstanding site from which to observe the annual spring migration of hawks, eagles, falcons, and other raptors.

Hondo Canyon. Spanish, "deep."

Jaral Cabin Trail. Jaral in New Mexico Spanish refers to a willow thicket. Here the name likely refers to limbs used in the construction of a long-abandoned ranger cabin along the route.

Juan Tabo Canyon/Picnic Area. The identity of the man for whom this canyon—and numerous other features in Albuquerque—was named remains a mystery. The name first appears in a 1778 petition using Cañada de Juan Taboso as a landmark. It's been suggested this person belonged to the Taboso Indian group, a tribe akin to the Lipan Apaches, and though their traditional territory was far to the southeast, it's not impossible that one of their members settled here. At least one legend attributes the name to an Indian sheepherder who grazed his flocks in the canyon. Another legend is that Juan Tabo was a priest who lived here; the name is absent from church records. But Juan Tabo is likely to remain the stuff of legends.

Kiwanis Cabin/Meadow. In the late 1920s, the Kiwanis Club of Albuquerque built a log cabin here. This later burned. In the late 1930s the Civilian Conservation Corps (CCC) built the present stone structure, but it retained the name Kiwanis Cabin. A campground was at the meadow, but when bighorn sheep were introduced to the Sandias the campground was abandoned because the meadow was in their summer range.

According to Kirk Douglas . . .

The Movie Canyon acquired its name when the trail in it was constructed in 1962 in connection with the making of the movie *Lonely Are the Brave*, starring Kirk Douglas. He claimed the film was among the best movies he appeared in–and certainly the most demanding!

Lagunita Seca. The perfect descriptive name, "dry little lake" exactly describes this small meadow southeast of Palomas Peak.

La Luz Mine/Trail. Juan Nieto is said to have discovered this lead-silver deposit in 1887. Colonel Bernard Ruppe and others bought the claim in 1907, and it was called the Ruppe Mine until La Luz Trail was built. Several stories explain the name La Luz, "the light." One is that lights from the mine's cabin sometimes were visible from Albuquerque. It also is possible that, as with other La Luz names in New Mexico, the name honors *Nuestra Señora de la Luz,* "Our Lady of the Light," one of the names for the Virgin Mary.

Las Huertas Canyon. This well-watered valley is ideally suited for the orchards (Spanish, *huertas*), some still here, for which the early Spanish village of Las Huertas also was named. Though the canyon was visited by Coronado in 1540, settlement dates from the eighteenth century.

Lorenzo Canyon. Origin unknown, but this was once an important water source for grazing allotments, and Lorenzo possibly was a permittee.

Madera Canyon/Cañon Madera. Spanish, "wood, lumber." This name and that of the nearby village of La Madera recall logging operations that existed here as late as the 1950s and 1960s.

Mano Trail. A prehistoric hand-grinding stone, or *mano,* is said to have been found along this route. Perhaps the accompanying *metate* is still there.

Media Spring/Cañon Media. Probably originally *medio,* Spanish, "middle," because the canyon is between Las Huertas and Osha Canyons.

Movie Trail. Originally constructed for the filming of *Lonely Are the Brave,* 1962, starring Kirk Douglas.

North Sandia Peak. At 10,447 feet, the main summit of the northern Sandias.

Ojo del Orno. See *Tunnel Spring.*

Osha Spring/Cañon Osha. This is the New Mexico Spanish name for the medicinal plant *Ligusticum porteri,* known in English as "lovage." The Osha Loop Trail was named by New Mexico Mountain Club member John Southwick because from the 10K Trail it descends almost to Osha Spring and then climbs to the North Crest Trail. The Osha Spring Trail climbs to the spring from Las Huertas Canyon.

Oso Corredor Trail. Spanish, "running bear." When this trail was completed in the fall of 1989, U.S. Forest Service workers voted on a name, and this won because that fall a drought had driven an unprecedented number of bears out of the mountains to run about the foothills.

Oso Pass. Spanish, "bear," for reasons unknown (see *Bear Canyon*), though Oso Pass would be used by bears to pass between Embudo Canyon and Embudito Canyon.

Pa'ako. When the Spaniards came here, they found a large Tiwa Indian pueblo on the east side of the Sandias; its name was *Pa'ako,* said to mean "root of the cottonwood," likely for the cottonwoods around the nearby spring and the stream it feeds. The Spaniards established a mission called San Pedro del Cuchillo, "Saint Peter of the Ridge," but the mission and the pueblo were abandoned before 1670. The ruins now are used for archaeology field work.

Palo Duroso Canyon. Spanish, "hard wood."

Palomas Peak. Spanish, "doves," though here it is said to refer to bandtail pigeons, perhaps nesting here, or to the limestone ledges surrounding the top being evocative of the light bands on the pigeons' tails.

Piedra Lisa. Spanish, "smooth or slick rock," usually derived from water flowing over a lip of granite. At least two canyons in the Sandias have this name.

Pino Canyon. Spanish, "pine," likely for a stand of ponderosas in the canyon.

Post Pass. A U.S. Forest Service trail sign is on a post here.

Pyramid Peak. Think of a Mayan rather than an Egyptian pyramid when looking for the resemblance that inspired the descriptive name of this 8,134-foot peak at the head of Juan Tabo Canyon.

Rincón. Spanish, "corner, secluded place, box canyon."

Rincón Peak. At 8,201 feet, this is the highest point on Rincón Ridge, the north-south ridge that forms the western boundary of Juan Tabo Canyon.

Rozamiento Trail. This is a fairly recent hiker name, which perhaps explains the nonstandard spelling of the Spanish *rosamiento,* meaning "friction," referring to the granite slabs along the route, where only the friction of shoe soles on the rock allows a hiker to continue.

U.S. Forest Service volunteer Gerry Sussman on patrol in Rozamiento Canyon.

Sandia Mountains. Spanish, "watermelon." As *The Place Names of New Mexico* says,

One explanation attributes this name to watermelons, or at least watermelon-resembling gourds, growing in canyons here. Another attributes it to being transferred from El Corazón de la Sandia, *a mountain in the Spanish Sierra Nevada resembling the heart of a watermelon. The most popular explanation is that the Sandia Mountains, especially when viewed from the northwest at evening, resemble a sliced watermelon, the granite pink with alpenglow, capped by a white limestone layer and covered with dark-green vegetation resembling a rind. But the most likely explanation is the one believed by the Sandia Indians: the Spaniards, when they encountered the pueblo in 1540, called it Sandia, because they thought the squash growing there were watermelons, and the name Sandia soon was transferred to the mountains east of the pueblo. The Tiwas call the Sandia complex* Bien Mur, *"big mountain." The Tewas call it* Oku Pin, *"turtle mountain," for its shape. The Navajo name for the Sandia Mountains means "revolving (in a horizontal plane) mountains." The Sandia Mountains figure in the mythology of all the Indian groups.*

Sandia Cave. Archaeological excavations revealed evidence of humans being here at least ten thousand years ago, and possibly much earlier.

South Sandia Peak. At 9,782 feet, the highest summit of the southern Sandias.

South Sandia Spring. Usually reliable spring, high on the brow of the southern crest of the Sandias.

Smelter Trail. Unofficial trail leading toward ruins of a smelter in Tecolote Canyon likely used to process non-local metallic ores.

Stripmine Trail. The scars of early attempts to stripmine this area are visible along this route.

Sulphur Canyon. Origin unknown, but possibly related to a mine on the ridge separating this canyon from the one in which the Doc Long Picnic Area is located.

Tecolote Peak/Canyon. Spanish, "owl."

Tejano Canyon. Spanish, "Texan," origin unknown.

10K Trail. This had previously been called the Osha Spring Trail, but this name was confusing and inaccurate because of a mislabeling on maps of several canyons in the northeastern Sandias, so John Southwick of the New Mexico Mountain Club proposed the name *10K Trail,* because the trail begins and ends at 10,000 feet (K = 1,000).

Three Gun Spring. This name originally appeared in Spanish as *Tres Pistoles,* and local lore tells that three pistols from the Spanish conquistadors were found here. More recently, someone had carved the outline of three pistols into a wooden water tank, now gone, at this spring, possibly to commemorate the earlier discovery.

Tijeras Canyon. Separating the Sandias from the Manzanita Mountains, Tijeras Canyon originally was known as Carnuel Canyon, for the settlement located at its west end (see *Carnuel Peak*). Now it takes its name from the village at its east end. *Tijeras* is Spanish and means "scissors," and it is widely believe the locality was named because two canyons come together here, like the blades of scissors.

Tree Spring Trail. Long before the road here was paved, travelers had noticed a spring issuing from a huge tree stump. Although the stump is gone, the spring and the trail named for it remain, though the spring actually is about 0.5 miles before the trailhead, on the north side of NM 536.

Tunnel Spring. Many years ago miners drove a tunnel into the mountainside here, but their mining was impeded when the tunnel hit an aquifer. The spring issuing from the tunnel later fed a fish hatchery, but when the U.S. Forest Service acquired the site they dynamited the tunnel for the public's safety, and now the water issues from a metal pipe. A smelter resembling a beehive-shaped *horno* was associated with the mine, and the nearby Cañon Ojo del Orno recalls this.

Waterfall Canyon. In wet times, a scenic waterfall is here.

Whitewash Trail. Patches of light-colored rocks and soil resemble splotches of lime-based whitewash along this steep, rocky route.

Names Used by Climbers

Unknown to most visitors to the Sandias are the names climbers use among themselves and in their writings. Here are their names for major rock formations along the western face of the Sandias: Beastie, Lady, The Three Pigs, Shield, Prow, Needle, Tombstone, Mummy, Castle, Cake and Candle, Chimney, Sentinel, Lost Spectacle, Yataghan, Chaos Crag, Mexican Breakfast, Fire Hydrant, Whiskey Peak, Beer Peak, and many more. The names of the climbing routes are also wonderful in their whimsy and irreverence. A sample: Clarks Cramps, Labor Day Route, Warpy Moople, Short but Thin, Masochist Variant, Fantasia, Out to Lunch—and that's on just one cliff!

CHAPTER 17
Hiking Trails

Don Carnicom

Whether you are a newcomer or a seasoned hiker, the Sandia Mountains will provide you with a diversity of hiking experiences, from desert hiking in the foothills to subalpine at the crest, drier on the west side and wetter on the east. These factors, combined with the normal seasonal changes and over 140 miles of trails, will give most hikers almost any combination of hiking conditions they may be looking for any time of the year. Although the Sandias are surrounded by communities totaling more than half a million people, a visitor can still experience a sense of solitude by hiking slightly more than a mile on most trails.

A log fence along Kiwanis Meadow.

The Sandia Mountain Wilderness, designated by Congress in 1978, makes up a major portion of the Sandias. This includes about 37,200 acres and more than 110 miles of trails on which a variety of recreational activities take place. Within the Wilderness certain restrictions apply: mechanized vehicles, including bicycles, and motorized equipment are prohibited. Numerous signs indicate when you are entering the Wilderness.

Although no developed campgrounds are found in the Sandias, backcountry camping is permitted outside of picnic areas. Bicycles are permitted on most trails outside the Wilderness; popular routes include trails in the foothills, the Sandia Peak Ski Area trails, and trails in the Manzanita Mountains south of I-40. Trails also are open to horseback riding, and several trailheads accommodate horse trailers, though horses are not recommended on the Crest Spur, Embudito, and upper Embudo Trails.

The trail system of the mountains is composed of a main north-south trail along the ridge (Crest Trail 130), with side "feeder trails" coming up from the east and west. Paralleling the Crest Trail but at lower elevations are two north-south trails connecting many of the feeder trails: Foothills Trail 365 on the west side and Faulty Trail 195 on the east. The Foothills Trail runs through both National Forest and City of Albuquerque Open Space land. While numerous unofficial trails exist in the Sandias, only the most popular and maintained trails are described in this book.

227

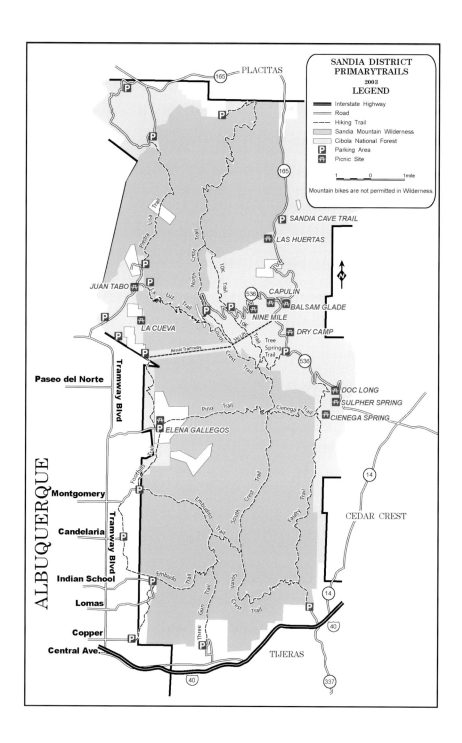

Switchbacks along the La Luz Trail

When you're hiking the La Luz Trail, the switchbacks may seem endless, but in fact they are finite. If you consider a switchback to be any place where the trail makes a bend of at least 120 degrees, you encounter thirty-eight switchbacks hiking the 7.7 mile trail.

Some general comments applicable to various locations in the mountains are:

Parking Fees are applicable at many trailheads.

Occasionally backcountry travel is limited due to high fire danger.
Please contact the Sandia Ranger District at 281–3304.

Proper trail ethics encourages trail users to use designated trails.
By doing so users reduce erosion, the creation of confusing unofficial side trails, and the possibility of getting lost or injured.

The trails are maintained by the Forest Service trails staff, Forest Service volunteers, organizations within the Adopt-A-Trail Program, New Mexico Friends of the Forest, and City of Albuquerque Open Space.

In the following trail descriptions, all directions are from Albuquerque.
Please refer to the accompanying map (p. 228) for trail locations relative to the mountains and other trails.

Foothills Trail 365

Easy: 13 miles, 800-foot elevation change. This popular trail stretches from the Lower Sandia Peak Tram Terminal south to I-40 and serves pedestrians and bicyclists, as well as providing access to several forest trails.

Piedra Lisa Trail 135

Difficult: 5.8 miles, 2,099-foot elevation change. The southern trailhead is at the parking lot 0.25 mile past the turnoff to the Juan Tabo Picnic Area. The northern trailhead is on FR 445 south of NM 165 in Placitas. This trail offers very good views of the sheer cliffs on the west face of the Sandias.

La Luz Trail 137

Difficult: 7.7 miles, 3,775-foot elevation change. A favorite of many hikers, the La Luz Trail begins at the Juan Tabo Picnic Area and ends at the Upper Tram Terminal. The Crest Spur Trail 84 near the top goes to the Crest.

The Most Remote Place in the Sandias

According to research by environmental Geographic Information Systems (GIS) specialist Kurt Menke, the most remote point in the northern Sandias is 1.96 miles from the wilderness boundary, at coordinates 35.11593 north, 106.42693 west. The most remote in the southern Sandias is 2.24 miles from the wilderness boundary, at coordinates 35.26114 north,106.44456 west.

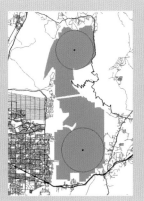

Pino Trail 140
Difficult: 4.7 miles, 2,798-foot elevation change. Access to the Pino Trail is from the Elena Gallegos Picnic Ground, in the City of Albuquerque Open Space. This is a pleasant alternative to the La Luz Trail but is steadily steeper and within the forest most of the time. It ends at the Crest Trail 130.

Embudito Trail 192
Difficult: 5.6 miles, 3,039-foot elevation change. Embudito begins at the end of Trailhead Road. Go east on Montgomery Boulevard past Tramway Boulevard, turn left on Glenwood Hills Drive, then right on Trailhead Road. This trail, which ends at the Crest Trail 130, is the most direct route to South Peak from the west side. The lower half is exposed, rocky, and steep while the upper half is also steep but forested.

Embudo Trail 193
Difficult: 3.2 miles, 1,749-foot elevation change. Access to Embudo Trail is from the City of Albuquerque Open Space trailhead facility at the end of Indian School Road. The Embudo Horse Bypass Trail, just south of Embudo Trail, reconnects to Embudo Trail above the narrow, rocky part of the canyon. The "box" at Embudo Spring (near the canyon entrance) is an easy and very popular hike. The Embudo Trail ends at Post Pass and the junction with the Three Gun Spring Trail 194.

Three Gun Spring Trail 194
Moderate: 4.0 miles, 2,133-foot elevation change. To access Three Gun Spring Trail, take I-40 to Exit 170. Travel east on NM 333 1.5 miles to Monticello subdivision. Follow hiking symbols to the trailhead. This trail, excellent in winter, provides scenic views to the south and makes for an interesting hike through the Upper Sonoran life zone. At the Wilderness boundary, you will see the Hawk Watch Trail going east to an observation point for spring counts of migrating raptors.

The Best Vantage Point from Which to View Aspens in the Fall
The consensus among longtime hikers in the Sandias is that the view of fall aspens from the Del Agua Overlook on the north Crest Trail has no peers.

Crest Trail 130
Difficult: 26.5 miles, 4,118-foot elevation change. To access the south trailhead, take I-40 to the Tijeras Exit 175. Go under I-40, turn right on the paved road through Canyon Estates subdivision. The north trailhead at Tunnel Spring in Placitas is accessed from FR 231 south of NM 165. The trail can also be accessed near its middle at the crest parking lot. The length and wide range of elevations and life zones along the Crest Trail results in it having a greater variety of wildlife, plants, and geology than any other trail in the Sandias.

Faulty Trail 195
Moderate: 9.0 miles, 808-foot elevation change. To begin hiking from the south, follow the directions to the south end of the Crest Trail described above. Hike the South Crest Trail 130 for 0.8 miles to the intersection with the Lower Faulty Trail. About 1 mile farther on the South Crest Trail is the junction with the Upper Faulty Trail, which joins the Lower Faulty Trail after 1.25 miles. To find the Faulty Trail's north trailhead, hike northwest on the Bill Spring Trail 196 from the Doc Long Picnic Area on the Crest Highway. Staying between about 7,000 feet and 7,800 feet for 9 miles in heavy timber makes for a great day hike, but you'll need a car at the other end if planning a one-way hike.

Cienega Trail 148
Difficult: 2.2 miles, 1,659-foot elevation change. The trail can be reached from the Crest Highway by going to the west end of the Cienega Canyon Picnic Area. This is the only trail to the South Crest Trail from the three popular picnic grounds in this area.

Tree Spring Trail 147

Moderate: 2.0 miles, 1,039-foot elevation change. The trailhead is on the west side of the Crest Highway, about 6 miles from NM 14. It is the shortest route to the crest from the highway for hikers, bikers, and equestrians.

10K Trail 200

Moderate: 4.9 miles, 572-foot elevation change. The trailheads for the north and south sections of this trail are located on the Crest Highway, which intersects the middle of the trail about 12 miles from NM 14. The 10K Trail intersects numerous trails, making it easy to plan short and long loop hikes.

Note: *The U.S. Forest Service strongly discourages private groups and individuals from clearing or creating trails on their own initiative. Doing so can result in hikers becoming lost, as well as intrusion upon sensitive wildlife areas and cultural sites.*

To Learn More:

The following publications were used as references for this section and provide more detailed trail information.

Coltrin, Mike. *Sandia Mountain Hiking Guide.* Albuquerque: University of New Mexico Press, 2005.

High Desert Field Guide, 1997.

Julyan, Robert. *The Mountains of New Mexico.* Albuquerque, the University of New Mexico Press, forthcoming 2006.

Sandia Mountain Trails. Cibola National Forest, 2001. Available at the Ranger Station.

Sandia Mountain Wilderness Map, 1991. Available at the Ranger Station.

Sandia Mountains Visitors Guide. Public Lands Interpretive Association, 1994.

Trail Map of the Elena Gallegos Picnic Area and Sandia Foothills. (Albuquerque Open Space).

CHAPTER 18
Cross-country Skiing and Winter Recreation

Sam Beard

Cross-country Ski Trails

The Sandias' cross-country ski-trail system consists of six major marked but ungroomed routes, within or radiating from the Sandia Crest–Upper Tramway Terminal area. Although not machine-groomed, all these trails and part of the North Crest Trail 130 are tracked by skiers during or shortly after each storm. Most of the routes lie on east- and north-facing slopes in the trees to minimize snow melt due to the intense solar radiation at the high elevations.

All the trails were cleared and marked by New Mexico Cross-country Ski Club volunteers, under the leadership of the Trails Committee Chair, Sam Beard, in cooperation with the U.S. Forest Service. To minimize environmental impact, volunteers were given permission to clear routes by pruning branches and removing fallen trees. Felling mature trees and digging trails were not permitted. A natural trail tread of organic forest duff has gradually developed on these trails as hikers, deer, and other animals have walked over them during the months without snow.

The marked trails were cleared between 1970 and 1990 by club members as part of the Adopt-A-Trail Program on the Sandia Ranger District. Initially only hiking trails and unplowed picnic areas and forest roads, such as the service road to the upper tramway terminal, were available for skiing. As cross-country skiing became more popular in the early 1970s, club members began looking for additional routes and soon found a one-lane buried cable route leading from the crest parking lot to Kiwanis Meadow. The Forest Service granted permission to clear this route, which was named Buried Cable Trail.

Three other early trails were routed along existing clearings formed by a survey right-of-way, logging roads, and an abandoned highway clearing. Tom Mayer found a proposed highway survey right-of-way running from the service road to the north across the Crest Highway to the 10K Trail. Volunteers used chainsaws to clear the Survey Trail, because the area had not yet been designated wilderness. The original Challenge Trail leading from the Ellis Trailhead parking area down the mountain to the base of the Sandia Peak Ski Area was planned by John Southwick and generally followed existing timber-sale roads to minimize the amount of clearing required. Art and Katherine Arenholz nailed blue plastic diamonds on trees to mark this original route. Sections of this trail were later rerouted to the present location parallel to the Crest Highway for better snow conditions and to reduce maintenance. The Ellis Trail follows a wide clearing for an earlier

planned highway from the upper mountain to Placitas. Protests by conservationists eventually led to the project's cancellation, and the cleared route was designated a hiking trail, which is skied in the winter.

Three other marked trails were planned as narrow routes leading from the service road to specific destinations to give the skier a wilderness-like experience on a more difficult trail with very good snow conditions and an interesting destination. The combination of the Rocky Point and Gravel Pit Trails leads the skier over four limestone outcroppings to the restaurant near the upper tramway terminal and past the Gravel Pit Overlook to Kiwanis Meadow. Lynn Asbury and John Thomas helped plan the Rocky Point trail. These trails permit the skier to bypass the busy and usually hard-packed service road. The Switchback Trail takes the skier from the service road through four major switchbacks to the crest parking lot.

All of the marked cross-country ski trails are maintained for year-round use by Ski Club and Friends of the Forest volunteers.

Groomed Cross-country Ski Trails and Snow Play Areas

Each winter the University of New Mexico cross-country ski team obtains a permit to groom selected wide routes in areas between Capulin Spring Picnic Ground and Sandia Crest. A snowmobile pulls equipment that sets tracks for traditional diagonal-stride skiing and also smoothes and packs a track for skating. The Norski racing club also groomed trails for several years for citizen races. Other groups interested in skating may groom trails from time to time.

Tubing and sledding are permitted, but not encouraged, at several locations along the Crest Highway. Snow play on the dangerous, steep slopes at the 10K Trailhead parking areas and inside the highway switchback below Tree Spring Trailhead is not permitted. A better location is the Capulin Snow Play Area, operated by the U.S. Forest Service.

Snowshoeing and Snowboarding

The number of snowshoers in the Sandia Mountains has increased greatly in the past several years due to a desire for year-round outdoor activities and modern lightweight snowshoes with much-improved bindings. Snowshoeing is permitted in the forest and on all hiking and cross-country ski trails. Snowshoers should walk to the side of cross-country ski trails to avoid damaging the tracks set by skiers.

In recent years, backcountry snowboarding has gained popularity in the Sandias, outside the Sandia Peak Ski Area. Especially popular are the steep gravel-pit slopes on the service road (FR 488). Snowboarders should watch for snowshoers and cross-country skiers in these areas—and vice versa.

Scientific Classification

Throughout this book we have used scientific classifications of plant and animal names. To help you gain familiarity with these systems, here is how our state butterfly, the Sandia hairstreak *(Callophrys mcfarlandi)* and the alligator juniper *(Juniperus deppeana)* are placed within the system of scientific classification. Note: Within this system, the genus and species names always are italicized.

example: Sandia Hairstreak butterfly, Callophrys mcfarlandi
Kingdom • Animal
    Phylum • Arthropoda
        Class • Insecta (other examples include: Aracnida, Chilopoda, Diplopoda, Crustacea)
            Order • Lepidoptera (other examples include: Hymenoptera, Coleoptera, Araneida, Scorpionida)
                Family • Nymphalidae (other examples include: Pieridae, Pompilidae, Theridiidae, Gerridae, etc.)
                    Genus • *Callophrys*
                    Species • *Callophrys mcfarlandi*
                    Common Name • Sandia hairstreak

example: alligator juniper, Juniperus deppeana
Kingdom • Plantae – Plants
    Subkingdom • Tracheobionta – Vascular plants
        Superdivision • Spermatophyta – Seed plants
            Division • Coniferophyta – Conifers
                Class • Pinopsida
                Order • Pinales
                    Family • Cupressaceae – Cypress family
                    Genus • *Juniperus* (L. juniper)
                    Species • *Juniperus deppeana*
                    Common Name • alligator juniper

Key to Some Plants of New Mexico

Use this key to unlock the identity of trees you see. Start with the first set of statements to determine what leaf type of the tree you are trying to identify. The number at the right directs you to the next step in the key. For example, if the specimen is a broadleaf tree go to line 5. Continue down the key until you identify the tree or find that it doesn't fit the key. This key only identifies *some of the trees in the Sandias*, not all of them. Above all have fun testing your skills.

1. a. Needle-leaf trees; leaves retained in the winter • 2
   b. Broadleaf trees; leaves lost in the winter • 5
2. a. Needle-leaf trees; bear seeds in cones with scales that open • 3
   b. Short, scale-like leaves; bear seeds in cones that resemble hard berries • 10
3. a. Needles separate; not in bundles • 4
   b. Needles in groups of two or more • 12
4. a. Rough "fish-scale" bark; needle cross section square • **Engelmann Spruce**
   b. Smooth or furrowed bark; needles flat • 14
5. a. Leaves simple (only one "leaf" on a leaf stem) • 6
   b. Leaves compound (3 or more "leaflets" on the same leaf stem) • 9
6. a. Leaves at least two times longer than wide • 7
   b. Spade-shape leaves; white to gray-green bark • **Aspen**
7. a. Leaves with wavy edges forming "leaf lobes" or prickles • 8
   b. Leaves long, slender, separate, with mostly smooth edges • **Willow**
8. a. Leaves deeply indented along each side • **Gambel Oak**
   b. Leaves slightly indented, sharp points along edge • **Wavy Leaf Oak**
9. a. Three leaflets; leaf stems dark green, paired seeds with wings • **Box Elder**
   b. Many oval, paired leaflets; seeds pods long and furry; thorny •
      New Mexico Locust
10. a. Bark stringy, not in squares • 11
    b. Bark very rough, in squares • **Alligator Juniper**
11. a. Yellow-green leaves, bunched toward the end of branch •
       One-Seed Juniper
    b. Gray-green leaves; weepy branches • **Rocky Mountain Juniper**
12. a. Needles grow in groups of less than five • 13
    b. Needles in bundles of five • **Limber Pine** or **Southwestern White Pine**
13. a. Needles short (2 inches), in groups of two, edible seeds • **Piñon Pine**
    b. Needles long (4-8 inches), in groups of three • **Ponderosa Pine**
14. a. Needles shorter than 1.5 inches • 15
    b. Needles curved, longer than 1.5 inches; grey bark • **WhiteFir**
15. a. Dark, furrowed bark; cones with "mouse tail" bracts • **Douglas-fir**
    b. Light-grey bark, usually soft or spongy; cones fall apart when ripe •
       Corkbark Fir

APPENDIX 3
Checklists

Butterflies of the Sandia Mountains
Family Danaidae
❑ Monarch, *Danaus plexippus*—appear in August and September
❑ Queen *Danaus gilippus*—foothills only

Family Papilionidae
❑ Pipevine swallowtail, *Battus philenor*—foothills only
❑ Black swallowtail, *Papilio polyzenes*
❑ Old World swallowtail, *Papilio machaon*—not common
❑ Anise swallowtail, *Papilio zelicaon*
❑ Giant swallowtail, *Papilio cresphontes*—fringe areas only, urban
❑ Western tiger swallowtail, *Papilio rutulus*—canyons
❑ Two-tailed swallowtail, *Papilio multicaudata*
❑ Pale swallowtail, *Papilio eurymedon*—extreme northern Sandias

Family Lubytheidae
❑ North American snout butterfly, *Libytheana bachmanii larvata*—foothills, open scrub

Family Nymphalidae
❑ Variegated fritillary, *Euptoieta claudia*—foothills only
❑ Great spangled fritillary, *Speyeria cybele*—northern Sandias
❑ Northwestern fritillary, *Speyeria hesperis*—mountain meadows
❑ Mormon fritillary, *Speyeria mormonia*—mountain meadows
❑ Bordered patch, *Chlosyne lacinia*—piñon juniper–oak woodland
❑ Silvery checkerspot, *Chlosyne nycteis*—streamsides
❑ Pearl crescent, *Phyciodes tharos*—roadsides
❑ Northern crescent, *Phyciodes cocyta*—streamsides
❑ Tawny crescent, *Phyciodes batesii*—rocky hillsides
❑ Field crescent, *Phyciodes pratensis*
❑ Painted crescent, *Phyciodes picta*
❑ Mylitta crescent, *Phyciodes mylitta*
❑ Question mark, *Polygonia interrogationis*
❑ Satyr comma, *Polygonia satyrs*
❑ Hoary comma, *Polygonia gracilis zephyrus*—Las Huertas Picnic Area (adults early spring, lay eggs, caterpillars and pupae until late July, adults emerge)
❑ California tortoiseshell, *Nymphalis californica*
❑ Mourning cloak, *Nymphalis antiopa*

Family Nymphalidae (continued)

❏ Milbert's tortoiseshell, *Nymphalis milberti*
❏ Virginia painted lady, *Vanessa virginiensis*—forest edges
❏ Painted lady, *Vanessa cardui*—roadsides
❏ West Coast lady, *Vanessa annabella*—foothills
❏ Red admiral, *Vanessa atalanta*—moist woods, urban parks
❏ Buckeye, *Junonia coenia*—open, bare, and grassy areas
❏ Viceroy, *Limenitis archippus*
❏ Weidemeyer's admiral, *Limenitis weidemeyerii*—canyons, streams
❏ California sister, *Adelpha bredowii*—canyons, streams
❏ Goatweed leafwing, *Anaea andria*—deciduous woods, open fields

Family Satyridae

❏ Canyonland satyr, *Cyllopsis pertepida*—piñon juniper–oak woodland
❏ Ringlet, *Coenonympha tullia*—grassy open areas
❏ Wood nymph, *Cercyonis pegala*—open meadows
❏ Mead's wood nymph, *Cercyonis meadii*—piñon juniper–oak woodland
❏ Small wood nymph, *Cercyonis oetus*—open meadows

Family Pieridae

❏ Pine white, *Neophasia menapia*—alpine only
❏ Spring white, *Pieris sisymbri*
❏ Checkered white, *Pieris protodice*
❏ Western white, *Pieris occidentalis*—rare, northern areas only
❏ Margined white, *Pieris napi marginalis*—rare, northern areas only
❏ Cabbage white, *Pieris rapae*—foothills, open areas
❏ Large marble, *Euchloe ausonides*—foothills only
❏ Southern Rocky Mountain orangetip, *Anthocharis julia*
❏ Clouded sulphur, *Colias philodice*—foothills, open areas
❏ Orange sulphur, *Colias eurytheme*—foothills, open areas
❏ Queen Alexandra's sulphur, *Colias alexandra*—northern Sandias, mountain meadows
❏ Southern dogface, *Zerene cesonia*—foothills only
❏ Cloudless sulphur, *Phoebis senna* sp.—foothills only
❏ Mexican yellow, *Eurema mexicana*—foothills only
❏ Sleepy orange, *Eurema nicippe*—foothills only
❏ Dainty dwarf, *Nathalis iole*—mountain meadows, roadsides

Family Lycaenidae

- ❑ Tailed copper, *Lycaena arota*—open woodland
- ❑ Blue copper, *Lycaena heteronea*—northern areas only
- ❑ Purplish copper, *Lycaena helloides*—northern areas only
- ❑ Colorado hairstreak, *Hypaurotis crysalus*—oak woodland (Colorado state butterfly)
- ❑ Great purple hairstreak, *Atlides halesus*—oak woodland, larvae feed on mistletoe
- ❑ Coral hairstreak, *Satyrium titus*—shrubby areas along trails
- ❑ Behr's hairstreak, *Satyrium behrii*—piñon-juniper woodland
- ❑ Banded hairstreak, *Satyrium calanus*—edge of forest
- ❑ Western green hairstreak, *Callophrys affinis*—northern Sandias
- ❑ Sandia hairstreak, *Callophrys mcfarlandi*—yucca agave desert, foothills only
- ❑ Thicket hairstreak, *Callophrys spinetorum*—piñon-juniper forest
- ❑ Juniper hairstreak, *Callophrys gryneus*—piñon-juniper woodland
- ❑ Western pine elfin, *Callophrys eryphon*—pine forests
- ❑ Gray hairstreak, *Strymon melinus*—open disturbed weedy areas
- ❑ Western pygmy blue, *Brephidium exile*—foothills only
- ❑ Marine blue, *Leptotes marina*—foothills only
- ❑ Ceraunus blue, *Hemiargus ceraunus*—open woodland, roadsides
- ❑ Reakirt's blue, *Hemiargus isola*—meadows, creeksides
- ❑ Western tailed blue, *Everes amyntula*—open woodland and low shrub areas
- ❑ Arizona "spring azure" blue, *Celastrina argiolus cinerea*—forest edges, muddy areas
- ❑ Western square-spotted blue, *Euphilotes battoides*—open woodlands
- ❑ Rita spotted blue, *Euphilotes rita*—foothills only
- ❑ Silvery blue, *Glaucopsyche lygdamus*—moist woods and meadows
- ❑ Melissa blue, *Lycaedes melissa*—foothills, open weedy areas
- ❑ Greenish blue, *Plebeius saepiolus*—roadsides, stream edges, northern Sandias
- ❑ Boisduval's blue, *Plebeius icarioides*—northern Sandias
- ❑ Lupine blue, *Plebeius lupini*—alpine slopes to desert chaparral
- ❑ Arctic blue, *Agriades glandon*—alpine fields and meadows

Reptiles and Amphibians of the Sandia Mountains

Snakes
Non-venomous
- ❑ Coachwhip, *Masticophis flagellum*
- ❑ Striped whipsnake, *Masticophis taeniatus*
- ❑ Bull snake/Gopher snake, *Pituophis melanoleucus*
- ❑ Wandering garter snake, *Thamnophis elegans*
- ❑ Mountain patchnose snake, *Salvadora grahamiae*
- ❑ Lined snake, *Tropidoclonion lineatum*
- ❑ New Mexico milk snake, *Lampropeltis triangulum*
- ❑ Great Plains rat snake, *Elaphe guttata*
- ❑ Smooth green snake, *Liochlorophis vernalis*
- ❑ Longnose snake, *Rhinocheilus tesselatus*
- ❑ Glossy snake, *Arizona elegans*
- ❑ Hognose snake, *Heterodon nasicus*
- ❑ Texas blind snake, *Leptotyphlops dulcis*
- ❑ Ringneck snake, *Diadophis punctatus*
- ❑ Night snake, *Hypsiglena torquata*
- ❑ Plains black-headed snake, *Tantilla nigriceps*

Venomous
- ❑ Western diamondback rattlesnake, *Crotalus atrox*
- ❑ Blacktail rattlesnake, *Crotalus molossus*
- ❑ Prairie rattlesnake, *Crotalus viridis*

Lizards
- ❑ Prairie lizard, *Sceloporus undulatus*
- ❑ Short-horned lizard, *Phrynosoma douglasii*
- ❑ Collared lizard, *Crotaphytus collaris*
- ❑ Great Plains skink, *Eumeces obsoletus*
  Whiptail lizards
  - ❑ New Mexico, *Cnemidophorus neomexicanus*
  - ❑ Chihuahuan spotted, *Cnemidophorus exsanguis*
  - ❑ Checkered, *Cnemidophorus grahamii*
  - ❑ Little striped, *Cnemidophorus inornatus*
  - ❑ Plateau striped, *Cnemidophorus velox*
- ❑ Tree lizard, *Urosaurus ornatus*
- ❑ Leopard lizard, *Gambelia wislizenii*
- ❑ Lesser earless lizard, *Holbrookia maculata*
- ❑ Roundtail horned lizard, *Phrynosoma modestum*
- ❑ Side-blotched lizard, *Uta stansburiana*
- ❑ Many-lined skink, *Eumeces multivirgatus*

Amphibians
❏ Tiger salamander, *Ambystoma tigrinum*
❏ New Mexico spadefoot toad, *Spea multiplicata*
❏ Couch's spadefoot toad, *Scaphiopus couchii*
❏ Plains spadefoot toad, *Spea bombifrons*
❏ Great Plains toad, *Bufo cognatus*
❏ Red-spotted toad, *Bufo punctatus*
❏ Woodhouse's toad, *Bufo woodhousii*
❏ Bullfrog, *Rana catesbiana*

Turtles
❏ Box turtle, *Terrapene ornate*

Birds of the Sandia and Manzanita Mountains

The following checklist was compiled from *Birds of the Sandia and Manzanita Mountains,* which is more comprehensive and is available free from the Sandia Ranger District in Tijeras. The following list does not include occasional, accidental, or transient species.

New World Vultures
❏ Turkey vulture

Geese and Ducks
❏ Mallard
❏ Green-winged teal

Hawks and Eagles
❏ Northern harrier
❏ Sharp-shinned hawk
❏ Cooper's hawk
❏ Northern goshawk
❏ Swainson's hawk
❏ Red-tailed hawk
❏ Ferruginous hawk
❏ Golden eagle

Falcons
❏ American kestrel
❏ Merlin
❏ Peregrine falcon
❏ Prairie falcon

Grouse and Turkeys
❏ Wild turkey

New World quail
❏ Scaled quail

Cranes
❏ Sandhill crane

Sandpipers
❏ Spotted sandpiper
❏ Common snipe

Pigeons and Doves
❏ Rock dove
❏ Band-tailed pigeon
❏ Mourning dove

Cuckoos and Roadrunners
❏ Greater roadrunner

Typical Owls
❏ Flammulated owl
❏ Western screech owl
❏ Great horned owl
❏ Northern pygmy owl
❏ Burrowing owl
❏ Long-eared owl
❏ Northern saw-whet owl

Goatsuckers
❏ Common nighthawk
❏ Common poorwill
❏ Whip-poor-will

Swifts
❏ White-throated swift

Hummingbirds
❏ Black-chinned hummingbird
❏ Calliope hummingbird
❏ Broad-tailed hummingbird
❏ Rufous hummingbird

Kingfishers
❏ Belted kingfisher

Woodpeckers
- ❏ Red-naped sapsucker
- ❏ Williamson's sapsucker
- ❏ Ladder-backed woodpecker
- ❏ Downy woodpecker
- ❏ Hairy woodpecker
- ❏ Northern flicker, red-shafted form

Tyrant Flycatchers
- ❏ Olive-sided flycatcher
- ❏ Western wood-peewee
- ❏ Hammond's flycatcher
- ❏ Dusky flycatcher
- ❏ Gray flycatcher
- ❏ Black phoebe
- ❏ Say's phoebe
- ❏ Ash-throated flycatcher
- ❏ Cassin's kingbird
- ❏ Western kingbird

Shrikes
- ❏ Loggerhead shrike

Vireos
- ❏ Gray vireo
- ❏ Cassin's vireo
- ❏ Plumbeous vireo
- ❏ Warbling vireo

Jays, Crows, and Ravens
- ❏ Steller's jay
- ❏ Western scrub jay
- ❏ Piñon jay
- ❏ Clark's nutcracker
- ❏ American crow
- ❏ Common raven

Larks
- ❏ Horned lark

Swallows
- ❏ Violet-green swallow
- ❏ Northern rough-winged swallow
- ❏ Barn swallow
- ❏ Cliff swallow

Chickadees and Titmice
- ❏ Mountain chickadee
- ❏ Juniper titmouse

Bushtits
- ❏ Bushtit

Nuthatches
- ❏ Red-breasted nuthatch
- ❏ White-breasted nuthatch
- ❏ Pygmy nuthatch

Creepers
- ❏ Brown creeper

Wrens
- ❏ Rock wren
- ❏ Canyon wren
- ❏ Bewick's wren
- ❏ House wren
- ❏ Winter wren

Kinglets
- ❏ Golden-crowned kinglet
- ❏ Ruby-crowned kinglet

Gnatcatchers
- ❏ Blue-gray gnatcatcher

Thrushes
- ❏ Western bluebird
- ❏ Mountain bluebird
- ❏ Townsend's solitaire
- ❏ Hermit thrush
- ❏ American robin

Thrashers and Other Mimics
- ❏ Northern mockingbird
- ❏ Sage thrasher
- ❏ Curve-billed thrasher
- ❏ Crissal thrasher

Starlings
- ❏ European starling

Wood Warblers
- ❏ Orange-crowned warbler
- ❏ Nashville warbler
- ❏ Virginia's warbler
- ❏ Yellow warbler
- ❏ Yellow-rumped warbler
- ❏ Black-throated gray warbler
- ❏ Townsend's warbler
- ❏ Grace's warbler
- ❏ Northern water thrush
- ❏ MacGillivray's warbler
- ❏ Wilson's warbler

Tanagers
- ❏ Hepatic tanager
- ❏ Western tanager

Towhees and Sparrows
- ❏ Green-tailed towhee
- ❏ Spotted towhee
- ❏ Canyon towhee
- ❏ Rufous-crowned sparrow
- ❏ Chipping sparrow
- ❏ Clay-colored sparrow
- ❏ Brewer's sparrow
- ❏ Black-chinned sparrow
- ❏ Vesper sparrow
- ❏ Lark sparrow
- ❏ Black-throated sparrow
- ❏ Sage sparrow
- ❏ White-crowned sparrow
- ❏ Golden-crowned sparrow
- ❏ Dark-eyed junco

Grosbeaks and Buntings
- ❏ Rose-breasted grosbeak
- ❏ Black-headed grosbeak
- ❏ Blue grosbeak
- ❏ Indigo bunting

Blackbirds and Orioles
- ❏ Red-winged blackbird
- ❏ Eastern meadowlark
- ❏ Western meadowlark
- ❏ Brewer's blackbird
- ❏ Brown-headed cowbird
- ❏ Bullock's oriole
- ❏ Scott's oriole

Finches
- ❏ Gray-crowned rosy finch
- ❏ Black rosy finch
- ❏ Brown-capped rosy finch
- ❏ Pine grosbeak
- ❏ Cassin's finch
- ❏ House finch
- ❏ Red crossbill
- ❏ Pine siskin
- ❏ Lesser goldfinch
- ❏ American goldfinch
- ❏ Evening grosbeak

Old World Sparrows
- ❏ House sparrow

Mammals of the Sandia Mountains

❏ Virginia opossum, *Didelphis virginiana*
❏ Desert shrew, *Notiosorex crawfordii*
❏ Merriam's shrew, *Sorex merriami*
❏ Montane shrew, *Sorex monticolus*
❏ Dwarf shrew, *Sorex nanus*
❏ Little brown bat, *Myotis lucifugus*
❏ Southwestern myotis, *Myotis auriculus*
❏ Fringed myotis, *Myotis thysanodes*
❏ Long-legged myotis, *Myotis leibii*
❏ Yuma myotis, *Myotis yumanensis*
❏ Silver-haired bat, *Lasionycteris noctivagans*
❏ Big brown bat, *Eptesicus fuscus*
❏ Hoary bat, *Lasiurus cinereus*
❏ Townsend's big-eared bat, *Plecotus townsendii*
❏ Pallid bat, *Antrozous pallidus*
❏ Spotted bat, *Euderma maculatum*
❏ Brazilian free-tailed bat, *Tadarida brasiliensis*
❏ Big free-tailed bat, *Nyctinomops macrotis*
❏ American black bear, *Ursus americanus*
❏ Ringtail, *Bassariscus astutus*
❏ Northern raccoon, *Procyon lotor*
❏ Striped skunk, *Mephitis mephitis*
❏ Hog-nosed skunk, *Conepatus mesoleucus*
❏ Western spotted skunk, *Spilogale gracilis*
❏ Ermine, *Mustela erminea*
❏ Long-tailed weasel, *Mustela frenata*
❏ Black-footed ferret, *Mustela nigripes*
❏ American badger, *Taxidea taxus*
❏ Red fox, *Vulpes vulpes*
❏ Kit fox, *Vulpes macrotis macrotis*
❏ Gray fox, *Urocyon cinereoargenteus*
❏ Coyote, *Canis latrans*
❏ Wolf, *Canis lupus*
❏ Puma, *Puma concolor*
❏ Bobcat, *Lynx rufus*
❏ Thirteen-lined ground squirrel, *Spermophilus tridecemlineatus*
❏ Spotted ground squirrel, *Spermophilus spilosoma*
❏ Rock squirrel, *Spermophilus variegatus*
❏ Texas antelope squirrel, *Ammospermophilus interpres*
❏ Black-tailed prairie dog, *Cynomys ludovicianus*
❏ Gunnison's prairie dog, *Cynomys gunnisoni*

- Colorado chipmunk, *Tamias quadrivittatus*
- Least chipmunk, *Tamias minimus*
- Red squirrel, *Tamiasciurus hudsonicus*
- Abert's squirrel, *Sciurus aberti*
- Botta's pocket gopher, *Thomomys bottae*
- Yellow-eared pocket gopher, *Pappogeomys castanops*
- Silky pocket mouse, *Perognathus flavus*
- Hispid pocket mouse, *Chaetodipus hispidus*
- Rock pocket mouse, *Chaetodipus intermedius*
- Banner-tailed kangaroo rat, *Dipodomys spectabilis*
- Ord's kangaroo rat, *Dipodomys ordii*
- American beaver, *Castor canadensis*
- Northern grasshopper mouse, *Onychomys leucogaster*
- Mearns' grasshopper mouse, *Onychomys arenicola*
- Western harvest mouse, *Reithrodontomys megalotis*
- Montane harvest mouse, *Reithrodontomys montanus*
- Deer mouse, *Peromyscus maniculatus*
- White-footed mouse, *Peromyscus leucopus*
- Brush mouse, *Peromyscus boylii*
- Piñon mouse, *Peromyscus truei*
- Northern rock mouse, *Peromyscus nasutus*
- Tawny-bellied cotton rat, *Sigmodon fulviventer*
- Southern plains woodrat, *Neotoma micropus*
- White-throated woodrat, *Neotoma albigula*
- Mexican woodrat, *Neotoma mexicana*
- Long-tailed vole, *Microtus longicaudus*
- Mexican vole, *Microtus mexicanus*
- Muskrat, *Ondatra zibethicus*
- Brown rat, *Rattus norvegicus*
- Black rat, *Rattus rattus*
- House mouse, *Mus musculus*
- North American porcupine, *Erethizon dorsatum*
- Black-tailed jackrabbit, *Lepus californicus*
- Eastern cottontail, *Sylvilagus floridanus*
- Mountain cottontail, *Sylvilagus nuttallii*
- Desert cottontail, *Sylvilagus auduboni*
- Elk, *Cervus elaphus*
- Mule deer, *Odocoileus hemionus*
- Pronghorn, *Antilocapra americana*
- Bighorn sheep, *Ovis canadensis*
- Horse, *Equus caballus*

Sandia Field Guide Team and Contributors

Project manager:
Gerry Sussman

Editorial coordinators:
Robert Julyan
Mary Stuever

Special editorial reviewer:
Ellen Ashcraft

Editorial committee:
Mary Bean
Sam Beard
Dana Howlett
Robert Julyan
Mary Stuever
Gerry Sussman
Mary Voldahl

Steering committee:
Dick Traeger, Chair
Mary Bean
Sam Beard
Don Carnicom
Dana Howlett
Gerry Sussman
Mary Voldahl

Fund-raising committee:
Richard Becker
Don Carnicom
Gerry Sussman
Dick Traeger

Administrative support:
Margaret Furman

Guide contributors:
Rich Anderson—reptiles and
 amphibians
Art Arenholz—birds
Jenny Arenholz—birds
Jayne Aubele—geology
Sam Beard —fire ecology,
 cross-country skiing
Jeanette Buffett—wildflowers
Pearl Burns—wildflowers
Don Carnicom—trails
David A. Conklin—tree diseases
Larry Crumpler—geology
James Deal—geology
Tom Ferguson—wildflowers
Ernie Giese—arthropods

Helen Haskell—fungi, mosses,
 grasses, etc.
John Hayden—human presence
Robert Julyan—ecology, human pres-
 ence, introduction, place names
David Lightfoot—arthropods
Spencer Lucas—geology
Sue Bohannan Mann—introduction
Paul Polechla—mammals
Damon Salceies—reptiles and
 amphibians
Paul Stubbe—weather, geology
Mary Stuever—trees and shrubs
Eugene Van Arsdel—tree diseases

Technical reviewers:

Kelly Allred—grasses
Sandra Brantley—arthropods
Irwin Brodo—lichens
Ruth Bronson—fungi
Chuck Buxbaum—grasses, etc.
Mike Coltrin—trails
Dick Frederiksen—overall review
Jerry Goffe—digitized bird photos
Dana Howlett—ecology, fungi,
    human presence
Robert Julyan—human presence,
    trails
James Karo—birds
Spencer Lucas—geology
Phyllis Martinez—introduction,
    human presence

Carol Mochel—geology
Charlie Painter—reptiles and
    amphibians
Lynn Ruger—digitized text
Christopher Rustay—birds
Damon Salceies—reptiles and
    amphibians
Hart Schwarz—birds
Robert Sivinski—flora
Jim Stuart—reptiles
Mary Stuever—fire, wildflowers
Dick Traeger—trails
Dirk Van Hart—geology
Mary Voldahl—fungi, trails,
    fire ecology

Other friends and contributors:

Cliff Dils—former District Ranger, Sandia Ranger District
Scott Dunn—Outdoor Editor, *Albuquerque Journal*
Robert DeWitt Ivey—author and plant illustrator,
    Flowering Plants of New Mexico
Kurt Menke—GIS Specialist, Earth Data Analysis Center, UNM
Jean Szymanski—U.S. Forest Service

University of New Mexico Press staff:

David Holtby—editorial consultation
Sonia Dickey—editorial consultation and photo editing
Sarah Ritthaler—editing and proofreading
Kathleen Sparkes—book design and production management
Danielle Rodgers—production assistance

Illustrations:
Mike Brown—trails
Larry Crumpler—geology
Robert DeWitt Ivey—wildflowers,
    trees and shrubs
Helen Haskell—grasses
Adair Peterson—wildflowers
Jeff Segler—trees and shrubs

Photo contributors:
J. Scott Altenbach—mammals
Heidi Anderson—reptiles and
    amphibians
Rich Anderson—reptiles
Jenny Arenholz—birds
Jane Aubele—geology
Roger W. Barbour—mammals
Troy L. Best—mammals
David Brock—mammals
Jeannette Buffett—wildflowers
Pearl Burns—wildflowers
Steve Cary—arthropods
David Conklin—tree diseases
Larry Crumpler—geology
Sharyn Davidson—arthropods
J. des Lauriers—mammals
Vladimir Dinets—mammals
Jerry W. Dragoo—mammals
Jon L. Dunnum—mammals
Richard B. Forbes—mammals
William S. Gannon—mammals
Jerry Goffe—birds
David J. Hafner—mammals
J.G. Hall—mammals
Justine Rebecca Hall—sidebars

HawkWatch International—birds
Robert Julyan—human presence,
    introduction, lichens,
    sidebars, trails
James Karo—birds
David Lightfoot—arthropods
Don L. MacCarter—mammals
Pat O'Brien—birds
Cathy Pasternak—birds
Paul J. Polechla Jr.—mammals
Rio Grande Nature Center
    State Park—birds
Damon Salceies—reptiles and
    amphibians
Sevilleta National Wildlife Refuge,
    Long-term Ecological
    Research—mammals
William Stone—cover, back,
    frontispiece
Paul Stubbe—geology
Gerry Sussman—sidebars
US Forest Service, Sandia Ranger
    District—throughout
Mary Voldahl—lichens, birds

Acknowledgements and Credits

There are many volunteers who helped to bring this project from concept to reality. Don Carnicom, a dedicated U.S. Forest Service volunteer, first suggested that there was a real need for a natural history and human history guide to Albuquerque's defining natural resource, our treasured Sandia Mountains. He brought this idea to the attention of colleagues at the New Mexico Friends of the Forest, a nonprofit organization of volunteers formed to work in partnership with the Forest Service. As our organization is committed to education and conservation, it was an ideal project for us, especially since there is nothing available in book form that offers information about flora, fauna, geology, ecology, human presence, and recreational opportunities in the Sandias.

With the leadership of Sam Beard, president of the Friends of the Forest; the guidance of Dick Traeger, who chaired our steering committee and developed plans to move this project forward; and the major contributions of Paul Stubbe, Margaret Furman, Don Carnicom, and Richard Becker, we started working on the guide. With us every step of the way were our wonderful friends with the Forest Service: Mary Bean, Dana Howlett, and Mary Voldahl. They served on many committees, read and edited every section of the guide, and made invaluable contributions with their ideas and suggestions that added so much to this book. Many thanks also to Cliff Dils, Sandia District Ranger, for his encouragement over the many months of this undertaking. Very early on, Mary Stuever, coauthor of the *Philmont Field Guide,* came on board as editorial coordinator, to give her expert advice on organizing the project and planning the editorial work. Mary pulled us through the very difficult early months with clarity, grace, and energy. More recently, after Mary took a position in Arizona, Robert Julyan, author of many books, including *Place Names of New Mexico,* took on responsibilities as editorial coordinator. We are so very fortunate that he agreed to add this to his very busy schedule. Bob and Mary put in untold hours, checking details, getting photos, working with our contributors, rewriting material, and molding the many parts of the guide into a cohesive and engaging book.

Special thanks go out to all of the volunteer writers, the heart and soul of this enterprise, whose wonderful expertise and hours of work and meetings have given us this guide. For them, this was a labor of love. Of particular note, Art Arenholz, who wrote the bird chapter, and Pearl Burns, Jeanette Buffet, and Tom Ferguson, who wrote the wildflower chapter, moved this venture forward early and set the pace for our other contributors.

After all of the chapters had been completed, we called on specialists in many fields to review them and give us their expert advice. We are especially grateful to David Lightfoot and his colleagues at the Arthropods Division in the UNM Department of Biology, who made available not only their experience and knowledge but also their photographs. Similarly, we are deeply indebted to Robert DeWitt Ivey, who graciously gave us permission to use his superb drawings from his book *Flowering Plants of New Mexico.*

Other technical experts included the staff at the Sandia Mountains Natural History Center, Kelly Allred for Grasses, Dr. Irwin Brodo for Lichens, Ruth Bronson for Mushrooms, Mike Coltrin (author of the new *Sandia Mountain Hiking Guide*) for Trails, Charlie Painter and Jim Stuart for Reptiles, Christopher Rustay for Birds, Robert Sivinski for Wildflowers, and Dirk Van Hart for Geology. When these reviews were completed, the entire manuscript was sent to Dick Frederiksen, Emeritus Professor at Texas A&M (who now lives in Albuquerque and spends hours hiking in the Sandias) for a final review. All of these professionals did a wonderful job, and we are indebted to them for their help. Of course, any errors in the book remain our sole responsibility.

One of the major challenges that we faced in preparing the guide was the need for funding. Our fundraising committee, which included Richard Becker, Don Carnicom, Dick Traeger, and me, were very gratified at the wonderful response that we received. We want to express our great appreciation to all of the donors, listed within, both corporate and private. Without their assistance, we would not have been able to bring you the guide as you see it, with all of the color photos.

I am certain that our *Field Guide to the Sandia Mountains* would not have seen the light of day without the very professional and sure hand of David Holtby, editor-in-chief and associate director of the University of New Mexico Press, and his superb staff. We are very thankful for their early recognition of the importance of this work and their unswerving commitment to copublish it with us. This gave us the final impetus to move ahead with the work to be done. We went to them for advice often during the book's gestation period, to the guide's great benefit.

It was my great pleasure to work with and get to know all the remarkable people who produced our guide. They are as magnificent as the mountains.

—*Gerry Sussman*
Project Manager

Geology
Jayne Aubele

A great debt is owed to Vincent C. Kelley, the "father" of modern New Mexico field geology, and to the many hundreds of geologists laboring in the field of New Mexico geology who have increased our understanding of this geologically dynamic area. The chapter authors thank Helen Haskell and Carol Mochel for reading and reviewing early versions of the chapter. I also would like to thank Mary Stuever, Dick Traeger, Gerry Sussman, Jim Deal, and Paul Stubbe for inviting me to be involved with this great project! Larry Crumpler designed and created all graphics in this chapter.

Grasses, Fungi, Lichens, Mosses
Helen Haskell

I need to recognize Robert Sivinski and Kelly Allred for their help with the grasses. Bob also read over the text of all the sections. Also thanks to Dr. Irwin Brodo for information regarding lichens. The staff of the Sandia Mountain Natural History Center and Charles Buxbaum at Sandia Preparatory School also reviewed the contents.

Wildflowers
Pearl Burns, Jeanette Buffett, and Tom Ferguson

We are indebted to Robert Sivinski, for his thorough and thoughtful review of our section, and to Adair Peterson for illustrations.

Trees
Mary Stuever

Jeff Segler dug through years of accumulation to share original artwork from the *Philmont Fieldguide* for the conifers. I also extracted details from that book which include a bit of Dan Shaw's wit and keen observations. Robert DeWitt Ivey not only provided drawings for the deciduous chapter, but has provided years of inspiration and enthusiasm and the best "coloring book" in the Southwest. Pearl Burns and Tom Ferguson shared shrub research. Phyllis Martinez is here in spirit for her love of Sandia trees. John Hayden and Joe Price once again assured me of my facts.

Arthropods
David Lightfoot

I'd like to mention Sharyn Davidson, a local photographer who lives in Cedar Crest, who provided some of the arthropod photographs. Sandra Brantley also helped me with the text. Sandy also is Senior Collection Manager, Division of Arthropods, Museum of Southwestern Biology, University of New Mexico.

Reptiles

I would like to express my sincere appreciation to Helen Haskell and my wife, Heidi Anderson, for reviewing and offering suggestions for improving the manuscript. I would like to thank my brother, Chris Anderson, who also made helpful comments on the manuscript—I doubt I would have developed an interest in these fascinating and beautiful animals had it not been for the childhood encouragement of my brother and his contagious love of reptiles and amphibians.

Birds
Art Arenholz

My acknowledgments go to: James Karo, for photography; Jerry Goffe, for digitizing all my bird slides and donating several bird photos; Lynn Ruger, who did the data entry for all my text; Cathy Pasterczyk, for photography; HawkWatch International, for photography; Rio Grande Nature Center State Park, for photography.

Mammals
Paul Polechla

More recently, Gary Morgan has contributed to the knowledge of the smaller mammals of this site and time. Recent mammals of the area have been described by Vernon Bailey, Robert Parker, Ronald Clothier, Robert DeWitt Ivey, the U.S. Forest Service (especially the files of Beverly DeGruyter), James Findley and his students, and Terry Yates and his students and personnel. I have drawn from the works of these people as well as the Museum of Southwestern Biology (M.S.B.) collection and the Zoonotic Disease Program studying Hantavirus and rodents near Placitas, both housed at the University of New Mexico. In addition, I have drawn from my own observations recorded in field notes deposited at the M.S.B.

Trails
Don Carnicom

Gratitude is due to Mike Coltrin, for his review of this section, and also to Dick Traeger and Mary Voldahl, who also reviewed the manuscript.

Our Corporate and Individual Donors

Crest ($5,000+)
High Desert Investment Corporation
Intel Corporation
Public Service Company of New Mexico
REI

Spruce-Fir ($4,000+)
Albuquerque Community Foundation

Conifer ($1,000+)
Lockheed Martin–Sandia National Laboratories

Ponderosa ($500+)
Blue Cross/Blue Shield
Exerplay, Inc.
New Mexico Mountain Club
New Mexico Quilters Association
Presbyterian Healthplex
Southwest Airlines
Jim Bewley
Don and Mina Carnicom
Bob and Sally Lowder
Patrick O'Leary Memorial
Paul and Sueshila Stubbe
Jeff and Patti Young

Piñon ($250+)
Adair Peterson
Buffett's Candies
Skyleidoscope Hot Air Balloon
Smokey Bear Balloon
Mary Sweet
Bill and Debbie Velasquez

Juniper ($100+)
TJ's Camera
Turquoise Trail Association
Sam and Edwina Beard
Richard W. Becker
Mark Chavez
Karen Davenport
Glenn and Theresa Wertheim
Gerry and Arla Sussman

Grassland ($50+)
The Creamery, Inc.
Mike the Printer
Tinkertown Museum
J.Wheeler, Ltd.
Sam Benia and Kathy Kirsling
Anne Hickman
Thomas and Ellen Mendelsohn
Donald and Susan Partridge
Betty Smith
Charles and Marcia Wood

Notes

Notes

Notes